Foreclosure Defense

Foreclosure Defense

A PRACTICAL LITIGATION GUIDE

Rebecca A. Taylor

15 14 13 12   5 4 3 2

Library of Congress Cataloging-in-Publication Data
Foreclosure defense : a practical litigation guide / Rebecca A. Taylor.
    p. cm.
    Includes index.
    1. Foreclosure—United States—Handbooks, manuals, etc. 2. Mortgage loans—Law and legislation—United States—Handbooks, manuals, etc. 3. Actions and defenses—United States. I. Title.
KF697.F6T39 2011
346.7304'364—dc23   2011019674
ISBN: 1-978-61632-993-8

Dedication

To the soldiers fighting on the side of justice in this battle; you create hope and new possibilities with everything you do.

Contents

Acknowledgments

Sincere thanks to Erin Nevius, who worked with me from the beginning on this project; your professionalism, support, and talent have made this book possible.

Thank you to Manatee County, Florida, for granting free online access to court documents; this will be an invaluable tool to those fighting foreclosure, as they can view thousands of foreclosure documents, obtain templates, and spend less time reinventing the wheel.

Thank you to my mother, Jeanne Boyer, for always praising and encouraging my writing.

Thank you to my stepfather, Chuck Holdeman, for your constant interest and support.

Thank you to my husband, Jim, who has stood by me no matter what; your love has sustained me.

Thank you, Carl; one day you will know how much the patience, understanding, and space you gave me helped others; you are wise and lighthearted beyond your years. You will always be a Batman, Robin, Superman, Buzz Lightyear, Spiderman, and every superhero to me.

Introduction

The goal of this book is to assist attorneys throughout the country in their practice of foreclosure defense law. As most Americans know, our country is in the midst of a foreclosure epidemic which has settled more in certain states than others but affects us all nonetheless. This book is about how homeowners all across this country can save their homes and how we as lawyers can help them. There are things we can do for homeowners that they cannot do for themselves.

I have worked in litigation for almost 14 years and am going on my third year in the foreclosure field. I am not a mortgage broker, a title examiner, or a financial expert, and I don't pretend to be one. I was an American Studies major at Rutgers College and have always been fascinated by American culture; this crisis seems to be a crucible that reveals who we really are. That is not to say that everyone working for the banks to prosecute foreclosures wants to be on that side; I know, as I used to be one of them. I have been on all sides of this mortgage crisis in Florida, one of the worst foreclosure war zones. I have represented banks and handled as many as 500 litigation foreclosure files at a time.

What This Book Is and Is Not

I am only licensed to practice in Florida, so what applies here may not apply in your state, and none of the information or proposed forms contained in this book are legal advice, as everyone's situation is different; all content in this book is supplied for informational purposes only. For each issue, consult the rules and law of the appropriate jurisdiction, which may also be constantly changing. Readers are also cautioned to review any subsequent history, whether positive or negative, of all authorities cited herein.

The book includes sample forms that are intended to assist attorneys nationwide and serve as templates for your own foreclosure defense documents. Many of the court forms are obtained from the Manatee County, Florida, website, which is one of the few counties in the country at this time that permits free online access to court-filed documents. It is truly a wealth of free information. The website Pacer.gov is a one-stop portal to federal cases from all 50 states; it charges a fee for downloading and viewing of documents.

For several years now, we have heard numerous theories about how this foreclosure crisis arose. I will not attempt to offer theories about how we got into this predicament. My purpose here is to offer the benefit of experience I have gained as a litigation attorney in the foreclosure industry. This book does not encompass all available law applicable to foreclosure defense, and it should not be relied upon as your only tool in this field. The book does focus on a number of issues raised in recent law or news or issues that often recur in foreclosure cases. As a caveat, some of the cases discussed in this book are virtually brand-new law and are still subject to appeal or reconsideration. I also make a point to discuss legal issues that have come up frequently in my own foreclosure experience.

This book is written from a foreclosure defense perspective, and my goal has been to provide current relevant law to assist homeowners and their attorneys. As such I do not present many cases for the proposition of supporting the banks' arguments.

My focus is on litigation practice in the court where the plaintiff files the initial foreclosure complaint. General principles of appellate practice and bankruptcy are discussed, but these are complex fields of law requiring special expertise and discussion beyond the scope of this book. The book also does not focus on actual trial procedure, as this area of law also requires special expertise, and trial procedures vary greatly among jurisdictions.

This book endeavors to assist you in navigating alternative dispute resolutions to avert a foreclosure action from even being filed against your client. If an action is filed, howver, it will help guide you through possible litigation strategies and defenses in the court where the foreclosure action is initially filed, which is usually state court (see flowchart, page xvi). Federal practice is also very complex, and litigants must follow numerous rules and procedures established by the appellate rules of civil procedure, the particular court, and judges themselves. Banks[1] are usually looking to get their judgments as quickly and easily as possible and find that state court is the easier route for them.

Right now, multiple government investigations into the foreclosure crisis are ongoing, which hopefully will eventually give us a remedy for the epidemic of bank fraud and sloppiness in foreclosure filings. Law professor Kurt Eggert commented on the December 2010 Senate hearings regarding the foreclosure crisis where federal agencies testified about problems they have experienced with servicers:[2]

> At the recent Senate testimony where all the federal agencies came forward and testified about servicer problems, it was telling that they didn't talk about what they have already done about it. . . . Instead they talked about the investigations they are conducting that they hoped would inform them on what to do next. How many years are we into this crisis? We are long past the point of where we should be investigating to see what's happening.[3]

Professor Eggert indicates that we should have had more solutions from the government by now; the foreclosure crisis has been dragging on for years. When in the news we hear of a token homeowner receiving a happy ending to a mortgage nightmare, it

---

1. When I use the term "bank" in this book, I am aware that the terms bank, investor, servicer, plaintiff, and owner of the loan are not always interchangeable, although they sometimes can be one and the same. However, for the sake of convenience, unless stated otherwise in this book, I use the term "bank" to denote the party who claims authority (whether validly or not) to own the loan, file the foreclosure action, and grant a loss mitigation solution.

2. Defined as "the person responsible for servicing of a loan (including the person who makes or holds a loan if such person also services the loan)," except for certain federal agencies. 12 U.S.C. § 2605(i)(2).

3. Gretchen Morgenson, *A Mortgage Nightmare's Happy Ending*, N.Y. Times, Dec. 25, 2010.

Litigation Strategies and Defenses in Foreclosure Actions

is still too much of a rarity—like a lottery-winning story. These results need to become commonplace. We are seeing many good results for homeowners from the judicial branch of government and there are a number of legislative programs in place, such as Home Affordable Modification Program (HAMP), that are also yielding results. But the courts will not have to do as much judicial legislating if we have more decisive guidance from state and federal legislatures.

One might think that some banks possess mens rea in their frenzy to push baseless foreclosures through the system. The banks' conduct, while nonviolent, is reminiscent enough of an established criminal law principle to seem like "depraved-heart" foreclosure: "[e]xtremely negligent conduct, which creates what a reasonable man would realize to be not only an unjustifiable but also a very high degree of risk of . . . injury to another or to others—though unaccompanied by any intent to . . . do serious [] injury—and which actually causes the [injury] of another."[4] However, real estate developers continue to receive money despite defaulting on their loans.[5] So why has all this money floating around eluded most homeowners who need help to avoid foreclosure? Millions have begged for aid from the government and their pleas remain largely unanswered. Any loan modification program that a bank might participate in is strictly voluntary: No bank has been forced to help any homeowner, except by the courts.

Occasionally there will be David-versus-Goliath stories of individual triumph by individuals fighting the banks on their own. A remarkable story is of one Florida woman who has faced off against the banks for 25 years.[6] The end to this foreclosure saga has not yet come, but this woman, Patsy Campbell, has no intention of giving up: "They're not going to take this house. . . . I intend to stay in this house and maintain it as my residence until I die." Ms. Campbell is currently handling her case pro se, and the legal theories on which

---

4. *See* WAYNE LAFAVE & AUSTIN SCOTT, SUBSTANTIVE CRIMINAL LAW, Vol. 2.

5. *See* Charles V. Bagli, *Real Estate Developers Prosper Despite Defaults*, N.Y. TIMES, Jan. 1, 2011.

6. Robbie Whelan, *The 25-Year "Foreclosure from Hell*," MSN REAL ESTATE at http://realestate.msn.com/article.aspx?cp-documentid=27145486 &page=0, Jan, 27, 2011.

she is fighting the foreclosure are not specifically explained, although the article mentions that she has raised issues of standing, improper loan transfer, improper debt, forged documents, laches and discovery violations, and bankruptcy. Other homeowners have been heartened by her example and have hired attorneys in an attempt to buy time, the article says.

However, this article should not be interpreted as carte blanche for homeowners to attack foreclosure without competent legal counsel. The numbers—and almost anyone who attends foreclosure court hearings on a regular basis—will tell you that Ms. Campbell's story is a definite exception to the rule. The fact that Ms. Campbell's case has lasted this long may well be mostly by virtue of the judges assigned to her case, their willingness to consider her continued arguments and grant her relief. The article describes Ms. Campbell as a "stern, confident woman who can quote Florida civil-procedure statutes by reference number," which must certainly help. Another homeowner in similar circumstances as Ms. Campbell could very well experience a very short foreclosure case resulting in the bank's favor, depending on any number of factors, including the judges, court procedures, opposing counsel, personal relations, and the way that the facts and law are presented to the court.

Ms. Campbell's case, however, is also an example of how raising articulate, legally supported arguments in the court system is always an effective method of foreclosure defense for both attorneys and pro se litigants alike. Many judges grant relief to the banks only because the law presented to them does not leave room for any other alternative—for example, when the bank has presented a motion for summary judgment and the defendant has no papers in opposition. This is where parties and their attorneys must come in and present a different story to the courts.

Part I

Ethical
Considerations

1

Inside the Bank Foreclosure Defense Industry

In the legal business, change is a fundamental rule of the game. If the federal laws aren't changing, the state rules are. There are certain principles that are more constant, such as the canon of stare decisis, whereby courts still adhere to a legacy of case law and long-standing legal policies. From stare decisis, we may develop strategies that can be somewhat uniform, no matter where you practice law. However, there are so many issues of first impression in the foreclosure field of law that every time a new issue is decided, it will change the game; then the rules may change again if the decision is overturned on appeal and new statutes are enacted.

Although this is less the case than perhaps at the beginning of the foreclosure crisis, many bank representatives have no previous experience with litigation or any court matters, and legal principles are foreign to them. They may not understand or might just claim ignorance as to why a homeowner is entitled to receive any of the materials requested in discovery. Bank representatives often resist even more vehemently having to appear for a deposition, and are often shocked at the inherently grueling nature of this proceeding.

3

Yet the banks must not forget that in filing all of these foreclosure actions, they are no different from any other litigation plaintiff, and "litigation has a tendency to make public the sort of information that individuals otherwise would prefer to keep private."[1] Although the banks are multibillion-dollar financial behemoths, as so succinctly put by New York Judge Arthur Schack,[2] it is individuals who must answer discovery on behalf of the banks, and often they are in for a rude awakening to the fact that their private information may become public.

Attorneys for banks often endeavor to shield their clients from the rigors of discovery. The competition for banks' business among foreclosure firms and attorneys is fierce. In the midst of a flailing economy, the foreclosure industry is one of the few job fields that is on the rise today. Thanks in part to the TARP funds, which bailed out many banks, these corporations now have abundant financial resources to dedicate to obtaining foreclosures, and law firms and attorneys everywhere are fighting for a piece of the pie. Law firms that never previously dealt with foreclosures happily opened their doors to the business, drawn in by the irresistible profits.

---

1. Ragge v. MCA/Universal, 165 F.R.D. 601, 605 (C.D. Cal. 1995).
2. CitiMortgage, Inc. v. Nunez, 2010 N.Y. slip op. 52142 (U) at *1 (N.Y. Sup. Ct. 2010).

Banking is an industry in which the legal business can be controlled far too much by the judgment of non-lawyers. It's an often-prevailing practice among foreclosure plaintiffs to wash their hands of defaulting borrowers, never mind the reason the borrowers supposedly defaulted in the first place. Bank foreclosure firms, servicers, and client systems will often assume the philosophies and modus operandi of their clients. Attorneys know that they are usually hired by clients to perform stated objectives but expect to use their knowledge and ethics to direct their clients to recommended legal avenues. For bank foreclosure attorneys, customer service must often win out over professional judgment if they wish to keep their clients, and those who do not will lose the business or be fired, whether or not the attorney has a flawless track record (in his professional judgment).

These attorneys know that some of the pitfalls of discovery, such as the highly adversarial direct confrontation, intimidation, and fear (particularly for those unfamiliar with the litigation arena) associated with a deposition can be disastrous for client relations. Therefore, bank attorneys will often expend much more energy to fight foreclosure defense discovery than they will in any other area of the litigation process. Foreclosure law firms often do not even consider a foreclosure action to be "litigated" unless it becomes "contested," and only at that point do some foreclosure firms refer a case to their litigation department. This is why some banks fail to address litigated issues for quite some time, or even ever—simply because they have not routed a case to the right department, and it just sits in the hands of personnel.

As we can see from a litany of recent case law and investigation results, it is banks that are often directing their attorneys' professional judgment. It may also be that some clients go over or around the lawyer until they get the answer they want. I don't believe that most people in the foreclosure industry enjoy putting people out of their homes; it's merely something to pay the bills. The foreclosure firms are just representing a client that wants to assert a legal position; everyone has the right to counsel, from people injured in a car crash to those accused of murder—even terrorists. Attorneys often do not share the views or philosophies of their clients; they simply have a job to do.

Also, the foreclosure industry often does not take a great deal of interest in the human aspects of their employees to the extent that employees are sometimes not able to produce or deliver the product expected of them. There is so much work to be done and so many foreclosure sales that are expected to be closed that the foreclosure industry has little patience for anything that deviates from a robotic ability to just produce, produce, produce. This is the expectation of the banks; they are all about numbers. In the trend as of late, much work gets farmed out overseas because many companies are opting to receive mechanical product like clockwork. This makes perfect sense for the foreclosure industry; however, banks do need locally licensed attorneys to get their judgments.

Chapter 2

Advertising

The rules of your local bar association will likely govern how you may advertise your service in your area; the following points may already be required, but whether they are mandatory or not, they are good principles to follow. Good, extremely ethical advertising helps to establish your reputation as one of the good guys. In your advertisements directed at struggling homeowners, you should distinguish yourself from the sharks. For example, if your jurisdiction permits you to send direct-mail advertisements to homeowners, tell them how you got their information—through public court filings, for instance. The homeowner is less likely to feel like someone's prey if you let them know you obtained their information through public records and not in an underhanded manner. Homeowners should be wary of anyone who asks them to relinquish title to their house or directs them to sign any kind of contract. Such contracts will often insulate the consultant or attorney from liability if he or she is unsuccessful in granting the homeowner a solution, and in such a case may also leave the borrower exposed to a deficiency judgment. The sharks usually make offers that seem too good to be true and appeal to a homeowner's emotions rather than logic.

You should then make clear to your prospective clients that you, like any other attorney, cannot guarantee a result to anyone. It is now virtually common knowledge that no loan solution, or any result in litigation, for that matter, is guaranteed. The rules of the game are complex, and as of this writing there is no general law that will compel a lender to modify loans. Therefore, if a case is handled properly, it will require many hours of hard work on both you and your client's part to maximize the chances for your client to prevail.

You should also use caution in the use of testimonials, if your jurisdiction permits them at all. Avoid creating the expectation that just because you obtained a particular result in one case, you will be able to do the same for everyone. Your jurisdiction may also not permit any celebrity endorsements, or statements that you are a "specialist," or "certified," or allow solicitation of prospective clients in person.

There are many different ways of structuring the fee agreement, whether you and your client agree on a reasonable hourly rate or a flat monthly fee, as many foreclosure defense attorneys do. One thing I would not suggest is to enter into an arrangement where the subject of the litigation (your client's home or property) becomes part of the fee arrangement. At least one attorney has been subject to scrutiny by the local bar association due to his practice of attaching a second mortgage to a client's home if he obtains a favorable outcome in the foreclosure case.[1] If you and your client are both fighting to obtain a property interest in the same thing, it is hard to imagine how a conflict of interest would not arise sooner or later.

As discussed later on, distressed homeowners are often the target of swindles and scams that prey on human desperation to save their home. Be part of the solution, not part of the problem. If you work out a fee agreement that takes the client's financial situation into account and then you are able to work out a favorable solution, that client will likely give glowing reviews about you to anyone he thinks you might be able to help, which is priceless advertising. That will build your practice faster than a few unscrupulously high fees would.

---

1. Diane C. Lade & Harriet Johnson Brackey, *Bar Investigates Attorney Who Offers Clients Second Mortgage to Pay Lawyer Fees*, SUN-SENTINEL (Fort Lauderdale, Fla.), Nov. 9, 2010.

Chapter 3

Conduct Toward Opposing Counsel and Parties

Bank attorneys often get pleas to cancel or continue a hearing on the bank's motion for summary judgment after opposing counsel had just appeared in the case. Many bank's lawyers might want to say yes to this request, but then of course there is the matter of justifying such a decision to the bank. If you ask to cancel simply because you've just appeared in the case, the bank's counsel is likely to tell you to take it up with the judge. It serves defense attorneys well to consider such requests in this light: give the bank attorney a reason for cancelling the hearing that is justifiable to their chain of command. Such reasons include:

- if the particular judge's procedures required the hearing to be coordinated with opposing counsel and it was obvious that it had not been;
- if the notice of hearing was sent to the wrong address;
- if bank's counsel scheduled the hearing during the period of a previously issued notice of unavailability; and
- if the motion was scheduled without the underlying documents required to be filed therewith, such as the affidavit of indebtedness, costs, and attorney's fees.

Diplomacy with opposing counsel is key in all cases but particularly in foreclosure cases, where your client's emotions and stakes are high. The practice of law can be draining enough as it is, and when a personal battle with the other side enters the mix, it can wear you down to the point of taking you out of the game altogether. There are many advantages to a diplomatic relationship with your opponent:

1. Professional courtesies are more likely to be granted, such as agreed orders, rescheduling of hearings, and positive peer ratings;
2. You will develop valuable professional contacts and possibly even friendships;
3. The other side will be more amenable to open communication with you and your client and possibly an amicable resolution of the case;
4. You are more likely to enjoy your work rather than dread it; the latter will eat away at your career;
5. The judge will look upon both of you more favorably. Most judges hate to be in the middle of attorneys' personal feuds. When you show the court that you are working amicably with the other side, you demonstrate the utmost professionalism and raise yourself above the crowd. This is welcome relief for the court and its staff.

Sometimes, there will be attorneys who seem to fight an amicable relationship at every turn, despite your best efforts. Some attorneys will lie about you and your client. Some will commit clear violations of your local ethics rules to the point where you want more than anything to file a bar complaint against them. Bring the conduct to the court's attention, in as professional and non-emotional a manner as possible. Just present the facts and let the court decide what should be done with them.

Do not accept the invitation to engage in personal attacks and childish complaints. If opposing counsel begins such attacks, nine times out of 10 the judge will swiftly deal with the unprofessional conduct without your even having to say a word. There are certain things that judges expect attorneys to handle on their own, such as reasonable deadline extensions, coordinating hearing dates, complying with reasonable discovery requests, and working together to comply with the judge's guidelines when necessary. Most judges are perturbed when they are called upon to baby-sit practicing adult attorneys; this is time they could be spending granting results to either you or other parties desperately waiting for the court's attention.

In most situations, the conduct of antagonistic attorneys does not rise to a sanctionable level but only complicates your case. For example, they might be aggressive litigators. You may wonder why this case is even in court, the issues may be so simple to you. Maybe your client is well able to reinstate the loan or resume making payments, but the adversary insists on pursuing foreclosure. This may make no sense to you, as usually a bank will obtain much less money for a property upon sale than it would receive if your client resumed making payments. The answer to this tactic, and a general rule for any attorney, is to overprepare. When you know your case better than the opponent, you stand a better chance of convincing the court to see the case the way you do.

As a foreclosure defense attorney you may already have an advantage over your adversary simply by virtue of the team you are on. Many courts now frown upon bank foreclosure attorneys in general.[1] Courts will almost always hold a lawyer accountable rather than his or her client because the lawyer is an officer of the court and usually the one who brings the matter before a judge in the first place, utilizing valuable court resources and time. Although most attorneys have traditionally been permitted to file a complaint simply on the good-faith belief that a true factual basis exists for their clients' claims,[2] a greater burden has now been placed on foreclosure attorneys in filing banks' complaints. New York, together with many other jurisdictions, requires attorneys to attest to the factual basis underlying each residential foreclosure case filed.[3] New York Deputy Chief Administrative Judge Ann Pfau explained one reason for this rule: "If you

---

1. John Schwartz, *Judges Berate Bank Lawyers in Foreclosures*, N.Y. TIMES, Jan. 10, 2011.

2. *See* FED. R. CIV. P. 11(b).

3. *Id.*

can't get good information, you shouldn't be filing the cases in the first place."[4] And as New York University legal ethics professor Stephen Gillers noted, "[w]hen the consequence of a lawyer plying his trade is the loss of someone's home, and it turns out there are documents being given to the courts that have no basis in reality, the profession gets a very big black eye."[5]

Lawyers in general are, unfortunately, easy targets for anything that goes wrong, because anyone can hold our feet to the fire by simply complaining, or threatening to do so, to the state bar—a potential nightmare situation for any lawyer. Bank foreclosure attorneys are much easier to blame than an amorphous, infinitely large banking entity, where assignment of blame can so easily be swept under the carpet or lost in the shuffle.

However, any attorney, no matter whom they represent, may go further with the court by practicing simple civility. In general, judges and court staff care less about who you actually represent than the quality of their personal experience with you. By treating the court staff with the same respect as you would give the judge; familiarizing yourself with the judge's and local jurisdiction's rules and procedures; and always being punctual, professionally dressed, and cordial to the court, teammates, and opponents alike, you will establish yourself as someone whom others enjoy running into and working with, including those on the opposite side of the table.

---

4. *Id.*
5. Foreclosures, N.Y. TIMES, Jan. 10, 2011.

Part II

Trial Basics

Chapter 4

Written Arguments

Good writing is an essential element of your law practice. Sometimes a well-written argument with abundant citation to legal authority will obviate the necessity for oral argument of a matter, or will at least make your job much easier at the hearing. Sometimes a judge will decide whether to grant you a hearing based on what you submit in writing first, as in appellate practice, but many trial courts are now following certain procedures on this as well; for example, one judge requires that you submit a motion for rehearing for his review first, and he will then decide if he will grant hearing on the motion or simply deny it without further hearing.[1]

In foreclosure defense circles, you will often see boilerplate forms circulating that may have no factual relation to your specific case. Avoid using such forms without tailoring the forms and allegations contained therein to your case. Use of these forms will often tip off the courts that your papers are filed solely for delay purposes, which is usually not an effective strategy.

In preparing a written argument, begin by determining all of the issues you need to research. The entire time you are doing research, you will be learning more about your case and forming your argument in your head. You don't want to start writing before

---

1. Civil Division (09) Procedures, Hon. David Krathen, *available at* http://www.17th.flcourts.org/div09procedures.pdf at p.11.

your research is done; there may be something out there that can change your whole argument.

Once you are done with your research, you can either organize your authorities by issue or by your outline and write from beginning to end, or you can start going through your cases in no particular order and just jump between sections of your writing. For the latter approach, Microsoft Office 2010 really assists you to write in any way and any order you want—you can create headings in the left-hand navigation pane and click on them to jump between sections in the document. There are also very easy tools that allow you to create any kind of table, graph, chart, or demonstrative aid you want.

Create a new heading for each issue that a case raises, and just add to or create more headings with each subsequent case. This is where the case-briefing skills you learned in law school come in handy. Most everyone has heard of the IRAC theory for case briefing; I=Issue, R=Rule, A=Analysis, C=Conclusion. Be sure to include all of those elements in your discussion of a case.

Once your mini case briefs are all included in one document, you can begin the analysis portion of the writing—explaining what you think all the cases mean, tying the facts of this particular case in, and weaving an argument. Learn as you write and let the process stir up new ideas, maybe even further areas of research. Once this analysis is done, it should be relatively easy to compose the conclusion.

In a foreclosure case, of course, everything you are arguing should generally show how your defenses preclude granting of relief to the bank: how the court should find that the complaint is legally insufficient, how the bank has not acted in good faith, how the bank is not entitled to a judgment of foreclosure, why the property cannot go to sale, etc. Though more law is coming out all the time in this area, many issues may still be matters of first impression for a court. With issues where there has not yet been a case that proscribes the action the court should take in a specific instance, you can still defer to older, well-settled principles of law, which quite often lead to equitable defenses. A foreclosure action is an equitable as well as legal proceeding, and the bank should not receive a foreclosure judgment unless it has done equity.[2] Clearly this has not been the case with many loans, and though there may not be a favorable case on all fours with your situation, you may still be able to make an equitable argument which cites the specific facts of your situation and demonstrates how the bank cannot be entitled to relief.

One lawyer's adage advises: "If you don't have the law, pound the facts. If you don't have the facts, pound the law. If you don't have the facts or the law, pound the table." Making a forceful, confident argument will usually get the attention and respect of a court (although some judges might find literal table-pounding contemptuous). When confronted with a challenging document from the other side, dissect every legal issue, research everything, and prepare a well-organized and reasoned argument, counter-argument, or brief for both the benefit of the court and yourself. When you have written out and charted your argument, you have also better organized it in your mind. Be sure to write out and answer most questions that the court is likely to ask.

Preparation is obviously important in every kind of case; however, it's particularly important in foreclosure cases, as it's an advantage you are likely to have over the bank's attorney. With hundreds of cases usually assigned to every attorney, they generally do not have the time to examine, research, and craft their best argument. However, an advantage the bank attorneys are likely to have is the wealth of collective knowledge they share with their colleagues, since most bank foreclosure firms are large and have many attorneys. The bank attorneys will constantly be comparing notes and results on what worked and what did not in court. Most of them will quickly have encountered virtually every legal defense argument in one form or another.

What the bank attorneys will be less prepared for is your careful application of perhaps familiar law to the unique facts of your client's case to craft a case and argument that they cannot defeat by just shooting from the hip. Many bank attorneys are accustomed to

---

2. *See* Centex Home Equity Co., LLC v. Jarrett, No. CV-03-0195133S (Conn. Super. Ct. April 28, 2004); Emigrant Mortgage Co., Inc. v. Corcione, 28 Misc. 3d 161, 169 (N.Y. App. Div. 2010).

dealing with boilerplate motions and, likewise, formulate boilerplate responses which they hope will cause a judge to summarily dismiss a borrower's defenses. It is much more rare for bank attorneys to receive homeowner filings that itemize the particular facts of their case and apply the law to those facts. These sorts of papers usually require more preparation in opposition, and that kind of time is usually not on the bank attorney's side. For example, do not simply allege generally that the bank has no standing to foreclose on the loan. Thoroughly research the chain of title and specifically assert facts, if any, to show there is no indication that this particular loan has been transferred to the plaintiff (Chapter 16). If you contend that service was improper, have your client submit an affidavit specifying facts that contradict those alleged in the return of service (Chapter 15). If summary judgment is improper, allege specific facts and law, and present evidence to show that genuine issues of material fact exist that prevent entry of summary judgment for the bank, or that prompt entry of summary judgment is in the borrower's favor (Chapter 21).

Foreclosure judges are often weary of boilerplate foreclosure defense positions, and most likely will find it refreshing to hear a defense that is tailored specifically to the circumstances of your particular client and appreciate a written embodiment of your argument, which will make their job easier. Judges often ask what authority will permit them to grant particular relief, and if you give them that authority on a silver platter, you will make it easier for them to decide for your client.

Of course, this does not mean that even if you present that well-crafted argument, which you may consider a *magnum opus*, that you will always win, whether the bank attorney is shooting from the hip or not. As all litigation attorneys know, other factors come into play when judges render their decision: sometimes it is political—they know opposing counsel better than you; perhaps they did not like the color of your tie or shoes, or your demeanor; or the decision may just be seemingly arbitrary. This is a primary reason why you always need to have a court reporter with you, so that if a decision is rendered that is directly opposite to what the legal result should be, you can file a prompt appeal.

Chapter 5

Preparing for Hearings

When you submit motions to the court that cite to a voluminous amount of case law or other authorities, be early and organized (actually, this approach is always needed in the practice of law; it is the lack of doing so that often gets attorneys in hot water). Either you or your legal assistant need to print out all the cases and authorities, then tab and index them. You should make sure that a copy of your motion, brief, and/or binder of authorities is in the judge's hands on the day that particular judge requires that motions be received in advance of a hearing. Many judges require that they receive a copy of any motion set for hearing a week to 10 days in advance. Make sure that opposing counsel receives a mirror image of anything you send to the judge, highlighting and document markings included. Some judges will consider even one yellow highlight on a document to be a sanctionable ex parte communication if the identical highlight does not exist on opposing counsel's copy.

A court reporter should attend every hearing in your case, especially for any dispositive hearings. Have his or her cell phone number handy so you can call if need be. If they don't appear, sometimes there will be another court reporter in the vicinity of the courtroom you may be able to hire. Failing that, you may want to request a continuance rather than risking not having a good record in case you need it. You never know when the opposing party or the court will say something that could make or break your case, and you will need a record of it. Due to the slipshod manner in which so many banks handle their foreclosure cases, and in which they insist they should be granted relief, having a record of everything may become important at any stage in the litigation. Hearings and everything that happens in court are a sort of discovery as well. Every time the parties are before the judge, there is a chance to gain new information about your case, often unexpectedly and without even having to ask. Based on what happens in court, you may have grounds to seek summary judgment or judgment on the pleadings in favor of your client. Conversely, if the trial court enters an unjust ruling that is fatal or damaging to your case, you may want to appeal immediately.

At least one week before your hearing, you should have your court reporter scheduled and confirmed for that day and time. Make sure the court reporter's office has a copy of your notice of hearing with the judge's name, address, and room number on it. For that matter, when you send out notices of hearing, double-check the judge's name, address, and room number. This can often work to the homeowners' advantage: when the bank sends out a notice of hearing with an inaccurate location and the homeowners (usually pro se) eventually show up, the bailiff sometimes tells them that the hearing has been cancelled because the bank did not put the proper location on the court notice and that the bank will have to reschedule the hearing.

If you receive an unfavorable ruling, determine as soon as possible whether you should file a motion for rehearing or reconsideration of the ruling. The time in which you have to do this is very limited, often as short as 10 days from the date of the ruling.[1] The purpose of a motion for rehearing "is to afford a party an opportunity to demonstrate that the court overlooked or misapprehended the law or facts pertinent to the original motion," not to "serve as a vehicle to permit the unsuccessful party to argue once again the very questions previously decided."[2] File the motion for rehearing on or before the deadline; it should not matter when the

---

1. *See* FLA. R. CIV. P. 1.530.

2. Bankers Trust Co. of Cal., N.A. v. Payne, 188 Misc. 2d 726, 728–29 (N.Y. App. Div. 2001).

motion is actually set for hearing as long as you filed on time. Some courts may not permit you to just set your motion for hearing automatically; they may want to review your motion to ascertain whether you have asserted proper grounds.[3] Depending on the nature of the ruling, you may decide to appeal the ruling as well (see Chapter 22).

3. Civil Division (09) Procedures, Hon. David Krathen, *available at* http://www.17th.flcourts.org/div09procedures.pdf at p.11.

Chapter 6

The Initial Client Interview

Your client may be a longtime friend or acquaintance, or someone who just walked through your door for the first time. The world of foreclosure defense may be completely new to both of you. How do you begin to solve the problem that has already cost millions of Americans their homes? You conversation might begin with a question attorneys may ask their clients in any number of settings: What do you want to achieve? The answer from your client will be essential to the strategy you develop (a sample client intake form is included on the form CD in the back of the book). The strategy for a foreclosure case may be less obvious than in other fields of law. In a personal injury suit, the plaintiff generally wants to recover the maximum amount of damages possible. In a criminal defense action, the defendant wants to expel or minimize the charges and possible penalties. But in a foreclosure situation, whether actual or potential, your strategy will be determined by your client's goals for the property.

What Are Your Client's Goals?

Your client has just realized he will not be able to afford the mortgage payments. Maybe he has just lost his job, or there has been another financial emergency. He may be current now but knows he is on the brink of a late or missed payment. Many clients will come to you saying that they have already attempted to work things out with the bank, submitted and resubmitted paperwork, told they have been approved for loan modifications, and put on loan modification or forbearance plans, only to be told they are in default again. All your client knows is that he is spinning his wheels and just getting closer to losing his home.

One of the things both you and your client must do from the very first meeting in a foreclosure case (which probably goes without saying, but it cannot be stressed enough) is document and keep a record of every communication and contact with the bank, investor, servicer, or anyone regarding the subject loan or property. Countless parties have attempted to stop foreclosure on their home by telling the court that they are working something out with the bank and giving specific facts to support their assertions, but then foreclosure is entered anyway. You need to have all evidence of those negotiations every time you go before the judge. If everything was oral or over the telephone, have your client execute an affidavit as to what exactly transpired and what was said, and file this in a timely manner with the court.

Our job as attorneys should be to present all reasonable and viable options available to our clients based on the facts they have presented to us, and to let them decide which goal they would like to achieve. A client may change her mind about whether she wants to keep the property when presented with a variety of legal options. For example, a client may think she does not have enough income to keep the property and therefore wishes to give it up, but she may be eligible for Chapter 13 relief, which would allow her to keep the property, as discussed further in Chapter 23, Bankruptcy. Another client may have no income available at the present time and see no way that he can retain the property, but the party threatening foreclosure may have no standing or ownership interest in the loan to obtain summary judgment (Lack of Standing/Improper Plaintiff, Chapter 16).

On the other hand, sometimes giving up the property makes the most sense for a property owner. He or she may want to be relieved of the debt, change locations without trying to sell the property in a depressed market, or get a fresh start. When your client may have to make what may be a discouraging decision at first, our role as counselors at law becomes more important. Sometimes it is not fail-ure for your client to decide that she no longer wishes to keep the home or fight the foreclosure. Often it is just like a business deci-sion: there may be better opportunities for your client in which to invest her time, energy, and money. If too many other things in your client's life are suffering because she is desperately trying to keep the house, that could a sign for her to cut her line and move on. For homeowners who simply wish to be relieved of the mort-gage debt and turn the property back over to the bank, the primary issue for the attorney should be how to reach an amicable settle-ment of the lawsuit whereby their client will obtain a release from the bank and not be haunted by the threat of a deficiency judgment.

Often, the only parties who have the ultimate authority to grant your client a solution are the investors or the government. A court is one such branch of the government with that power. That is why it is important to not waste too much time trying to work with the servicer, whose only allegiance is to their investor-employers. When you start to get the runaround, simply continue to document every-thing and add it to the collection of evidence you bring to the court's attention.

Your prospective clients should bring all of their loan and other documents relevant to the case with them to their initial interview with you. The type of loan against the property your client initially executed will help determine the kind of relief for which she may be eligible. For example, many laws are designed to help borrowers re-tain only homestead or primary residences. Many jurisdictions pro-vide that mediation is mandatory for any foreclosure case involving homestead property. The courts will usually treat requests to retain homestead property with much more urgency than those to keep in-vestment property. Additionally, it is important to note whether the loan was a purchase money or a refinance; look at the loan applica-tion or the HUD-1 Settlement Statement to determine this. The an-swer to this question will help determine whether your client may be entitled to rescission under the Truth in Lending Act (Chapter 19).

A good approach may be for your clients to provide information to you as if they were preparing to file for bankruptcy, although they may not necessarily take this course. This will allow you to ascertain your clients' full factual and financial scenario and be able to best decide the wisest course of action. The disclosure required from all bankruptcy debtors requires them to provide extremely thorough and detailed accountings of their personal and financial status. As many attorneys know, it is often difficult to obtain all relevant facts from clients, particularly those they may find embarrassing or incriminating. However, there needs to be trust between attorney and client, and the confidentiality rules were enacted in part to foster that trust. An attorney is a fiduciary of her client and must use all information obtained to act in her client's best interest.

If a client clearly does not trust you, you should probably not represent him: even the seemingly smallest detail can change the proper strategy, goal, or result in a case, and particularly a foreclosure case. And the truth usually comes out. After you obtain a result, it may become apparent that this result was not the right one for your client, and you would have known that if you had gotten all the relevant information.

A recent *MSN Real Estate* article proposes tips to consumers in choosing a foreclosure attorney.[1] One thing the article suggests is that before a homeowner even hires an attorney, she should meet with a HUD-approved loan counselor. This is certainly a good component for a homeowner to pursue in addition to seeking legal counsel; later in the book Neighborhood Assistance Corporation of America (NACA), and what they are able to accomplish for many homeowners, are described in detail (Chapter 24). The homeowner may have defenses such as those provided by the Truth in Lending Act or tort claims that are subject to statutes of limitations on which a loan counselor cannot advise. Also, the availability of evidence may diminish with time, as well as claims of laches from the other side. Homeowners should consult with an attorney at the earliest stage of their loan dispute; often an attorney may be able to take preventive action that could stave off a foreclosure action in the first place. The article rightfully mentions that a loan counselor may be able to help a borrower organize and compile relevant paperwork prior to meeting with an attorney, but an attorney and/or her staff can help a homeowner do the same thing.

---

1. Holden Lewis, *8 Tips for Choosing a Foreclosure Attorney*, MSN REAL ESTATE, at http://realestate.msn.com/article.aspx?cp-documentid=27143247, Jan. 27, 2011.

The article also advises homeowners to "put on your game face" when they meet with an attorney, indicating that they should discuss their case without emotion and conduct themselves in a manner befitting a business meeting. While it is certainly helpful for a homeowner to have all relevant paperwork with them and organized in a way that will help an attorney quickly grasp key issues in their case, homeowners should not feel that they cannot display emotion about their circumstances. As attorneys, we cannot profess to be our clients' therapists, but we do possess knowledge and experience that compels us to understand the human side of the problems our clients present to us. And empathizing can help build trust with clients and help them disclose all the details of their situation, even the painful ones. Part of being an attorney should be being there for your clients and listening to the emotions that are part of their case. Though the law sometimes professes to make empirical decisions that are devoid of emotions, it is the emotions of people that fuel the evolution of law and often lead to significant changes. Therefore, while we must present our cases in a professional and organized manner to the court, an essential element to many cases is the acknowledgment of the emotions involved.

Have Your Clients Been Defrauded by "Foreclosure Consultants"?

Unfortunately, distressed homeowners are often seen as prey for opportunistic criminals. These people have preyed upon the desperation of homeowners to save their homes by telling them that they can only do it by paying exorbitant sums of money, which often proves to be for little or nothing.

In the game of foreclosure defense, there are usually two groups of players: attorneys and foreclosure consultants/loan counselors. Unscrupulous attorneys may take monthly payments from homeowners, claiming that they can keep the borrowers in their home for less than they were paying the bank. In reality, these people do not have a real knowledge of the applicable law or a desire to help the borrowers. The only result to the homeowners might be a time delay. A delay is not entirely meaningless, because it gives a borrower time to come to grips with reality, save money, work on a deal with the bank, or make other plans. However, a delay in and of itself is not the most meaningful result, because that time could be spent preparing a defense or plan which makes the most sense for that particular homeowner. There are inherent delays in most fore-closure cases anyway because of the backlog in the courts. Further-more, if the homeowners later on decide to advance a more well-reasoned defense, they may have prejudiced their case by the delay and the attendant inactivity. Many courts will not be persuaded by homeowners' excuses that they delayed because they did not know the consequences of a foreclosure action.

The other group of often-unethical players consists of non-law-yers generally called "foreclosure consultants." Many of them are to be avoided. Opportunistic swindlers have preyed on homeowners facing foreclosure with empty promises of loan modifications or rescuing them from foreclosure. Some consultants will approach a homeowner and ask him or her to pay a large up-front fee or monthly fees in exchange for the consultant to negotiate and reach a solu-tion with the bank. Often the consultants guarantee a loan modifi-cation; however, all they end up doing is collecting money for themselves. Others will ask homeowners to grant them title to the property, claiming that they will arrange a short sale with the bank and save the borrower from foreclosure. However, in many cases the consultants force homeowners to sign an agreement acknowl-edging that there is no guarantee that foreclosure will be avoided. Also, the agreements have often stated that the homeowners can still be sued for a deficiency judgment. The homeowners have gained nothing and are often worse off than they were before.

In an action filed by the Florida Attorney General against Out-reach Housing, LLC, Blair Wright, and Bryan E. Berry, the com-plaint alleged three causes of action against the defendants based on violations of Florida laws against deceptive and unfair trade prac-tices.[2] The defendants operated their scheme by soliciting homeowners facing foreclosure and inducing them to sign limited

---

2. Broward County Court Case No. CACE-08-049280 (07), http://myfloridalegal.com/webfiles.nsf/WF/MRAY-7PEQ5U/$file/Outreach HousingComplaint.pdf (case number obtained from the Broward County Court website Public Case Search).

powers of attorney granting defendant Wright powers as the homeowners' attorney-in-fact.[3] The limited power of attorney granted defendant Wright the power to, among other things, select attorneys for the homeowners.[4]

The Outreach Housing outfit also worked in concert with local Florida attorneys, which it needed in order to provide its solicited service of foreclosure defense in court.[5] Florida attorneys would be employed by Outreach Housing, signing a contract that granted Outreach the ability to remove any file from an attorney with two weeks' written notice.[6] Outreach falsely represented to the public that it did not split fees with attorneys, when in fact the defendants paid hired counsel directly from monthly payments collected from its "clients."[7]

The defendants would review mortgage documents and loan origination documents received from their homeowner customers and make determinations as to whether violations of any law had occurred.[8] The attorney general's complaint asserted that the defendants' document review and referral procedure, their employ of and control over attorneys, and fee-splitting with attorneys involved the unlicensed practice of law.[9] As of this writing, the Broward County on-line docket shows this case as still pending, but Outreach Housing and Mr. Wright have been dismissed as defendants.

A scheme almost identical to the Outreach Housing model was executed by foreclosure consultants in Ohio, who were ultimately sanctioned by the court and enjoined from further unlicensed practice of law.[10] In that case, the disciplinary counsel filed a three-count complaint against defendants Foreclosure Alternatives, Inc. and its officers.[11] The defendants' modus operandi was to find foreclosure

---

3. (Compl. ¶¶ 18–20).
4. (Compl. ¶ 20).
5. (Compl. ¶ 21).
6. *Id.*
7. (Compl. ¶¶ 23–24, 26).
8. (Compl. ¶ 27).
9. (Compl. ¶ 28).
10. *See* Disciplinary Counsel v. Foreclosure Alternatives, Inc., 2010 Ohio 6257 (Ohio Sup. Ct. 2010).
11. *Id.* at *1.

defendants through on-line databases, solicit those individuals, and induce them to execute contracts whereby the consultants would supposedly file documents in the foreclosure cases and negotiate with lenders.[12] The victims were charged $850 to $900 as an initial fee, after which they would make regular payments into their designated accounts until the funds reached a certain amount, which in one case was equivalent to four mortgage payments.[13]

Also similar to Outreach Housing, the *Foreclosure Alternatives, Inc.* defendants would employ attorneys, control their professional judgment on cases, and split fees with them.[14] The defendants represented to their customers that they had a "high success rate and could stave off foreclosure"; that the homeowners should stop making mortgage payments and should not file bankruptcy; that the foreclosure had been stopped by attorneys taking care of the cases; and that the consultant attorneys were right across the hall from the bank attorneys and would work things out with them, but the consultant attorneys were too busy to talk to the customers.[15]

The *Foreclosure Alternatives* court easily found that the defendants' activities constituted the unauthorized practice of law, which included, inter alia, proposing legal strategies to homeowners in foreclosure, advising them to cease mortgage payments, and dictating settlement terms for their customers.[16] The defendants were enjoined from further unauthorized practice of law, and civil monetary penalties were imposed against them.[17]

Another mortgage fraud scheme was revealed in a case where the defendant pled guilty to 25 counts of grand theft in connection with his practice of fraudulently converting the real estate of others to his own name.[18] In some cases, the defendant took money from investors under the pretense that he would use the money to flip houses and share the profits, but instead just used the money to

12. *Id.* at *6.
13. *Id.* at *7.
14. *Id.* at *7, *20, *22.
15. *Id.* at *20.
16. *Id.* at *24.
17. *Id.* at pp.38–39.
18. State of Ohio v. McClain, 2010 Ohio 6413 at **1–9 (Ohio App. 2010).

purchase properties for himself.[19] In other instances, the defendant offered the illusion of help to distressed homeowners by taking over the title to their properties and the responsibility for their mortgage payments, then often paid little or nothing on the mortgage, still leaving the original homeowners responsible for the loan.[20]

The wrong foreclosure defense agents may also cost a homeowner legitimate defenses that he is already pursuing, in the name of the consultant's best interest and in complete disregard for that of the homeowner. In one Maryland case, a foreclosure swindler claimed that if the homeowner would dismiss his bankruptcy case (thereby abdicating the protection of a bankruptcy stay against creditors) and allow the swindler to purchase the home, the swindler would grant the homeowner a rent-to-own agreement whereby the homeowner would pay the consultant, which would be applied towards the homeowner's repurchase of the property.[21] However, the consultant later alleged in court that he never told the plaintiff homeowner that he would assist the plaintiff with his credit or pay off the mortgage debt.[22] Instead, the defendant alleged that he approached the plaintiff as an investor whose only purpose was to purchase the subject property, and maintained that he never offered the homeowner any assistance or advice.[23]

Maryland statutes define a foreclosure consultant as someone who solicits a homeowner through any medium and represents that he will save a property from foreclosure or let the homeowner rent the home from the consultant, including a rent-to-own repurchase agreement.[24] One Maryland court found that this definition covers not only consultants who initiate the first contact with a homeowner, but also those who are considered to have been approached by a homeowner as well.[25] The appellate court found, contrary to the trial court's rulings, that the defendant was subject

---

19. *Id.* at *8.

20. *Id.* at *9.

21. Kargbo v. Gaston, 5 A.3d 1231, 1233 (Md. Ct. App. 2010).

22. *Id.* at 1233.

23. *Id.*

24. *Id.* at 1240, *citing* § 7-301 of the Protection of Homeowners in Foreclosure Act.

25. *Id.* at 1243.

to the provisions of the Protection of Homeowners in Foreclosure Act.[26] The trial court therefore had not even considered whether the defendant met the definition of a foreclosure consultant.[27] The appellate court remanded the case for a new trial, which inured to the benefit of the homeowner.[28]

When a homeowner has been defrauded by a foreclosure consultant or possibly another attorney and you are taking over the case, you should examine the facts closely to determine how their case may have been compromised by any wrongful or negligent actions and proceed to conduct damage control. In the case of a corrupt foreclosure consultant organization, you may report the organization to the local attorney general or other authorities, which may allow the homeowner to obtain monetary restitution. A request for an injunction may be appropriate if the activities are ongoing.

As a foreclosure complaint requests equitable relief, a court should consider the impact of inequities visited upon a homeowner who fell victim to a foreclosure scam. If the homeowner lost the only money he had available to hire an attorney in the scam, he might request that the court grant him a stay of the foreclosure case while he seeks alternative financial arrangements. If the foreclosure consultants utilized attorneys who committed malpractice in the homeowner's case, the new attorney should prepare a motion requesting that appropriate withdrawal or amendment of court papers be permitted. Homeowners should also request that the court rescind or release them from any contracts into which they entered with dishonest foreclosure consultants.

Do Your Clients Have Any Assets to Support an Offer?

If homeowners have any savings or financial resources that would allow them to cure the mortgage arrearage, they should do so right away. The demand letter should usually state the amount required from the borrowers to cure the default. If the demand letter has expired (meaning that the deadline stated therein for the borrowers

---

26. *Id.*
27. *Id.*
28. *Id.* at 1244.

to pay the arrearage has passed), the borrowers could contact the bank to request a reinstatement amount.

Sometimes a bank will consider and approve a loss mitigation plan submitted by the borrower or her attorney. Unless you have a specific contact at the bank who you know will give the proposal the proper attention, you may have to submit the proposal through the bank's foreclosure attorney. Bank foreclosure attorneys are extremely overwhelmed with work, and it is much more difficult for them to convey a verbal request to the bank than a written offer. A bank is more likely to respond to a written offer, because it shows that the borrower is serious and that she is willing to pay funds immediately to resolve the dispute; the bank is a business that is primarily concerned with making money. Also, if the wrong department receives the proposal at first, it is easier to transfer a written proposal between departments than to transfer hearsay, which can be lost in translation.

Begin by transmitting the proposal via e-mail and following up within a day by phone. The attorney or representative to whom you e-mailed the proposal may have to wait for approval from his chain of command, which in the bank world can take some time, as anyone who is experienced with completing short sales knows. If your proposal is accepted, make sure you find out whether the payment will resolve the foreclosure matter and bring the account current.

Chapter 7

Special Circumstances

Sometimes your clients will possess certain characteristics that distinguish them from the ordinary foreclosure defendant, such as a homeowner working to save his homestead property. Sometimes your client may not live in the property at all, or even be the homeowner of the property. Sometimes your client may not have executed the traditional mortgage, as there are increasing numbers of foreclosures that deal with reverse mortgages. Following are some examples of special circumstances that may describe your clients and that may change their available rights and the ideal strategy for those cases.

Military Status

The Soldiers' and Sailors' Civil Relief Act of 1940 (Civil Relief Act) protects homeowners in the military from losing their homes to foreclosure without certain conditions being met by the bank.[1] The Civil Relief Act is intended to assist service members in devoting "their entire energy to the defense needs of the Nation" and serves to temporarily suspend "legal proceedings and transactions which may prejudice the civil rights of such service members."[2] The Civil Relief Act

---

1. *See* 50 U.S.C.S. App. § 501 *et seq.*
2. *Sylph*, 42 F. Supp. 354–56 (E.D.N.Y. 1941).

"must be liberally construed for the benefit of the serviceman, and not the creditor" unless the court determines that a service member's ability to meet his obligation "is not materially affected by reason of military service."[3]

When a foreclosure action is filed against a service member during or within nine months after his or her military service (the Military Time Period), that service member may request that the court stay the foreclosure proceedings for an equitable period of time or "adjust the obligation to preserve the interests of all parties."[4] Furthermore, a "sale, foreclosure or seizure" of a service member's property during the Military Time Period is not valid unless a court order or agreement compliant with 50 U.S.C.S. App. § 517 states otherwise.[5]

However, if a court finds that "the ability of the defendant to comply with the judgment or order entered or sought is not materially affected by reason of his military service," the court will not grant a stay of the court proceedings to the service member.[6] In one case, the service member had stopped paying his debt and had taken the collateral automobile out of state without the mortgagee's consent.[7] The service member's bad-faith actions predicated the court's denial of a stay on the debt collection proceedings.[8]

The New York Times recently reported on the case of one soldier who lost his home seven years ago when the bank violated the Civil Relief Act and foreclosed on his home while he was deployed on active duty.[9] When the bank foreclosed in 2004, the soldier's wife and two small children were forced out of the property; the soldier, Sergeant James B. Hurley, who was also disabled while in Iraq, now fears that the whole ordeal may cost him his marriage.

Deutsche Bank Trust Company and its servicer, Saxon Mortgage Services, are still disputing whether the former homeowners

---

3. Brown Serv. Ins. Co. v. King, 24 So. 2d 219, 222 (Ala. 1945).

4. 50 U.S.C.S. App. § 533(b).

5. § 533(c).

6. Reese v. Bacon, 176 S.W.2d 971, 974 (Tex. Ct. Civ. App. 1943).

7. *Id.*

8. *Id.*

9. Diana B. Henriques, *A Reservist in a New War, Against Foreclosure,* N.Y. TIMES, Jan. 26, 2011.

are owed significant damages. They claim that Sergeant Hurley should recover no more than the fair market value of his lost home, but Hurley's attorneys assert that their client is entitled to punitive damages to, in addition to attempting to make the soldier and his family whole again, serve as a deterrent to further violations of the Civil Relief Act by banks. Unfortunately, the Hurleys' beloved home, where Hurley had a built a waterside gazebo surrounded by natural forest habitat, will probably never be theirs again, as the new owner has refused to entertain any offers for it and has also bought the adjoining lot.

Many courts may now require a bank to submit non-military affidavits together with their motion for summary judgment. These non-military affidavits may be on the court's checklist of items that must be present prior to the judgment being entered. In the affidavits, the bank's counsel usually attests that a party is not in the military. A court will also usually require that a non-military affidavit accompany a bank's motion for default against a party the bank has not yet been able to serve with the summons and complaint.

Foreclosure defense counsel should cross-check the non-military affidavit to verify whether any parties are in the military. Non-military affidavits from several jurisdictions are included on the form CD; there are varying requirements for what these affidavits must state. The Florida form requires that the affiant must state of her own personal knowledge that the subject defendant is not in the military and attach certificates supporting such testimony. Conversely, the New York and Wisconsin forms require that the affiant merely show grounds for his belief that a subject defendant is not in the military. This will be easy if your own client happens to be in the service, but it is sometimes more difficult to determine the military status of other parties. Often, a bank will rely on the information obtained from the Department of Defense Manpower Data Center website.[10] The bank or its counsel may not always have the Social Security number with the corresponding name; the name on which a search is based may be a very common name, or it may be misspelled; so the information obtained from the Department of Defense website may not always be foolproof, and a non-military

---

10. https://www.dmdc.osd.mil/appj/scra/scraHome.do.

affidavit relying on same could be inaccurate. If the bank has represented that parties to the foreclosure are not in the military and they in fact are, the foreclosure should not proceed unless the requirements of the Civil Relief Act are met.

Protecting Tenants at Foreclosure Act of 2009

Until December 31, 2012, tenants in a foreclosure property may still enjoy rights pursuant to the Protecting Tenants at Foreclosure Act (the Act).[11] The Act provides that no successor-in-interest shall take title in a foreclosed property without providing any bona fide tenant with a "notice to vacate at least 90 days before the effective date of such notice."[12] Furthermore, bona fide tenants are entitled to possession of the property for the full term of any bona fide lease executed prior to the date of the foreclosure notice, except for when the purchaser intends to use the subject property as his primary residence.[13] In that case, the purchaser must provide the tenant with the 90-day notice and afford the tenant the corresponding time period to vacate the property.[14] A bona fide lease or tenancy shall mean that the tenants are not children, spouses, or parents of the subject mortgagor; the tenancy resulted from an arm's-length transaction; and the rent is essentially market value.[15]

However, tenants in foreclosed properties should not construe the Act to grant them a private claim of action. "Federal courts have held that the Protecting Tenants at Foreclosure Act of 2009 does not create a federal private right of action, but indeed provides directives to state courts."[16] The objective of the Act "is to ensure that tenants receive appropriate notice of foreclosure and are not abruptly displaced."[17] One court emphasized that any remedy for

---

11. Pub. L. No. 111-22, § 702, 123 Stat. 1632 *et seq.*

12. *Id.* § 702.

13. *Id.*

14. *Id.*

15. *Id.*

16. Fannie Mae v. Lemere, No. CIV-S-10-1474-MCE GGHPS at *3 (E.D. Cal. July 6, 2010).

17. Nativi v. Deutsche Bank Nat'l Trust Co., No. 09-06096-PVT at *4 (N.D. Cal. May 24, 2010), *citing* Protecting Tenants at Foreclosure: Notice of Responsibilities Placed on Immediate Successors in Interest Pursuant to Foreclosure of Residential Property, 74 Fed. Reg. 30,106.

homeowners under the Act must come from the state courts or government, and that the Act is not a self-help statute.[18] Therefore, if a foreclosure defense attorney files a counterclaim on behalf of her client, she should not file a claim based on the Act. However, facts based on compliance or lack thereof can form powerful affirmative defenses that may preclude granting of the bank's motion for summary judgment.

As long as the tenants are not renting from anyone in their immediate family, they should be fine for the remainder of their lease. Many tenants feel scammed by the property owner if the owner had not told them that the property was in foreclosure, and they begin getting paper in the mail from the bank. However, the Act helps ensure that tenants get what they pay for, at least until the Act is automatically repealed on December 31, 2012. Tenants protected by the Act should keep very careful accounting of their rental payments. The Act is silent on the method tenants should use in making their rental payments and about security deposits. Tenants would be well-advised to guard their copy of the lease against loss, document the condition of the property through pictures, and keep a record of every payment they make.

Reverse Mortgages

In these difficult times, when many retirees have been forced to return to the workplace, some instead look to a reverse mortgage to provide them income from the equity in their home. A reverse mortgage is defined as:

> a nonrecourse transaction in which a mortgage, deed of trust, or equivalent consensual security interest is created against the consumer's principal dwelling—
> (1) securing one or more advances; and
> (2) with respect to which the payment of any principal, interest, and shared appreciation or equity is due and payable (other than in the case of default) only after—
> (A) the transfer of the dwelling;

---

18. *Id.* at *5.

(B) the consumer ceases to occupy the dwelling as a principal dwelling; or

(C) the death of the consumer.[19]

A reverse mortgage[20] may provide an income source to homeowners 62 of age and older by converting the equity in their home to cash flow.[21] Since reverse mortgages are federally insured, the homeowners will receive the income even if the lender goes under.[22] Once the homeowner passes away, however, the subject property will be sold by the lender to satisfy the debt.[23]

Most of us have seen the commercials about reverse mortgages on television, making them sound like a great way for the elderly to enjoy retirement and still put something away for their family. Having seen the ultimate effects of reverse mortgages from bank foreclosure work, however, the reality is not so rosy. Widows and widowers were granted a six-month stay of execution after the borrower passed away, and then foreclosure proceedings were launched to recoup the money advanced in the reverse mortgage. What often adds insult to injury is that the borrower may have received only a few months of income before he passed away and the bank still comes for the house. Or the elderly may be exploited and tricked into signing reverse mortgage documents by a swindler—sometimes one of their family members. In additional to just having lost a spouse, the homeowner left behind must face a foreclosure action and lose the home unless he or she can bring the arrearage current. These are some of the things that those commercials don't say, and some retirees have been misled by the way reverse mortgages are promoted: "It's a miserable thing

---

19. 15 U.S.C. § 1602(bb).

20. Also referred to as a home-equity conversion mortgage (HECM). Sandra Taliani Rasnak, *USTP's Civil Enforcement Activity Targets Mortgage Fraud and Mortgage Rescue Schemes*, 29-2 AM. BANKRUPTCY INST. J. 18, 72 (March 2010).

21. Allen Holzer, *Restructuring the Tax Treatment for Home Equity Draws: Implementing Consumption Tax Fundamentals to Preserve Home Equity*, 24 BYU J. PUB. L. 225, 243 (2010).

22. *Id.*

23. 29-2 ABIJ at 72.

to be thinking you're going to get kicked out after you're living here all this time and you're retired. . . . If I thought a reverse mortgage was going to set me up in a situation like this, I never would have participated."[24] In fact, a study conducted by the U.S. Government Accountability Office in 2009 reveals that "people interested in reverse mortgages were often told that such loans are foreclosure-proof and that they could never lose their homes."[25]

The Association for the Advancement of Retired Persons (AARP) has recently filed a lawsuit against the Department of Housing and Urban Development (HUD).[26] The lawsuit asserts that in late 2008, HUD changed its regulations that state that both spouses are liable for the full loan balance in a reverse mortgage, even if only one spouse signed the mortgage.[27] Reverse mortgages were intended to be nonrecourse loans, meaning that a borrower can never owe more than the property is worth, but under the new HUD rules, a reverse mortgage borrower must pay the full loan balance to keep the home, even if that amount exceeds the current market value.[28] Meanwhile, a third-party buyer need only pay 95 percent of the property's appraised value.[29]

A good approach for others residing in the home after the borrower has passed away may be to attempt to cure the default by reinstatement. Some attorneys have made challenges to reverse mortgage loan documents by stating that they are unconstitutional. For example, the Florida Constitution provides that property may not be conveyed by one spouse and that both must join in a transaction before their joint property may be conveyed.[30] If only one spouse entered into a reverse mortgage, recovery of the property by the bank upon the death of the borrower spouse may be unconstitutional.

---

24. David Streitfeld, *AARP Sues U.S. Over Effects of Reverse Mortgages*, N.Y. TIMES, March 8, 2011.

25. Richard Burnett, *Growing Reverse-Mortgage Defaults Put Homeowners at Risk of Foreclosure*, ORLANDO SENTINEL, Feb. 2, 2011.

26. David Streitfeld, *supra* note 24.

27. *Id.*

28. *Id.*

29. *Id.*

30. FLA. CONST., art. X, § 4(c).

Chapter 8

Inside Your Client's Loan

An ideal resolution to a loan dispute is always one that avoids the filing of a foreclosure action. Sometimes this might be accomplished by going to the top of the bank's chain of command to reach the person who has the ultimate authority to grant a solution. Sometimes you may be able to work with such an individual and settle things by just talking it out. Other times, you may still be able to obtain a loan modification through the servicer.

Find Out Who Owns Your Loan

The owner of or investor on your loan almost always hires a loan servicer to manage the loan, just as a landlord may hire a property management company to tend to the day-to-day issues relating to the property and its tenants. This is the company from which your client may have been receiving warnings about late payments or a demand letter, in which the borrower is basically directed to bring the loan current or face a foreclosure action.

However, the servicer may not be the owner of the loan. Sometimes they are the same; for example, Bank of America and Chase may service their own loans. In any case, the *investor* is the person or entity you want to speak with about finding a solution, as the buck stops with them (other than the government).[1]

You may also call the servicer and inquire as to who the investor is; if a foreclosure action has already been filed, the "plaintiff" in the action may be the investor. It is possible to spend years spinning your wheels with a servicer to get a loan modification and never get anywhere. The servicer may be able to stonewall a settlement, claiming that it does not have "authority" to take action. It will then tell you that it must present information to the investor and get back to you, yet never follow through. Cut to the chase and contact the investor. Perhaps the investor will be cooperative and work with you. Even if the investor is not cooperative, you should still be entitled to meet with them, as mediation is often ordered by the court if any party requests it.

You should ascertain the name of the owner or investor on the loan as quickly as possible so that you may begin reaching out to them regarding settlement proposals. (Hopefully they will not relegate the matter back to their foreclosure attorney or servicer; if that happens, you may need to seek a court order directing the investor to communicate with you directly regarding settlement or appear personally for mediation.) Most mortgages are executed using the Single Family–Fannie Mae/Freddie Mac Uniform Instrument applicable to your state.[2] Look at the name of the lender on page 1, paragraph (C). If this name is the same as the bank that claims to currently own your loan, or the current name is that of the original lender's successor-in-interest (which is usually the company that bought the original lender and, for the purposes of resolving the loan dispute, is the same as the old lender), you are most likely dealing with the investor, who is also the servicer in your particular case.

Some parties are still suspicious of the chain of title in cases where the original lender's successor-in-interest is claiming ownership of the loan. However, it is routinely a matter of public record

---

1. You may find out whether your mortgage is a federally backed loan and whether Fannie Mae or Freddie Mac is the investor on your loan by visiting http://www.fanniemae.com/loanlookup/ or https://ww3.freddiemac.com/corporate/.

2. Forms for each state are *available at* http://www.freddiemac.com/uniform/unifsecurity.html.

as to which banks bought what, such as the recent acquisitions of Washington Mutual by JP Morgan Chase, of Countrywide by Bank of America, of R-G Crown by Fifth Third, and of Wachovia by Wells Fargo. These acquisitions are also tracked by the Federal Deposit Insurance Corporation (FDIC), and the history of each banking entity can be examined on the FDIC website.[3] Such facts may qualify as evidence of which the court may take judicial notice.[4] "A judicially noticed fact must be one not subject to reasonable dispute in that it is either (1) generally known within the territorial jurisdiction of the trial court or (2) capable of accurate and ready determination by resort to sources whose accuracy cannot reasonably be questioned."[5] A court may take judicial notice of facts without being requested, or may be required to take judicial notice once a party has supplied the proper request and information.[6]

The FDIC is an "independent agency of the federal government" that "preserves and promotes public confidence in the U.S. financial system by insuring deposits in banks and thrift institutions for at least $250,000; by identifying, monitoring and addressing risks to the deposit insurance funds; and by limiting the effect on the economy and the financial system when a bank or thrift institution fails."[7] The information from the FDIC website may therefore already be within the scope of the court's knowledge and recognition, or it is reasonable that such information be considered by the court to be a source that can "accurate[ly] and read[il]y" confirm the information and "whose accuracy cannot readily be questioned."[8] The bank may thereby prove its ownership of the loan by judicial notice; this is an instance where it's likely best not to exert much energy attempting to prove otherwise, except when it is questionable whether the successor-in-interest acquired the asset loan at issue.

In such a scenario, if you are simply trying to get in touch with the owner of the loan for settlement purposes, it should be sufficient to contact your servicer and submit your proposal. However,

---

3. *See* http://www2.fdic.gov/idasp/main.asp.
4. *See* Fed. R. Evid. 201.
5. Fed. R. Evid. 201(b).
6. *Id.* at (c)–(d).
7. http://www.fdic.gov/about/learn/symbol/index.html.
8. Fed. R. Evid. 201(c)–(d).

you should still make sure that your proposal is being routed to the correct department. If you are not receiving an adequate response and have not been directed to communicate only with the bank's foreclosure counsel, you may attempt to move up the bank's escalation matrix. This is usually internal information where the chains of command and individuals at each level of management are listed, together with their contact information. If you cannot obtain this information from the bank voluntarily, you may be able to obtain it through discovery. This is useful information that could lead to the dispute being resolved more efficiently and properly; sometimes the delay in resolving a case results from it being mishandled by employees who lack the training or knowledge that upper management may have. Banks will probably raise objections based on privilege in response to discovery requests for escalation matrices, but courts may look favorably upon such requests, as they may assist in narrowing the triable issues sooner and, hopefully, lead to a more prompt and amicable resolution of the case.

Loan Modifications

It seems there should be no reason to deny a loan solution to willing homeowners who can support monthly payments and will work as long and hard as necessary to save their home. Yet it is still happening left and right. A recent story in *The New York Times* relates that there are some real estate companies that are employed fulltime by Fannie Mae and Freddie Mac, reselling foreclosed properties.[9] These properties are often sold for less than 60 percent of what the homeowner owed. While this is a winning situation for the real estate companies and for the new buyers, it is not for the people who lose their homes and most likely cannot purchase another property because of their credit. Foreclosure has cut across all loan products, from subprime to, more recently, prime.

Loan modifications can be a solution that does not end with the bank obtaining a judgment of foreclosure, selling the house,

---

9. Binyamin Appelbaum, *Cost of Seizing Fannie and Freddie Surges for Taxpayers*, N.Y. TIMES, June 19, 2010.

and ousting the homeowners. However, the number of people who want loan modifications has been vastly greater than those who receive them:

> As of mid-December, HAMP had processed almost 520,000 permanent loan modifications. The panel estimated that by the time the program is finished, it will have prevented only 700,000 foreclosures overall—quite a contrast to the three million to four million modifications that the Treasury anticipated when it rolled out its plan. Up to 13 million foreclosures are expected to have occurred by 2012, the [Congressional Oversight Panel] said.[10]
>
> House Representative Brad Miller has recognized the inherent conflict of interest by having loan servicers have so much authority over whether a homeowner receives a loan modification or not, and urged "that loan servicers be separated from the institutions that hold a borrower's loan."[11] This is because, [a]s the report from the Congressional Oversight Panel noted, loan servicers can profit significantly by pushing borrowers into foreclosure. It gives the servicers more opportunities to keep charging lucrative fees and little incentive to seek a modification.[12]

As discussed, many borrowers must communicate with a servicer who is not the owner of the loan, but merely manages the loan on the owner's behalf. When the servicer is also the originator of the loan, theoretically more possibilities for loan modifications should exist, because the middleman and the servicing fees are cut out of the picture. Also, the borrowers would then be dealing with the party who has the authority to grant a modification. A servicer who is not the owner of the loan has no authority to grant a modification, and would probably have little incentive to convey a settlement offer from the borrower to the owner if, in doing so, it would cheat itself out of default servicing fees.

---

10. Gretchen Morgenson, *A Mortgage Nightmare's Happy Ending*, N.Y. Times, Dec. 25, 2010.

11. *Id.*

12. *Id.*

Though permanent loan solutions are still relatively rare, servicers will more commonly place a borrower on a "trial modification," "trial forbearance," or similar temporary plan. The arrangement requires the borrower to make several payments, often much larger than her or his original payment. The borrower is enticed to do this by the bank's representation that the borrower may be approved for a permanent loan modification at the end of the trial period. However, this plan often turns out to be a ploy on the bank's part to wring more money out of a desperate homeowner without any intention to end the foreclosure or reinstate the borrower's loan. Therefore, if the bank has been rejecting your payments but offers your client a trial modification, keep this possibility in mind. In deciding whether to accept the bank's offer of a trial solution, realize that the bank may still deny your client a permanent solution even if she makes all of the required trial payments. If your client loses the case, she may have to consider these payments as a loss, when the money could have been used for a more beneficial purpose. However, if your client makes the payments and is still denied, the court may order that the bank grant the homeowner a permanent modification over the bank's objections, as some courts have already done.[13]

Also be careful about signing any modification agreement prepared by the bank. Many settlement agreements drafted by the bank will attempt to use the settlement to issue a suspended sentence. The agreement might contain a forbearance or reduced payments for a certain term, and maybe purport to resolve all of the outstanding arrearage and interest. But these agreements may contain provisions stating that the borrower waives all defenses present or future to the foreclosure action, and that the borrower consents to judgment, releases all claims against the bank, etc. Especially if the agreement is not a full and complete settlement of the foreclosure action where both parties benefit, the option to proceed with the litigation may be a preferable alternative to signing such a contract of adhesion.

If the bank does attempt to have your client sign an unconscionable agreement, the court may hit the bank where it hurts, as did

---

13. PHH Mortgage Corp. v. Barker, 2010 Ohio 5061 (Ohio Ct. App. 2010); Emigrant Mortgage Co., Inc. v. Corcione, 28 Misc. 3d 161, 169–70 (N.Y. App. Div. 2010).

one New York court when a bank attempted to have homeowners sign a settlement agreement which forever stripped them of any defenses to foreclosure and branded them as financially insolvent.[14] Courts may not always hold banks accountable in the way that this particular court did, so a borrower should not count on the courts to save them from all bad agreements.

In this particular New York case, the homeowners had entered into an adjustable-rate mortgage in 2007 and had defaulted on their payments in 2008 due to loss of employment.[15] The homeowners strenuously attempted to reach an amicable resolution of the default with the bank, which had refused such relief and waited 14 months after the default before filing a foreclosure action.[16] The court saw no reason for the length of time between the default and the foreclosure filing other than for the bank to "indubitably increase the amount of interest Plaintiff could exact from Defendants."[17]

In reviewing the bank's motion for summary judgment, the court found greatly disturbing the terms of the loan, which provided for the interest rate to be increased annually and for the interest rate to be set at 18 percent upon default by the borrowers.[18] The court was familiar with the customs and practices in the mortgage-lending industry and found it was "a virtual certainty that Defendants were not afforded the opportunity to freely bargain and negotiate in reaching the operative terms that [were] subject to the Court's scrutiny," and that the loan documents were contracts of adhesion.[19]

When referred by the court to settlement conferences, over the "vociferous and inexplicable objections of Plaintiff's counsel,"[20] the bank presented a loan modification agreement that it alone had drafted in which it proposed to recoup the principal sum together with interest at $132.54 per diem for almost two years and almost

---

14. Emigrant Mortgage Co., Inc. v. Corcione, 28 Misc. 3d 161, 169–70 (N.Y. App. Div. 2010).

15. *Id.* at 162.

16. *Id.* at 162–63.

17. *Id.* at 163.

18. *Id.*

19. *Id.* at 164.

20. *Id.* at 163.

$20,000 in "other charges," which the bank's counsel initially refused to itemize for defense counsel.[21] Only after the court questioned the plaintiff about these "other charges" was it revealed that these charges included legal fees of almost $8,000 for a "paucity of services" and tax and insurance advances of $10,000 when the actual costs for these items were a fraction of that amount.[22]

Even more shocking to the court were the terms of the bank-proposed settlement agreement itself, which included inter alia:

1. Borrowers unconditionally, knowingly, voluntarily, intelligently, and after having obtained the advice of counsel or having been given ample opportunity to obtain the advise [sic] of counsel and declined to do so, waives any claim, counterclaim, right of recoupment, defenses, affirmative defenses or set-off of any kind or nature whatsoever with respect to the Existing Default, the Loan Documents, and/or the Indebtedness.[23]

2. Borrowers submit to the jurisdiction of the Court and confirm that all contractual and statutory conditions precedent to such foreclosure proceedings have been satisfied. . . . BORROWERS ACKNOWLEDGE THAT ALL PAYMENTS MADE UNDER THIS AGREEMENT ARE MADE WITHOUT PREJUDICE TO THE LOAN ACCELERATION OR THE PENDING FORECLOSURE PROCEEDINGS AND SHALL NOT CONSTITUTE A WAIVER OF ANY OF LENDER'S RIGHTS TO FORECLOSE.[24]

3. Emigrant shall, among other things, be immediately entitled, without any notice to the Borrowers, to exercise any and all remedies available to it and shall be entitled to collect all sums due under the Loan Documents as if this Agreement had not been made . . . the Borrowers shall have no right to cure said default, and Emigrant will be free to pursue all of

---

21. *Id.* at 165.
22. *Id.*
23. *Id.* at 165–66.
24. *Id.* at 166.

its rights and remedies under the Loan Documents and this Agreement, at law and at equity.[25]

4. [The Borrowers and all of their heirs, successors and assigns] . . . release[] and discharge[] the [Plaintiff and their heirs, successors and assigns] from . . . (a) any and all claims for violation of the Truth In Lending Act ("TILA"), 15 U.S.C. § 1601, et seq., or its implementing regulations; (b) any and all claims for unfair and/or deceptive trade practices; (c) any and all claims for consumer fraud or for fraudulent and/ or predatory lending practices; (d) any and all claims for attorney's fees and costs of any kind or nature, by statute or otherwise; (e) any and all claims that could have been asserted in any legal proceeding or action; and (f) any and all claims that are relating to, concerning, or underlying the Loan, and the brokering, closing, servicing or administration of the Loan.[26]

5. Borrowers hereby acknowledge, represent and warrant that if they cannot perform in accordance with the terms of this Agreement, they will never be able to perform in accordance with the Loan Documents, nor will they be able to reorganize under the provisions of the United States Bankruptcy Code or any similar law. Accordingly, in consideration of this Agreement and in recognition of Emigrant's willingness to enter into this Agreement, Borrowers hereby agree that if a petition in Bankruptcy is filed by or against them, as debtor and debtor-in-possession (if applicable), Borrowers hereby consent to immediate and unconditional relief from the automatic stay of 11 U.S.C. § 362 (the "Stay") in favor of Emigrant, waives their right to oppose a motion for relief from the Stay, waives the benefits of the Stay, and hereby admits and agrees that grounds to vacate the Stay to permit Emigrant to enforce its rights and remedies under this Agreement, the Loan Documents and/or any other documents executed in connection therewith exist and shall continue to exist, which grounds include, without limitation,

---

25. *Id.*
26. *Id.* at 166–67.

> the fact that Emigrant's interests in the Property cannot be adequately protected.[27]

The court was shocked and distressed by these provisions, especially the last, which "effectively attempt[ed] to deprive Defendants of any ability, now or at any future date, to act in a legitimate manner to save their home by invoking the protection of the United States Bankruptcy Code."[28] The court remarked that never before had it been presented with such a proposal, especially one "accompanied by absurd representations . . . that Defendants presently are and will forever be insolvent."[29]

Instead of complying with court settlement guidelines to "act and negotiate in good faith," the court found that the bank had instead "created a scenario whereby it is a virtual certainty that Defendants will ultimately be irreparably damaged and . . . gone to extraordinary lengths in an attempt to insulate itself from liability while at the same time ensuring that it will not sustain any pecuniary loss and that all cost will be borne by the Defendants."[30]

The court declared that "the conduct of Plaintiff in this matter has been over-reaching, shocking, willful and unconscionable, is wholly devoid of even so much as a scintilla of good faith and cannot be countenanced by this Court."[31] When the conduct of a party is "unconscionable, shocking or egregious," a court has the discretion to award punitive damages.[32] In light of the reprehensible conduct of the bank in this case, the court issued rulings that punished the bank and brought redemption and justice to the homeowners. The court ruled first that the bank's motion for summary judgment was denied and that it was forever barred from collecting any interest on the loan or legal fees for the almost two-year period in question, and that the homeowners' debt was determined to be no more than the principal balance.[33] Best of all, the court

---

27. *Id.* at 167.
28. *Id.*
29. *Id.* at 168.
30. *Id.* at 169.
31. *Id.*
32. *Id.*
33. *Id.* at 169–70.

ordered that the bank pay $100,000 in exemplary damages to the homeowners.[34]

The Power of the Media

Bank of America employees are mandated to "transfer callers from people like members of Congress, officials from regulatory agencies, attorneys general offices and the news media 'to your team or unit manager . . . no exceptions.'"[35] When the government or media talk, the banks listen. Often, media and the attendant public scrutiny have the effect of magically transforming a no-solution loan into a permanent solution loan. In January 2011, scrutiny of Bank of America from *The New York Times* caused the bank to transform one of their files previously "in the category of unavoidable foreclosure" to a permanent loan reinstatement.[36] The journalist on the story, Joe Nocera, calls this the "Heisenberg Journalism Principle," after the Heisenberg Uncertainty Principle, which "states that the process of observing subatomic particles," or banks, in this case, "affects their behavior."

The homeowner at the center of this and a previous story by Mr. Nocera was Lilla Roberts, a 73-year-old retired physical therapist. Bank of America had foreclosed on Ms. Roberts' home in the summer of 2010 and she was now facing eviction proceedings. Ms. Roberts then hired a public interest attorney who found instances of possible fraudulent paperwork indicating Bank of America may not even have had foreclosure rights on the loan. Bank of America had given Ms. Roberts three temporary forbearances, but they never led to a permanent modification. The bank kept telling this homeowner that a modification "was in the works" right up until it foreclosed on her house.

All this changed after Mr. Nocera wrote his first story about Ms. Roberts.[37] Eviction proceedings stopped, and Bank of America "did

---

34. *Id.* at 170.

35. Nelson D. Schwartz, *Voices of Foreclosure Speak Daily About Desperation and Misery*, N.Y. Times, Nov. 16, 2010.

36. Joe Nocera, *Shamed into Altering a Mortgage*, N.Y. Times, Jan. 21, 2011.

37. Joe Nocera, *A Happy Ending to a Raw, but Common, Tale*, N.Y. Times, Dec. 3, 2010.

what it should have done in the first place: investigate whether Ms. Roberts was a good candidate for a loan modification. And whaddya know? She was!"[38] The bank agreed to give Ms. Roberts a fixed-rate mortgage at 2 percent, 40 years, and payments of $1,140 per month.[39] This saved Ms. Roberts from having to move to a shelter as she feared she would have to do. However, the modification included $12,000 in unexplained fees and a large balloon payment at the end which included almost $50,000 in accumulated interest. Ms. Roberts' attorney refused to accept the agreement with these terms and took the matter before the court.

Judge Duane Hart began by throwing out the mysterious $12,000 in fees, but ultimately permitted the balloon payment to remain. An attorney for Bank of America noticed Mr. Nocera in the courtroom and said to the judge that while he felt the modification plan was "'excellent,' his side was 'not comfortable discussing it publicly.' The judge responded angrily. 'We do things out in the open in this courtroom,'" and then summoned a court reporter so that not only would the modification plan be discussed publicly, the discussions "would be transcribed for posterity."

The bank's attorneys then stated the terms of the loan modification. Judge Hart responded that "[t]his is consistent with what I've been asking the banks to do ever since this crisis started. . . . And you'll do this for everyone even when *The New York Times* is not writing about it?" The bank's attorney "replied, lamely, 'There are different circumstances in every case.'"

A local South Florida paper has also come to the aid of homeowners, also grappling with Bank of America, whose house had gone to sale and who were facing eviction. The home went to foreclosure sale when the homeowners—who were housing extended family and grandchildren—were under the impression that they were under a loss mitigation plan with the bank.[40] Bank of America claimed that it was unable to stop the sale of the property in time.[41] Of course,

---

38. Joe Nocera, *supra* note 36.

39. *Id.*

40. Harriet Johnson Brackey, *Foreclosure: Even a Loan Modification Won't Always Stop a Foreclosure*, SUN-SENTINEL (Fort Lauderdale, Fla.), Oct. 25, 2010.

41. *Id.*

every case is different, but this seems to be a dubious claim. It is perfectly common for a plaintiff to file last-minute motions to cancel sales, and for those motions to be granted. Each court usually has specific procedures governing how it considers motions to cancel sales, taking into account that many plaintiffs do not realize a need to cancel a sale until hours beforehand.

Fortunately for this particular family, after the *Sun-Sentinel* had written about their home being sold out from under them when they thought they had a loan modification in place, Bank of America reversed the sale and placed the family back onto a loss mitigation plan.[42] Of course, this solution may not have been so easy to obtain if a third party had purchased the property at the sale and it had not gone back to the bank. A third party, usually purchasing a foreclosure property at a bargain, would not be so willing to give up its deal.

One Pennsylvania couple, Robert and Amy Ahleman, were also luckier than most, largely due to the aid of *The New York Times*.[43] The couple's long fight to save their home, though eventually successful, involved seemingly fruitless pleas for help from their bank, a bankruptcy filing, and hysterically crying to the bank over the phone. Ultimately, it seems that the primary thing that caused the homeowners to receive any relief was a call by *The New York Times* to their servicer, Litton Loan Servicing, to "ask why the Ahlemans' loan was stalled."[44] Only then did the servicer come forth with a proposal for a permanent loan solution: "[A reduction in interest] on their first mortgage from a variable rate of 9.3 percent to a fixed rate of 4.59 percent [and a waiver of] $38,332 in arrears on their loan, which included late fees and legal costs that had accumulated while the loan was in default."[45]

You may wish to network with members of the media and propose an offer where the media will receive something in return for favorable coverage of your client and her case, such as volunteer

---

42. Harriet Johnson Brackey, *Foreclosure: Shamjis Keep Their Home*, SUN-SENTINEL (Fort Lauderdale, Fla.), Oct. 27, 2010.

43. Gretchen Morgenson, *Loan Modification Ends a Mortgage Nightmare*, N.Y. TIMES, Dec. 26, 2010.

44. *Id.*

45. *Id.*

legal services if your local bar association so permits. Some newspapers endeavor to educate their readers as much as possible about the foreclosure process and how to avoid foreclosure themselves. You could offer to contribute articles or other material to the paper, which would help supply such information (while being careful to not offer general legal advice). Also, if you are able to offer pro bono services to distressed homeowners, the media may be interested in helping you promote such an event, as this may increase the media's viewership, and the media in turn may give favorable attention to your cases. In Florida, for example, one attorney whose cases are frequently covered by the media and who is largely credited with revealing the robo-signing crisis recently held a workshop where he selected 22 cases for pro bono foreclosure defense representation.[46]

Even if your local newspaper or other media does not cover your client's case, you can still incorporate news articles outlining successful loan solutions into arguments presented before the court, Though newspaper articles and other media sources are generally considered secondary authority and less persuasive than statutes and case law, many foreclosure news articles outline facts and stories that have not yet been considered or determined by the courts or legislature. Many courts are aware that banks fear bad press and that the media has helped influence the banks to grant homeowners favorable results; one judge asked a bank in open court whether they would help other borrowers as they helped the one before the court without the coverage of *The New York Times*.[47] Draw parallels in court between your client's case and a borrower who was aided by the media in obtaining a loan solution. Such arguments may well be persuasive to the court, which may have the power to order a loan solution for your client or ask the bank to justify why it has refused relief to your client when it granted relief to a similarly situated borrower.

Some homeowners employ independent efforts to promote a bank's wrongdoing, as a mother of two (including a son who is bipolar) has done by posting two signs—"one 25 feet by 18 feet and

---

46. Diane C. Lade, *South Florida Foreclosure Defense Firm Will Litigate 22 Cases for Free*, SUN-SENTINEL (Fort Lauderdale, Fla.), Feb. 7, 2011.

47. Joe Nocera, *Shamed into Altering a Mortgage*, N.Y. TIMES, Jan. 21, 2011.

another 15 feet by 20 feet"—announcing "The Bank is trying to steal my home, again" for all to see.[48] This borrower's efforts to promote her plight obviously succeeded in capturing the attention of the media. Ms. Luznar stated that she was current on her mortgage payments pursuant to a loan modification agreement executed in September 2008, when her March 2009 payment was rejected with a letter from the bank alleging that Ms. Luznar was now six months behind. The mortgage company acknowledged having received the payments but was "unclear" how the payments had been applied, according to the article.

Home Affordable Modification Program (HAMP)

If your client is eligible for HAMP, this is another loss mitigation option to pursue with the bank. President Obama introduced the Home Affordable Modification Program (HAMP) on March 4, 2009, whose goal was to reach "up to 3 to 4 million at-risk homeowners."[49] Loans eligible for HAMP are described as "first-lien mortgage loans originated on or before January 1, 2009, where the loan was secured by a one-to-four-unit property, one unit of which was the borrower's primary residence, and with the unpaid current."[50] The goal of HAMP is to reduce a borrower's monthly mortgage payment to 31 percent of the borrower's gross monthly income.[51] A servicer can earn up to $4,500 for completing a loan modification and keeping a borrower current on a modification over a three-year period, but the servicer is required to take the incentive money in lieu of, not in addition to, servicing contract charges, and it is unclear whether servicers in general have any greater financial incentive to complete modifications instead of receiving their usual contract charges.[52]

---

48. Arlene Satchell, *Pines Homeowner Protesting Bank Foreclosure*, Sun-Sentinel (Fort Lauderdale, Fla.), Mar. 4, 2011.

49. Jean Braucher, *Financial Products: Humpty Dumpty and the Foreclosure Crisis: Lessons Learned from the Lackluster First Year of the Home Affordable Modification Program (HAMP)*, 52 Ariz. L. Rev. 727, 748 (Fall 2010).

50. *Id.*

51. *Id.* at 749.

52. *Id.* at 752–53.

As of December 2009, 3.4 million borrowers were reported as being eligible for HAMP, with 940,000 in trial modifications and 67,000 in permanent modifications, just about 2 percent of the total borrowers eligible.[53] Twenty-five percent of the trial modifications were expected to convert to permanent status by March 2010.[54]

New York courts, which have been especially vocal in expressing the anger and frustration felt by so many in the foreclosure crisis, have demonstrated a lack of tolerance for banks that arbitrarily refuse to complete a HAMP modification.[55] In one case, a police officer who took a second job to pay the mortgage, and his wife, who was unable to work due to health reasons, contacted the bank to seek a loan modification.[56] At that time, the homeowners were not in default but feared they could be.[57] The wife testified that bank representatives told her that she would not be eligible for a modification unless she were three months late in her mortgage payments, and that she would have to default in order to qualify.[58]

The wife then followed this advice, made a down payment, provided a hardship letter and other documentation requested by the bank in furtherance of a modification, but the bank kept losing paperwork and the borrower had to constantly refax information to them.[59] Ultimately, the homeowners were notified by the bank that they qualified for HAMP and at first were told that they would have to make three monthly payments in the amount of $1,955.49 each, which the borrowers did.[60] After these first three payments were made, the bank advised that the trial period would have to be reset and reduced the monthly payments slightly.[61]

However, the day after the wife accepted the first modification in writing, the bank filed the foreclosure action.[62] The borrowers

---

53. *Id.* at 760.

54. *Id.* at 759.

55. Wells Fargo Bank, N.A. v. Meyers, 2010 N.Y. slip op. 20510 (N.Y. App. Div. 2010).

56. *Id.* at *1.

57. *Id.*

58. *Id.*

59. *Id.*

60. *Id.*

61. *Id.*

62. *Id.*

nonetheless kept on making all the payments demanded by the bank under the first two modifications.[63] However, after all this, the bank sent the homeowners letters stating that they were being denied for HAMP relief because their mortgage payment was greater than or equal to 31 percent of their monthly gross income, and that the investor on the loan had declined the modification.[64] Even still, during a court settlement conference, the bank proposed a new modification period where the monthly payments would now be $2,554, but the borrowers said they could not afford anything higher than the original amount of $1955.49.[65]

The court held a hearing to determine whether the bank had denied HAMP relief to the borrowers in bad faith.[66] The loss mitigation manager who testified for the bank had no personal knowledge about the borrower's case and testified that she reviewed the file for the first time the week of the hearing.[67] The bank witness could not explain why the bank had commenced the foreclosure action one day after the borrowers accepted the first modification, or how the bank arrived at the calculation that the homeowners' mortgage payment was equal or less to 31 percent of their gross monthly income.[68] As for the investor's purported denial of the modification, the court held that the investor, Freddie Mac, was not a party to the litigation, not the party seeking to foreclose the mortgage, and therefore such denial could not justify withholding HAMP relief from the homeowners.[69] The homeowners had also "complied with all the requirements of the trial modification and [had] appeared at all the conferences in [the] action."[70] In light of the evidence, the court ordered specific performance of the original modification agreement proposed by the defendants and dismissal of the foreclosure action.[71]

---

63. *Id.*
64. *Id.*
65. *Id.* at *2.
66. *Id.*
67. *Id.*
68. *Id.* at **2–3.
69. *Id.* at *3.
70. *Id.*
71. *Id.*

Chapter 9

Loss Mitigation

Waiver of Deficiency Judgments

A deficiency judgment is what a bank will often seek when it sells the property and the proceeds aren't enough to pay off the foreclosed loan. The bank will then pursue the former homeowner for the difference between what the home was sold for and what the borrower owed.

Unless there is a specific, binding agreement that prevents the bank from pursuing the homeowner for a deficiency judgment, the bank may very well do so. As noted in an *Orlando-Sentinel* column by Beth Kassab, a new collection industry focusing on recouping deficiency judgment funds is emerging.[1] Foreclosure attorney Matt Englett believes that in the coming years, banks will sell off these debts to collection companies, which will aggressively pursue the judgment funds.[2] Time is also on the banks' side in pursuing a deficiency judgment, as they have five years to seek the judgment and 20 years to collect.[3]

If your client is not seeking to keep her property, a good foreclosure defense settlement agreement will always include an agreement

---

1. Beth Kassab, *Walking Away From Home Isn't Risk-Free*, ORLANDO SENTINEL, June 2, 2010.

2. *Id.*

3. *Id.*

by the bank to waive any deficiency amount against her. If the bank does prepare a proposed settlement agreement, be sure to carefully review it and make corrections and revisions to it to protect your client's rights. Your client should not be worse off than she was before the settlement. Be sure that your client is not waiving all of her defenses to foreclosure if the settlement fails; that the bank cannot still pursue your client for a deficiency judgment; that the settlement agreement, if followed by your client, reinstates her loan, etc. It might be good to add an arbitration clause so that if there are future problems with the loan, the bank cannot file another foreclosure action at whim. Make sure the parties exchange mutual releases that resolve and dismiss the current foreclosure action. You may not be able to have the bank release all future claims against the homeowner in the event she defaults on the loan at some point down the road, but you can have the settlement agreement provide that the parties must exhaust alternative dispute resolution methods first.

Deed in Lieu of Foreclosure

A deed in lieu of foreclosure involves the tender of the subject property deed back to the lender in return for settlement of the case. The bank will often want to know whether there are any other liens against the property which would prevent it from receiving marketable title. If the title is clear and the bank is reasonable, a deed-in-lieu may be a better option for a homeowner who is not seeking to retain the property. A homeowner who wants to obtain a deed-in-lieu should obtain his own title report, which he can present to the bank in support of his proposal. Common sense would dictate that this would be a win-win situation in most cases; the bank gets to recover the house, and the borrowers can salvage their credit a bit and move on with their life.

Short Sale

A short sale is frequently sought as a solution to foreclosure by those homeowners who are willing to give up the property; they can sell it with the only consideration usually being release from the mortgage debt and any deficiency, and hopefully a better outcome on their credit report. A short-sale transaction usually involves a bank-approved sale of the property for less than what is owed on the mortgage. This procedure is often sought when the borrowers are "upside-down" in their loan, or when they owe more money than the current market value of the property. This is the case for many homeowners today who bought during the peak of the market, and now the value of the property is severely depressed from its original amount.

It can be just as difficult to obtain bank approval for a short sale as it is to gain any other kind of loss mitigation assistance. Many banks will simply refer a borrower or attorney inquiring about short-sale approval to their general customer service number, or a "loss mitigation" department number, which can be equally unresponsive and ineffective. Sometimes borrowers will simply proceed with a short sale without bank approval, but this approach is risky, as the bank still reserves the right to pursue the borrowers for any deficiency between the sale price of the home and the outstanding mortgage debt.

Ideally, borrowers who wish to conduct a short sale should, either personally or through their attorney, present to the bank a copy of a purchase contract between the homeowners and a buyer, as well as a HUD-1 Settlement Statement showing the amount that will be distributed to the bank at closing (a sample purchase contract and HUD-1 Settlement Statement are included on the form CD). The bank will then have an opportunity to either approve the amount or counter the offer, at which point the borrower can attempt to renegotiate the deal with the buyer.

The borrower should not close on the short-sale deal without obtaining a full release and waiver of deficiency from the bank. Otherwise, the bank will still be able to file lawsuits against the borrowers relating to the subject loan and seek a deficiency judgment against the borrowers. In a short sale, just as with any settlement, the homeowner must obtain the protection of mutual releases, including an agreement by the bank to waive any deficiency, acceptance of the short-sale fund as full and final settlement of the matter, and no negative reporting on the borrower's credit report. The borrower should compel the bank to report to the credit bureaus that the debt has been paid in full, if possible. At the very least, the credit report should reflect a short sale and not a foreclosure, so that one of the borrower's main objectives for seeking a short sale in the first place is obtained: the less severe repercussion of a short sale on a credit report as opposed to a foreclosure.

Conciliation Conference

Conciliation conferences are another alternative dispute resolution tool. They are often a less formal, less regimented version of mediation, as they are often conducted telephonically in Florida cases, but they may also be conducted in person or in court, as with a program devised by the city of Philadelphia, Pennsylvania. A conciliation conference is one component of the three-pronged system utilized in Philadelphia's Residential Mortgage Foreclosure Diversion Program.[4] This program assists families facing foreclosure by offering them a conciliation conference conducted as:

> [A] special court hearing where proposals to cure the mortgage default are presented to the lender's attorney and a judge *pro tem*. The homeowner is represented by a housing counselor and if available a *pro bono* attorney. In many cases, lenders may agree to loan modifications or the mortgage may be purchased and restructured under the Homeowners' Equity Recovery Opportunity (HERO)[5] Loan Program.[6]

The Philadelphia program also entails a Door-to-Door Outreach designed to raise homeowner awareness of the program. The outreach is extremely beneficial to discouraged homeowners who may have stopped opening their mail. The outreach teams have knocked

---

4. http://www.phila.gov/rda/residential%20mortgage%20foreclsure%20diversion%20program.htm.

5. "HERO Expansion is a mortgage program designed to support neighborhood stabilization by providing first mortgage financing to encourage first-time homebuyers and existing homeowners to purchase and/or purchase and rehabilitate foreclosed or abandoned properties including properties conveyed by deed in lieu of foreclosure or short sale." http://www.chfa.org/Homeownership/for%20Homebuyers/Homebuyer%20Mortgage%20%20Programs/HomeownersEquityRecoveryOpportunityLoanProgram.aspx.

6. *Id.*

on more than 2,400 doors since May 2008. Finally, the program provides a "Save Your Home Philly Hotline" staffed by lawyers and paralegals, which provides homeowners with more information about the program and schedules an initial face-to-face meeting between the borrower and a housing counselor. The Philadelphia program has resulted in many success stories, including forbearance agreements, decreased loan interest rates, and reduction of mortgage payments by hundreds of dollars per month. "Of the 2,331 households who have participated in a Conciliation Conference, 2,270 have averted foreclosure."[7]

In the 12th Judicial Circuit of Florida for DeSoto, Manatee, and Sarasota counties, banks must comply with the requirements of the Homestead Foreclosure Conciliation Program.[8] As the name indicates, the program is available only for homeowners who have filed for homestead property tax exemptions. The administrative order requires the bank to serve on the homeowner, together with the summons and complaint, a Notice to Homeowners Facing Foreclosure, which advises homeowners of the conciliation conference program. In the conciliation conference, the parties shall "have an open and frank discussion about the alleged default and [] consider realistic alternatives to foreclosure." The order further requires that:

> b. At the Conciliation Telephone Conference the lender shall arrange for the participation of knowledgeable persons, including attorneys, loss mitigation and others who can confirm the amount and type of default, and who are authorized to make binding commitments regarding alternatives to litigation, including refinancing, partial forgiveness of debt, approving sales to third parties, clarifying the amount required to reinstate or discharge the loan, requesting deeds in lieu of foreclosure, implementing procedures for the protection of the premises, and establishing a mutually agreeable date for relinquishing possession.

---

7. http://www.phila.gov/rda/residential%20mortgage%20foreclsure%20diversion%20program.htm.

8. Administrative Order Establishing Circuit-Wide Homestead Foreclosure Conciliation Program dated Nov. 25, 2008, http://12circuit.state.fl.us/LinkClick.aspx?fileticket=yaRGUDW%2BsWg%3D&tabid=114&mid=546.

Sanctions are imposed on banks that do not comply with this order in good faith. You need to find out what the conciliation requirements, if any, are in your jurisdiction. Even if a conciliation conference is not required, you could request one from the bank or court (if need be) in place of or in addition to a mediation.

Mediation

Mediations are an often effective alternative dispute resolution tool whereby parties may amicably resolve a dispute and enter a confidential written agreement that embodies the terms of their settlement. The mediation conference is managed and led by a neutral third party who acts as the mediator. A mediation typically begins with the parties, attorneys, and mediator in one room, where the parties may make opening statements similar to those made at trial. After these opening remarks, the parties and attorneys will often separate into "caucuses," with the mediator traveling in between. The mediator will convey the parties' offers and responses to each other. To facilitate settlement, the mediator may offer hypothetical situations if the case were to proceed to trial, strengths of the opposing party's case, and reasons why it would be beneficial for the parties to settle that day instead of leaving their fate to a judge or jury.

Mediations are now required by the courts in most foreclosure actions. Some court-ordered mediation programs are enjoying marked success, such as that implemented by Nevada legislation, which in its first full year kept nearly half its participants in their home and avoided foreclosure in nearly nine out of 10 cases.[9] The Nevada program credits much of its success to its requirement that bank representatives with full and complete authority to settle the case meet with borrowers in good faith.[10]

Other jurisdictions, such as Florida, now have the same requirement, but conversely have a dismal rate of success or lack thereof. According to a recent Florida report, only "a tiny fraction—6 percent—of eligible borrowers reached an agreement with their bank

---

9. Oskar Garcia, *Nevada's Foreclosure Mediation Kept Many In Home*, SEATTLE TIMES, Jan. 12, 2011.

10. *Id.*

as a result of mediation."[11] Mediations have been ordered by the Florida Supreme Court in virtually all new residential foreclosure actions. On December 28, 2009, the Florida Supreme Court entered a model administrative order to be adopted statewide governing a new foreclosure mediation program to help increase their success rate.[12] Among other things, the model order provides that all newly filed foreclosure actions against a homestead residence shall be referred to mediation no later than 120 days after commencement of the action. The order also provides that "only Florida Supreme Court-certified circuit civil mediators specially trained in residential mortgage foreclosure matters may be assigned to mediate cases referred to a managed mediation program." Therefore, only specially trained and certified mediators may preside over a managed mediation service. However, if the parties and court agree, any individual may serve as a mediator. The Florida Supreme Court has promulgated a list of mediators certified to handle foreclosure cases. Each case must have a court-appointed liaison as the go-between for the borrowers and lender. The liaison will provide an electronic database whereby the parties may post documents for each other's review.

However, many banks are not complying with the December 28, 2009, order and are "refusing to provide court-mandated documents showing they own the loan and its net value, or are filing faulty paperwork," thwarting thousands of mediations.[13] Borrowers who participate in these mediation programs are denied relief if they fail to comply with court procedures, but if banks violate the procedures they have not suffered the same consequences.[14] Borrowers are entitled to receive a "payment history, current appraisal of the property, the bank's estimate of the mortgage loan's present

---

11. Beth Kassab, *Foreclosure Mediation Helps Few So Far,* SUN-SENTINEL (Fort Lauderdale, Fla.), Jan. 13, 2011.

12. http://www.floridasupremecourt.org/pub_info/documents/AOSC09-54_Foreclosures.pdf.

13. Diane C. Lade, *Lawyers Say They're Forced to Cancel Mediations When Lenders Hold Back Disclosures,* SUN-SENTINEL (Fort Lauderdale, Fla.), Mar. 2, 2011.

14. *Id.* Naturally, excluding the banks from the mediation programs would not punish them, as many banks are seeking to avoid the mediation requirement anyway and would find excusal from mediation to be good news.

net value, and documentary evidence that the bank owns and holds the mortgage note" prior to the mediation.[15] Equal access to these documents by all parties can be critical to a successful settlement, as the numbers can determine whether the borrowers are eligible for the Home Affordable Modification Program (HAMP) or other possible solutions.[16]

The Mediation Bank Representative

The bank will usually want to dictate which representative will appear for the mediation. Although the courts have generally ordered that a lender representative at mediation must have authority to approve any solution, often the representative may not have true authority, or may not have all information with her necessary to finalize a settlement. A particular challenge presented in foreclosure mediations is obtaining a bank representative with authority to settle. Therefore, you should request that the investor be present in person for the mediation, even if you have to take the matter up with a court and present a motion for mediation requesting this specific relief.

Sometimes, the plaintiff in the foreclosure action will be the same entity as the originator of the loan. For example, Bank of America may generate a mortgage in-house, which means it is also the investor. However, Bank of America (or BAC Home Loans Servicing) may be merely the loan servicer, which means it is managing the loan on behalf of the true investor (often the plaintiff in the foreclosure action). It is crucial to ensure that whoever appears at a settlement conference has full authority to settle. Otherwise, a loan servicer may appear at a mediation and state that she or he does not have authority to agree to any solution that day because investor approval is required. A bank representative may not always state directly that they do not have full settlement authority, because that may indicate they have not mediated in good faith, which could be grounds for court sanctions. If your local jurisdiction has not already ordered that the bank representative have full and complete authority to settle, you should seek such an order from the court. Request that the court order that the bank have all authority and

---

15. *Id.*
16. *Id.*

resources (i.e., access to their case management system, laptop, full familiarity with the loan,[17] etc.) to consider all possible loss mitigation options, whether permanent or temporary, including reinstatement, forbearance, principal or payment reduction, short sale, deed-in-lieu, cash for keys, or any other solution proposed at the mediation.

Also, the homeowner should make every effort to require the bank to appear at the mediation in person. It is true that if a foreclosure judgment is entered against the homeowner, the travel costs incurred by the lender to attend the mediation may be assessed against the homeowner. However, these costs are minor compared with the overall principal balance, costs, and attorney's fees, which are included in final judgments anyway. There is a much greater chance for amicable agreements to be reached at mediation when all parties appear in person. Everyone will be able to meet face to face and is more likely to give the mediation the necessary time and attention. Also, it is much easier for someone to walk away from a mediation if he or she is on the phone. If the parties invest the time and energy to attend the mediation, the results are likely to be better. However, seek a court order that requires the bank to bring all documents, information, and computer access that might be needed to review and approve a solution.

Preparing for the Mediation

In the foreclosure setting, groundwork must be done beforehand to increase the chances of a successful mediation. You should contact the bank and obtain a list of all documents and information that the bank must receive prior to the mediation, such as loss mitigation applications, financial statements, bank records, tax returns, proposed or executed contracts, and so forth. Then you and the borrower should complete any forms and obtain all necessary information and furnish all requested documents and information to the bank as quickly as

---

17. Thorough and complete familiarity with the loan by both parties is essential for an effective mediation. Many courts have ordered that a bank representative have full and complete authority to settle at the mediation, but not necessarily full and complete familiarity with the loan. If your court has not implemented such a requirement, request it.

possible. In some cases, the parties may be able to hold an informal settlement conference over the phone prior to the mediation, often known as a conciliation conference. As always, the borrower must continue to follow up with the bank to make sure that the bank has received all documents and has everything it needs to offer a solution on the day of the mediation.

Many firms representing banks are attempting to push a foreclosure case to summary judgment and sale as quickly as possible. Do not let your case be treated like just another one in the mill. Insist on every single one of your client's rights. You may wish to hire a seasoned and experienced mediator who will pay attention to the details of your case. Investigate the overall success rate of the court mediation program in your area; it is certainly worthwhile if it is successful, like Nevada's, but if it suffers from a low settlement rate, you may want to explore an independent mediation. The right mediator can make all the difference. While it is true that no mediator can force a party to accept any settlement proposal, the right intermediary will have the proper knowledge, professionalism, and diplomacy to present each side with the strengths and weaknesses of their case and keep advocating settlement in an effective way. Conversely, a court-ordered mediation may not be as successful, because the conferences are being conducted in such bulk that, just like the court foreclosure filings, the main goal of the mediators is to get the cases pushed through quickly rather than helping carefully craft an agreement that is in the best interests of the respective parties.

If you are in an area where the court program still has a low success rate, seek the court's permission, if necessary, to use a different mediator. The court may ask your client to pay for it, or for at least half of the costs, if you are not using a program that is free of charge to the borrower, as some jurisdictions have now ordered mandatory mediation in residential foreclosure cases, with mediation costs to be borne by the banks.[18] In such court programs, borrowers may automatically qualify for a free mediation if they reside in the subject property or it is their homestead residence. The borrowers, of course, need to cooperate with the efforts of any court

---

18. http://www.floridasupremecourt.org/pub_info/documents/AOSC09-54_Foreclosures.pdf.

liaisons to reach out to them, to collect necessary paperwork from the borrowers, and to coordinate the mediation.

But if your client has the financial means to hire a mediator who will give your case the proper attention, this may be a worthwhile investment. Homeowners should seek a mediator whom they trust and who is known to be effective in facilitating solutions between banks and homeowners. Some jurisdictions will provide lists on their websites of mediators who have obtained a certification or approval from the courts to mediate foreclosure cases.[19] The website Avvo.com now lists and rates attorneys nationwide, and mediation is one of the categories provided by Avvo. An interesting feature of Avvo is that it permits you to pose questions to attorneys (and doctors), which is beneficial, as the attorney can promote her business and the prospective client can better weigh her options. Avvo is criticized by some who, for example do not agree with its method of rating attorneys. However, it is useful to consumers as another tool to obtain opinions about the quality of services a mediator may offer, and a shopper on Avvo may also determine the level of mediators' experience in their listed fields and how much mediation and foreclosure experience they have. Avvo also endeavors to list any disciplinary action against attorneys, but such information should also be cross-checked with the appropriate bar association.

You may also inquire with your local courts or bar association as to recommendations in selecting a mediator. Of course, there is no magic formula in selecting the right mediator. Some jurisdictions do not even require that a mediator be an attorney at all, or even have any formal training.[20] A layperson may even be able to obtain similar or better results than a professional, since mediation is more about diplomacy, people skills, and problem-solving than it is about arguing a case. But no matter whom you choose, you should exercise care to select a mediator who will give the mediation the time and attention it deserves, remain impartial, and help bridge differences between the parties.

---

19. http://www.ninthcircuit.org/programs-services/foreclosures/Downloads/Mediators-Osceola%20County.pdf; http://www.supremecourt.ohio.gov/JCS/disputeResolution/foreclosure/FAQ.asp; http://www.ord.uscourts.gov/alternative-dispute-resolution/volunteer-mediator-panel.

20. *See* FLA. R. CIV. P. 1.720(f)(1)(B).

In a case of mine that began in 2005, relations had unfortunately soured between myself and opposing counsel almost from the very beginning. We were ordered to mediation in 2007, which ended in an impasse. During the course of the case the first judge denied summary judgment to both parties; the case proceeded to trial, but a mistrial was declared because discovery issues were still outstanding. Almost immediately after the trial, the first judge retired. Nearly a year and a half later, we set a second summary judgment motion for hearing before the successor judge, who granted it. However, the issue of attorney's fees and costs payable to us was still highly contested. I scheduled a hearing on my motion for entry of final judgment, but the other side, in his cross-examination of our expert witness on fees, was delving into every detail of my fee affidavit. The time allotted for the hearing was soon extinguished, and the judge ordered the parties to mediation for a second time so that we could attempt to resolve the fees and costs dispute.

My co-counsel, who had only been on the case for six months, agreed to cover the mediation for me; I had a feeling that he would have a much better chance of resolving it than I would due to the history between opposing counsel and myself. Neither of us held out a lot of hope that it would be resolved due to opposing counsel's assertions that he intended to appeal the judgment and drag the case out for years longer, though it had now been over five years since the case had been filed.

However, our mediator, appointed by the judge, proved to be a very kindly, professional, and knowledgeable attorney who had been practicing for almost 40 years. He told me that he preferred to have parties to a case begin mediation at 10 a.m. and have the whole day free. He said that settlements more often occur if there is no arbitrary time limit for the mediation, because the parties do not feel that the negotiations have to switch off at a certain point. The mediator also said that he discouraged the use of opening statements, because they often put parties more on guard and in a combative stance at the beginning of the mediation, instead of letting the mediator set the tone.

I spoke with my clients and co-counsel by phone during part of the mediation, and my co-counsel shared my impression of the mediator. Of course, none of us knew what he said to opposing counsel, but the mediation was not over right away. As time drew on we saw that our cynicism about a second mediation was maybe not so appropriate; offers and counteroffers kept being exchanged. My co-counsel called me late in the evening to ask my position on another counteroffer and told me to stand by. Minutes later, the case had settled more than five years after inception.

You never really know what the outcome of any litigation is going to be, including the mediation that often goes along with it. However, the right mediator, who is good at diffusing situations, whom everyone respects, who brings the right knowledge to the table and, of course, gives your case the time and analysis required, may stand a better chance of settling your case than a rushed, volume-oriented mediator.

Therefore, as soon as you start to consider mediation, begin researching prospective mediators as soon as possible and, if feasible, reach an agreement with opposing counsel on the chosen mediator. Ascertain whether you are permitted to speak with the mediator without the opposing party present. Communicate with the mediator in an appropriate manner regarding his or her requirements and recommendations for preparation, and whether you need to bring any documents or other materials to the mediation. Also make sure you understand and comply with the mediator's payment procedures. Many private mediators charge from $250 to $400 per hour and ask that each party pay 50 percent of the total fee. The mediator usually expects to receive payment on the day of the mediation. Sometimes, as part of the mediation settlement, you may ask that the opposing party pay for the entire mediation, as we did in our case.

Mediating in Good Faith

Some red flags have recently been raised in relation to banks and mediation: whether banks have attended mediation when required, have been mediating in good faith, and whether the bank representative who attends actually has full authority to accept any settlement proposal made. Some banks may not want to tie themselves down to any mediation agreement because it can actually create more of a liability for them. They may give the appearance of complying with court directives only to the extent needed to avoid sanctions, but may not be mediating in good faith at all, or may refuse to consider that an agreement made at mediation is final. Some banks will not want to have to agree to any written agreement, because a mediation agreement often imposes tasks to be completed by both parties by certain deadlines, and the banks often do not want to open themselves to that kind of accountability and liability. Yet it can be difficult to prove that a bank representative did not mediate in good faith or have full and complete authority to settle, unless a bank representative lets something to that effect slip, as they sometimes do.

Agreements reached at mediation can include specific actions, such the submission of more documents from the borrower to the bank by a certain deadline; then the banks must do what they agreed to do at the mediation, such as reinstate the loan, complete the final review for a loss mitigation program, etc. The problem is that the mediation agreement may create an illusory promise on the part of the bank, because if it does not follow through later, it can blame the borrower for not providing the additional documents, or later say that the borrower still did not qualify for the program he or she was approved for at the mediation. The banks often hold allegiance to their internal guidelines first and foremost and to the law and court procedures second, even if they have been issued a direct order. A gargantuan bank does not face the same accountability that its homeowner opponent does.

It may be possible to prove the lack of the bank representative's full authority to settle if you ask whether your client could receive a deed in lieu of foreclosure and the bank representative does not have all information available to consider and determine such request right there at the mediation. This is why you should obtain a court order directing the bank representative to have a laptop available at the mediation that can grant access to all the programs necessary for him or her to determine any settlement request with full authority.

Court Enforcement of Mediation Requirements

If the bank representative does not attend the mediation, is not fully familiar with the case, and does not have full and complete authority to settle, you should consider filing a motion for sanctions. Many courts also provide for sanctions if any party fails to appear for a mandatory mediation. Mediations frequently fail to proceed because the bank has failed to appear. In such an instance, a motion for sanctions would be appropriate; there is always the chance that the case could have settled at mediation, and the non-appearing party has wasted court resources by missing this important settlement opportunity.

Again, sometimes the bank representative will appear at mediation but lack the full and complete authority to settle the case, as most jurisdictions require now. It is purposeless to hold mediation between parties who do not hold equal authority to settle the case. By now most people know that the responsibility to handle different aspects of foreclosure cases is fragmented into numerous departments at the bank. The bank should know the most appropriate department and representative to send to the mediation who will wield full settlement authority, whether it be for a short sale, deed-in-lieu, waiver of deficiency, reinstatement, etc. As mediations are confidential settlement discussions, you usually cannot record what is said. It is up to you whether you wish to continue with the mediation once you realize that the bank does not have full and complete authority to settle. Such mediations often end in an impasse anyway, because the bank is not mediating in good faith by not having the appropriate representative there, and demonstrates a lack of interest in amicable settlement. There is still a chance that a settlement could be reached in such a situation, but your client may not have the full range of options on the table needed to select the best solution.

Therefore, you will need to seek court relief if the bank has failed to comply with the court's mediation order or requirements. Obtain a certificate of noncompliance from the mediator, if possible, and use this or any other available evidence in support of your motion, keeping in mind any considerations of confidentiality. You may request that another mediation be conducted at the bank's expense, that the order specify and reiterate the requirements with which the bank must comply prior to and at the mediation, and sanctions that will result if it fails to obey the order. The court may even issue sanctions for the bank's disobedience at the first mediation, without the need of a second mediation or a chance for the bank to redeem itself. Examples of sanctions you could request might be those proscribed for discovery violations:

(A) An order that the matters regarding which questions were asked or any other designated facts shall be taken to be established for the purposes of the action in accordance with the claim of the party obtaining the order.

(B) An order refusing to allow the disobedient party to support or oppose designated claims or defenses, or prohibiting that party from introducing designated matters in evidence.

(C) An order striking out pleadings or parts of them or staying further proceedings until the order is obeyed, or dismissing the action or proceeding or any part of it, or rendering a judgment by default against the disobedient party.

(D) Instead of any of the foregoing orders or in addition to them, an order treating as a contempt of court the failure to obey any orders except an order to submit to an examination made pursuant to rule 1.360(a)(1)(B) or subdivision (a)(2) of this rule.

(E) When a party has failed to comply with an order under rule 1.360(a)(1)(B) requiring that party to produce another for examination, the orders listed in paragraphs (A), (B), and (C) of this subdivision, unless the party failing to comply shows the inability to produce the person for examination. Instead of any of the foregoing orders or in addition to them, the court shall require the party failing to obey the order to pay the reasonable expenses caused by the failure, which may include attorneys' fees, unless the court finds that the failure was justified or that other circumstances make an award of expenses unjust.[21]

Another mediation situation that may give rise to sanctions is when an agreement and a plan of action are formed at the mediation, but one of the parties does not comply. The bank will usually retain jurisdiction to enforce the settlement agreement. If the bank fails to comply with all terms of the mediation settlement agreement, the court

---

21. FLA. R. CIV. P. 1.380(b)(2).

might dismiss the foreclosure case with prejudice, as did a trial court in West Palm Beach, Florida.[22]

In a recent New York Case, the court imposed sanctions on a foreclosure plaintiff and plaintiff's counsel for failing to attend the court-ordered mediation.[23] In that case, the court mailed an order to the parties directing the plaintiff's attorney to appear for a settlement conference with a bank representative "fully familiar with the file and with authority to settle."[24] The order stated that sanctions may be imposed against any party who did not comply with its provisions.[25] An attorney for the plaintiff called the court-appointed referee shortly before the scheduled mediation, leaving a message which was returned by the referee but then not returned by plaintiff's counsel.[26]

Then, on the day of the mediation, plaintiff and its counsel failed to appear.[27] Plaintiff's counsel's only excuse was that she was unaware of the conference and that she had been playing "phone tag" with the referee.[28] The court found this excuse to be insufficient, noting that "[t]he order was mailed well in advance of the conference date to both plaintiff's counsel and the homeowner" and it is well-settled law that if a letter is properly stamped, addressed, and mailed, it is presumed to be delivered to its addressee.[29] The court then scheduled a hearing to determine whether sanctions should be issued against plaintiff and its counsel.[30]

Most courts will not tolerate lack of compliance with the local jurisdiction's mandatory mediation program. Court resources have been heavily taxed dealing with voluminous foreclosure filings, and the fewer foreclosures the court has to resolve, the better. If the parties refuse to appear for mediation, this circumvents the entire

---

22. Palm Beach County, Fla. Case No. 502008CA040810XXXXMB, *LaSalle Bank v. Briseus* (Fla. Cir. Ct. 2008).
23. BAC Home Loans Servicing v. Westervelt, 2010 N.Y. slip op. 51992U (N.Y. App. Div. 2010).
24. *Id.* at *2.
25. *Id.*
26. *Id.*
27. *Id.*
28. *Id.*
29. *Id.* at *3.
30. *Id.* at *6.

purpose of the mediation program. Some jurisdictions will permit telephonic appearance of the parties for mediation, but, as stated before, the mediation is more effective if everyone is there in person; when more time and energy is invested into the mediation, all parties are more likely to want a positive return.

Cash for Keys

If your client does not wish to keep the property, title of the property has already transferred to the bank, and your client is willing to vacate the property, you may request whether the bank will pay "cash for keys"; in other words, the homeowner will relinquish possession of the property in return for some monetary compensation, without the need for eviction proceedings. In one foreclosure case I handled, the homeowners had not filed any papers in defense to the foreclosure in the two years since it had been filed, until a summary judgment of foreclosure had been entered and the property had been ordered to sale. Only at that time did they hire an attorney who filed a motion to set aside the foreclosure sale. The bank filed a motion in opposition, which we set for motion calendar. The issue was highly contested, and the judge stated she would need to have the matter scheduled for a special set hearing, and the first available date was not until five months later.

The court ultimately denied the motion to set aside sale. I found out later that during the five months of waiting until the hearing, unbeknownst to me, the homeowners had been regularly visited by an agent of the bank who was offering them approximately $1,000 to surrender the title of the property. This apparently was one of the bank's "cash for keys" programs in action. Banks will frequently try to obtain a cash for keys deal with a homeowner to have them vacate the property before summary judgment; they will usually hire a contractor to go out and make repeated visits to a homeowner in furtherance of this goal.

As discussed earlier, you should not take a case if your client does not trust you. Your client needs to be fully committed to working with you. Another reason of why this is important is that your client needs to immediately inform you of any facts that could materially impact the case, including contacts from third parties attempting to make side deals with them, such as cash-for-keys offers. If your client does not trust or respect you, he or she might make a side deal and take a settlement without your knowledge, which could be detrimental to you if you proceed in the case without this knowledge; for example, you may ask the court for relief that is no longer warranted and waste court time and resources.

You may also seek a cash-for-keys settlement by, as with other loss mitigation proposals, contacting the investor if possible, or, if this is not possible, their servicer or attorneys. You might ask your client how much he would need for moving and living expenses for the immediate future and work off that figure in proposing an offer to the bank. You might consider a cash-for-keys negotiation when summary judgment has been granted, a sale of the property has been ordered, or title of the property has transferred to the bank and your client does not wish to appeal, or appeal is no longer an option.

Court-Ordered Modifications

One recent Florida case holds that borrowers who make good-faith representations to the court that they have been engaged in alternative dispute resolutions with the bank may be entitled to an evidentiary hearing where the truth of these assertions can be fully considered by the court before the foreclosure proceeds.[31] The presiding Florida court held that if "a moving party's allegations raise a colorable entitlement to relief, a formal evidentiary hearing and appropriate discovery is required."[32] The bank in that case did not even refute the borrowers' allegations that the parties had been cooperating in settlement negotiations.[33]

Sometimes the homeowners will show so much due diligence about getting the bank's allegations of default resolved that the court will grant the homeowners a loan solution where the bank will not, as was the case recently in Ohio.[34] In that case, one of the borrowers fell

---

31. Palacio v. Alaska Seaboard Partners Ltd. P'ship, 50 So. 3d 54, 56 (Fla. 1st DCA 2010).
32. *Id.*
33. *Id.*
34. PHH Mortgage Corp. v. Barker, 2010 Ohio 5061 (Ohio Ct. App. 2010).

ill, and both were not able to make payments or contact the bank for two months.[35] One of the borrowers then left several messages with the bank, none of which were returned.[36] Only after the borrower drove to a local branch of the bank did someone assist her and walk her through a loss mitigation assistance process in July 2007.[37]

In August 2007 the bank sent the borrowers a loss mitigation packet, which they completed, stating that the wife suffered from an illness that prevented her from working for long periods.[38] However, the borrowers advised that the wife had found a new job better suited to her medical condition and were now able to make mortgage payments.[39] The bank then sent the borrowers conflicting information; two notices of acceleration in August 2007 and a coupon book shortly thereafter listing a new monthly payment amount of $312.06.[40] The borrowers believed that this coupon book was in response to a loss mitigation approval and began making payments of $400 monthly.[41] However, in October 2007 the bank began returning the borrowers' payments to them, alleging that the loan was still in default and was being referred to the foreclosure department.[42] The wife then made another payment of $800 to a bank teller.[43] Despite this, the bank filed its foreclosure action against the homeowners on November 7, 2007, and later returned the $800 payment.[44]

The borrowers continued to make payments with the bank tellers and completed loss mitigation paperwork sent to them by the bank.[45] The bank continued with its foreclosure action and ultimately filed a motion for summary judgment in March 2008, which

---

35. *Id.* at *2.
36. *Id.*
37. *Id.* at *3.
38. *Id.* at *5.
39. *Id.*
40. *Id.* at **6–7.
41. *Id.* at **7–8.
42. *Id.* at *9.
43. *Id.* at *10.
44. *Id.* at *11–12.
45. *Id.* at *12.

the court denied due to a "genuine issue of material fact."[46] The borrower husband had filed an affidavit in opposition to summary judgment alleging, in part:

2. The Defendants . . . were reissued a payment book on October 1, 2007.
3. They understood that this was a redrafting of their mortgage and that they were to go forward in a current status.
4. They had already paid extra against their mortgage prior to having a default status prior to October 1, 2007.
5. The bank accepted their payments from October 2007 through January 2008, when the bank then returned a payment.
6. They believed that the parties had made their mortgage current as a result of the correspondence with the company and the issuing of the mortgage book in October of 2007.[47]

The trial did not take place until over a year later, in October 2009.[48] One of the bank's records custodians appeared and testified about the payment history.[49] According to her "letter log," she testified that three payments were returned to the borrowers but had no way of knowing if the bank had cashed the checks for those payments.[50] The records custodian also had insufficient knowledge regarding the borrowers' communications with the bank, stating that those would have been contained in another "letter log" kept by the loss mitigation department, which she did not have with her.[51]

The trial court essentially concluded that the borrowers had done everything in their power to meet their obligations with the bank until the bank had thwarted their efforts.[52] Accordingly, the

---

46. *Id.* at *15–17.
47. *Id.* at *27.
48. *Id.* at *18.
49. *Id.* at *18.
50. *Id.* at *19.
51. *Id.*
52. *Id.* at *20.

court found "it is equitable and in the best interests of justice" for the loan to be reinstated at the amount the borrowers owed as of October 2007.[53]

The appellate court noted that in Ohio, a foreclosure involves a two-pronged analysis: (1) a determination that borrowers have defaulted on a mortgage, and (2) a consideration of "the equities to determine if foreclosure is the appropriate remedy."[54] The trial court judge had commented on the record that the defendants:

> made every effort to get this loan back on track unlike the other ninety-nine percent of the foreclosure cases that I have. These people have tried to get back on track and get the thing reinstated and made what appears to me to be a good faith effort to do that.[55]

The bank's dissemination of conflicting directives to the homeowners was also a central issue in the case; on one hand the bank was sending the borrowers notices of default, and on the other, coupon books for payment, which the borrowers reasonably understood to be in furtherance of their loss mitigation requests.[56] Furthermore, while using the coupon books, the borrowers had made four payments totaling $2,000, which was more than the $1,288.64 the bank demanded to cure the alleged default.[57] The appellate court found that, in the interests of justice and equity, the lower court's decision to reinstate the loan was correct, over the bank's objections.[58]

---

53. *Id.*
54. *Id.* at *35.
55. *Id.* at *36, *citing to* Trial Trans., p.107.
56. *Id.* at *38.
57. *Id.* at *39.
58. *Id.* at *41.

Chapter 10

Motion for Sanctions

Courts are increasingly willing to grant a homeowner's motion for sanctions against a bank. There are numerous procedures and prerequisites to foreclosure that the banks must follow, and each of these directives to the banks opens more doors for sanctions against them if they fail to comply.

In announcing his investigations into three of the state's largest bank foreclosure firms, Florida Attorney General Bill McCollum stated, "I want law firms to really think about it before they go through this volume."[1] Going through this volume in such a rushed manner causes mistakes. As we have also found, some foreclosure firms and their employees, while rushing to meet bank time lines and motivated by financial rewards for faster foreclosures, have filed improper and fraudulent documents to expedite the court process.

These rushed mistakes and knowingly fraudulent acts usually inure to the detriment of the homeowner, sometimes fatally prejudicing his or her case. In every jurisdiction, however, procedures exist to deter and punish litigants from advancing frivolous claims and defenses, commonly encapsulated within a motion for sanctions.

---

1. Nirvi Shah, *3 South Florida Foreclosure Law Firms Probed*, MIAMI HERALD, Aug. 11, 2010.

In Florida, a statute commonly cited in support of civil litigation motions for sanctions when frivolous claims or defenses are raised is Fla. Stat. § 57.105, which provides in part:

> (1) Upon the court's initiative or motion of any party, the court shall award a reasonable attorney's fee to be paid to the prevailing party in equal amounts by the losing party and the losing party's attorney on any claim or defense at any time during a civil proceeding or action in which the court finds that the losing party or the losing party's attorney knew or should have known that a claim or defense when initially presented to the court or at any time before trial:
> (a) Was not supported by the material facts necessary to establish the claim or defense; or
> (b) Would not be supported by the application of then-existing law to those material facts.

A Florida court recently found that § 57.105 sanctions were appropriate against a bank that filed a foreclosure action, including a count for a lost note, when it could ultimately provide no evidence that it owned the note and mortgage or had standing to file the action.[2] In that case, another lien holder on the subject property took initiative in the case by filing an answer containing the affirmative defense that the bank lacked standing to maintain the foreclosure because it did not own the note and mortgage.[3] The lien holder propounded requests for admissions upon the bank in which, by virtue of the bank's failure to respond to same, it was deemed admitted that the bank "had no evidence to show that it owned or possessed the note and mortgage on the date that it filed the mortgage foreclosure action."[4]

Pursuant to the requirements of § 57.105, the lien holder served an unfiled copy of its proposed motion for sanctions on the bank,

---

2. Country Place Comm. Assoc., Inc. v. J.P. Morgan Mortgage Acquisition Corp., 51 So. 3d 1176, 1181 (Fla. 2d DCA 2010).
3. *Id.* at 1177.
4. *Id.*

granting the bank a safe harbor period in which to withdraw its frivolous claims prior to the finalized motion being filed with the court.[5] After receiving no response from the bank, the lien holder filed a motion for summary judgment seeking dismissal of the foreclosure, which was granted with leave for the bank to amend.[6]

After the granting of this summary judgment, the lien holder also scheduled its § 57.105 motion for hearing. The bank attempted to defeat this motion for sanctions by suddenly announcing that it possessed the original note and mortgage, even after the bank had filed an affidavit of lost original instruments about seven weeks prior, testifying that it could not find these original documents even after an extensive search.[7] The trial court agreed with the bank that it should not be subject to attorney's fees based on the fact that it could eventually assert a factually supported claim, even though no evidence existed for its claims of ownership when the first complaint was filed.[8]

The appellate court, however, distinguished the trial court's interpretation of § 57.105 which construed the statute according to its pre-1999 meaning, and the application of the statute since the 1999 revisions were made.[9] Under the pre-1999 version of § 57.105, "the determination of a party's entitlement to fees had to be made based on the entire action."[10] Put another way, a party could not be entitled to attorney's fees until the conclusion of the entire case and a party had exercised all of its options to amend its action or assert viable claims or defenses, regardless of whether it had ever made a frivolous claim at any point in the history of the case.[11]

However, pursuant to the 1999 revisions of § 57.105, the statute "authorizes an award of attorney's fees 'on any claim or defense at any time during a civil proceeding or action.'"[12] Now, a party need not wait until the conclusion of the entire action to assert

---

5. *Id.* at 1178; *see also* § 57.105(4).
6. *Id.*
7. *Id.*
8. *Id.*
9. *Id.* at 1179–80.
10. *Id.* at 1179.
11. *See id.*
12. *Id.* at 1180, *citing* § 57.105.

relief pursuant to § 57.105; a party may seek § 57.105 sanctions at any time a claim or defense is raised in violation of the statute's provisions.[13]

In this Florida case, the bank did not own or possess the note and mortgage when it filed the foreclosure action, and therefore lacked standing to pursue such action.[14] Therefore, the bank "knew or should have known that its action was unsupported by the material facts necessary to establish the claim."[15] Under the current version of § 57.105, it does not matter that the bank may eventually be able to assert a justiciable claim, only that it failed to do so when it first filed its action.[16] The appellate court thus found that the lien holder was entitled to attorney's fees as sanctions against the bank for filing a baseless claim.[17]

The Federal Rules of Civil Procedure reiterate the requirements of this Florida rule on sanctions, also extending sanctionable events to when legal action is pursued for purposes of harassment or delay:

> By presenting to the court a pleading, written motion, or other paper—whether by signing, filing, submitting, or later advocating it—an attorney or unrepresented party certifies that to the best of the person's knowledge, information, and belief, formed after an inquiry reasonable under the circumstances:
>
> (1) it is not being presented for any improper purpose, such as to harass, cause unnecessary delay, or needlessly increase the cost of litigation;
> (2) the claims, defenses, and other legal contentions are warranted by existing law or by a nonfrivolous argument for extending, modifying, or reversing existing law or for establishing new law;
> (3) the factual contentions have evidentiary support or, if specifically so identified, will likely have evidentiary support

---

13. *See id.*
14. *Id.* at 1181.
15. *Id.* at 1179.
16. *Id.* at 1181.
17. *Id.*

after a reasonable opportunity for further investigation or discovery; and

(4) the denials of factual contentions are warranted on the evidence or, if specifically so identified, are reasonably based on belief or a lack of information.[18]

In a federal case, a party may present a motion for Rule 11 sanctions, and a court may order such sanctions on its own initiative. The offending party and/or his attorney may be ordered to pay fees to the opposing side, and "[a]bsent exceptional circumstances, a law firm must be held jointly responsible for a violation committed by its partner, associate, or employee."[19]

Shotgun Foreclosures

Your client may be saving up the money to reinstate the loan, working on a short sale, or received representations from the bank that she will be approved for a loan modification. In the meantime, the homeowner tries to go on with her life, coming and going from her house as usual.

One day she comes home and the locks on the door have been changed. Or a stranger is coming on her property without her permission or knowledge. Perhaps someone keeps knocking on her door, maybe telling her that she needs to vacate her home. The court has not issued final judgment or scheduled sale of the property.

These events may be taking place because many banks, even after filing a foreclosure action, are also seeking a new brand of renegade justice to reclaim properties. A typical mortgage will allow the lender to take reasonable measures to preserve the collateral property if the borrower fails to do so. For example, the typical Fannie/Mae/Freddie Mac Uniform Instrument Mortgage provides in Paragraph 7:

Preservation, Maintenance and Protection of the Property; Inspections. Borrower shall not destroy, damage or impair

---

18. Fed. R. Civ. P. 11(b).
19. § 11(c)(1).

the Property, allow the Property to deteriorate or commit
waste on the Property . . .

Lender or its agent may make reasonable entries upon
and inspections of the Property. If it has reasonable cause,
Lender may inspect the interior of the improvements of the
Property. Lender shall give Borrower notice at the time of
or prior to such an interior inspection specifying such reasonable cause.

Nowhere in this clause does it state that the lender may take
possession of the property and oust the homeowner if the lender
considers the homeowner to be in default, without title legally pass-
ing to the lender. Yet this is exactly what has occurred, and continues to occur in some foreclosure cases. The lender will take the law
into its own hands and eject the borrowers from their property even
when title is still in the borrowers' names. In most cases there is no
legal justification for this.

A bank may instruct its property preservation department to "se-
cure" or "winterize" the property, which can involve the changing of
locks and directing the homeowners to leave. Sometimes these actions are purportedly brought under clauses in the mortgage, which
give the lender certain rights to preserve the property under certain
circumstances. Sometimes these acts are committed due to a discon-
nect between different departments of the servicer or banks. One
department may mistakenly believe that the property has gone to
judgment or sale and is not communicating with other departments
who are aware of the true status of the foreclosure action.

In either case, whether these acts are negligent or intentional,
the homeowner's rights are violated. If an individual enters the
homeowner's property without legal justification or permission, you
may have a valid action for trespass. Other legal remedies may be
available if the bank wrongfully changes the locks to your client's
home or destroys or damages any of her property. Unless and until
your client's house has been sold and the period of redemption has
expired, she is still the lawful owner of the home. As such, the bank
has no right to tell her to leave as long as she is the owner. If someone keeps coming to her door and offering her money to leave, or
using harassing or coercive measures to pressure her to vacate the

property, these are also violations of her rights. The bank may be committing criminal or civil violations, and it is important to bring them to the attention of the proper authorities. These facts may be beneficial to your defense when you file a motion for sanctions based on these events.

Due Process

Foreclosure defense attorneys should also be on the lookout for violations of homeowners' right to due process, which may form yet more grounds for sanctions. In their haste to push millions of foreclosures through the collective hopper, banks have often tried to push due process to the side. The Fifth Amendment of the United States Constitution provides that no person shall "be deprived of life, liberty, or property, without due process of law." The implication of the Fifth Amendment for foreclosure defense purposes is that no party can obtain a judgment of foreclosure without due process of law to the homeowner, which necessarily includes proper notice of all foreclosure proceedings. The banks have attempted to deprive borrowers of due process in foreclosure court proceedings. Sometimes a person's home has been taken away when he had no notice of the foreclosure action because the bank advanced fraudulent services of process to the court.[20] Other times, banks have submitted false documents to induce the courts to grant them summary judgment. The homeowners may have had notice but were falsely led to believe that the bank had the right to foreclose on their home.[21]

A paucity of due process is also apparent in the loss mitigation process. Many homeowners are at a loss as to why they have not qualified for borrower assistance programs through their banks, when according to the numbers they should qualify. Courts have interpreted the Fifth Amendment to mean that laws cannot be "void for vagueness," or fail "to give a person of ordinary intelligence fair notice that his contemplated conduct is forbidden" by a law.[22] In

---

20. *See* Bennett v. Christiana Bank & Trust Co., 50 So. 3d 43, 45 (Fla. 3d DCA 2010).

21. Wash. Mutual Bank v. Phillip, 2010 N.Y. slip op. 52034U at *2 (N.Y. App. Div. 2010).

22. Papachristou v. City of Jacksonville, 405 U.S. 156, 162 (1972).

one case, a federal court refused to defer to the Securities and Exchange Commission's (SEC) application of its own rules "if doing so would penalize an individual who has not received fair notice of a regulatory violation."[23] That court emphasized that regulations do not have to deal with criminal conduct in order for them to be void for vagueness.[24] To determine whether a law will pass the void-for-vagueness test, "the court must determine whether the enactment (1) provides sufficient notice of its proscriptions to facilitate compliance by persons of ordinary intelligence, and (2) is specific enough to prevent official arbitrariness or discrimination in its enforcement."[25] The banks' application of guidelines that determine which homeowners will qualify for and receive loss mitigation relief do neither in most cases.

Many homeowners facing foreclosure in America today have no idea what they would need to do to qualify for a loss mitigation program, or whether the banks are granting such relief to all parties who qualify. This is because the regulations of most banks that govern whether a borrower's home gets saved are void for vagueness. The criteria of the Home Affordable Modification Program (HAMP) are disclosed by the federal government,[26] but the way that many banks construe these criteria sometimes have the effect of nullifying these federal guidelines until they are virtually meaningless. The banks may sometimes tell homeowners that they initially qualify for HAMP, but at the end of the trial period arbitrarily decide that the borrowers do not qualify for relief after all, even after the borrowers have successfully made all payments required under the trial period. In some cases, courts have ordered the bank to make the trial modification permanent anyway.

Until the law changes so that homeowners everywhere have full, uniform due process in their rights to their home, perhaps the best method for us to fight is through the courts. Indeed, if the homeowners of today have any forum for demonstration, it is in the courts, but not in the traditional sense we think of when we picture

---

23. Upton v. SEC, 75 F.3d 92, 98 (2d Cir. 1996).

24. *Id.*

25. Columbia Gas Transmission Corp. v. Levin, 117 Ohio St. 3d 122 at *42 (2008).

26. http://makinghomeaffordable.gov/modification_eligibility.html.

demonstrations from the 1960s. Most judges do not want to see what is happening to the homeowners, and they are only doing what the law compels them to do. Here is the homeowners' chance to demonstrate before the court—to take all the facts and law and make the most compelling arguments possible. In general, the courts are listening to the homeowners far better than the banks. It is imperative that foreclosure defense attorneys tell homeowners' stories in the best ways possible; through our common-law system and with every good order, decision, and judgment, you will help create good case law.

Chapter 11

The Demand Letter

Though your client may have missed loan payments for months, there is usually one final warning before a foreclosure actually happens: the demand letter. The reason that your client receives a demand letter is typically because of the following paragraph from the Single Family-Fannie Mae/Freddie Mac Uniform Instrument with the Mortgage Electronic Registration Systems (MERS) or similar provisions of your client's mortgage:

> NON-UNIFORM COVENANTS. Borrower and Lender further covenant and agree as follows:
>
> 22. Acceleration; Remedies. Lender shall give notice to Borrower prior to acceleration following Borrower's breach of any covenant or agreement in this Security Agreement (but not prior to acceleration under Section 18 unless Applicable Law provides otherwise). The notice shall specify: (a) the default; (b) the action required to cure the default; (c) a date, not less than 30 days from the date the notice is given to Borrower, by which the default must be cured; and (d) that failure to cure the default on or before the date specified in the notice may result in acceleration of the sums secured by this Security Instrument, foreclosure by judicial proceeding

and sale of the Property. The notice shall further inform Borrower of the right to reinstate after acceleration and the right to assert in the foreclosure proceeding the non-existence of a default or any other defense of Borrower to acceleration and foreclosure. If the default is not cured on or before the date specified in the notice, Lender at its option may require immediate payment in full of all sums secured by this Security Instrument by judicial proceeding. Lender shall be entitled to collect all expenses incurred in pursuing the remedies provided in this Section 22, including, but not limited to, reasonable attorneys' fees and costs of title evidence.

This standard mortgage language essentially provides that the lender must send the borrower a demand letter granting a period of at least 30 days to cure any default on the loan. The demand letter must set forth the exact sum the borrower must provide in order to cure the default. The lender cannot later accelerate the loan and begin foreclosure proceedings unless it gives warning in the letter that it will take such actions if the default is not cured in time.

The whole foreclosure process basically begins with the demand letter. The only reason homeowners usually get this letter before getting served with a complaint is that the mortgage, like the one quoted above, typically requires the bank to give the borrower notice before accelerating the loan. The letter will be titled Notice of Default, Notice of Intent to Accelerate, or something similar. Some mortgages, such as for some commercial and residential loans, do not contain such a clause requiring notice prior to acceleration. If your client receives a foreclosure complaint and did not receive a demand letter first, you should immediately review the mortgage to ascertain what notice of default and right to cure, if any, is included. The mortgage is usually attached to the complaint, but if it is not, and your client does not have a copy, the mortgage will usually be recorded in the local public records. Many localities now offer online viewing of their public records.

If your client can bring the loan current, have him do it. The foreclosure process can be very hard to end in the borrower's favor once it has started, and favorable results will require a good deal of work and, often, more attorney's fees and costs to your client. You may also submit a payment that is less than the amount being demanded, which may also forestall the bank from proceeding with foreclosure. However, at this point the bank may reject any amount less than the demand total.

Once your client pays the amount required to reinstate the loan contained in the demand letter, you need to follow up with the bank and confirm that the payment was received, properly credited, and that the loan is now current, and obtain written confirmation of same.

When clients receive a clear, unambiguous demand letter that sets forth the amount required to bring the loan current, and clients can pay, they should certainly do so if they wish to avoid foreclosure. However, sometimes the demand letter will be so ambiguous that the homeowner cannot be assured that the purported default will be resolved even if she does pay. It may not provide the exact amount required to pay the arrearage, or it may not advise the borrower of her continuing right to reinstate the loan even if acceleration is commenced. If your client is in a position to pay the claimed arrearage and intends to do so, you should contact the bank for clarification of the amounts due and owing. However, it may be advisable for your client not to pay the claimed amounts (especially if she is financially unable to do so) if the deficient demand letter, left as is, may help your litigation strategy. For example, you may choose to file a motion to dismiss for lack of condition precedent (Chapter 16), assert this deficiency as an affirmative defense (Chapter 19), or raise this issue at the summary judgment stage (Chapter 21).

In Mississippi, it is unlawful for a bank to proceed to a foreclosure sale without accounting "to a mortgagor for the amount it would take to bring the loan current before foreclosing on the property."[1] The borrower there asserted that she never received an accounting from the bank as required by law, and the bank rebutted that the borrower was not entitled to one as she was in default, notwithstanding its provision of a purported statement in discovery.[2] However, the documents produced by the bank did not provide an

---

1. West v. Nationwide Trustee Servs., Inc., No 1:09CV295-LG-RHW at *7 (S.D. Miss. Aug. 4, 2010).
2. *Id.*

appropriate accounting, as one of the two documents was illegible and the other was incomplete and unauthenticated.[3] Therefore, the court upheld the borrower's statutory claim of wrongful foreclosure.[4]

Connecticut law also directs that the demand letter must also clearly advise the borrowers of the amount needed to cure the default and cannot be ambiguous.[5] In a relevant case, the defendant asserted that the notice of acceleration preceding the foreclosure action was insufficient because it sought collection on payments not yet due and misrepresented the required amount to bring the loan current.[6] The court agreed with the borrower and found that the demand letter was ambiguous as to the amount needed and actions required of the borrower in order to avoid acceleration of the loan.[7] The language of the demand letter inaccurately indicated that the borrower would have to pay two different sums to cure the default.[8] Accordingly, the court denied the bank's motion for summary judgment, finding that a genuine issue of material fact existed.[9]

When a bank failed to comply with the provisions of the mortgage requiring notice of default to the homeowners prior to acceleration of the loan, one court reversed an entry of summary judgment.[10] The mortgage in that case contained the standard paragraph 22 language regarding notice of default provisions.[11] The homeowners filed a brief in opposition to the bank's motion for summary judgment, arguing that the bank failed to provide them with notice pursuant to paragraph 22 prior to filing the foreclosure action.[12]

---

3. *Id.*

4. *Id.* at *10.

5. U.S. Bank, N.A. v. Suvemay, No. CV08-5014358S (Conn. Super. Ct., Oct. 4, 2010).

6. *Id.*

7. *Id.*

8. *Id.*

9. *Id.*

10. LaSalle Bank, N.A. v. Kelly, 2010 Ohio 2668 at *14 (Ohio Ct. App. 2010).

11. *Id.* at *10.

12. *Id.* at *9.

The court held that the requirements of paragraph 22 do not constitute an affirmative defense, but rather a condition precedent to a foreclosure action.[13] As the bank had not made any attempt to show that it had complied with the notice provisions of paragraph 22, a genuine issue of material fact remained, making summary judgment for the bank improper.[14]

Occasionally, your client will be in a situation that is fatal to the bank's case. One such situation is when the homeowners have made payments on the loan after the demand letter was sent and the bank accepted the payments. It does not matter whether the bank applied the payment to the principal and interest or placed the payment in a suspense account; the bank has still accepted a payment, and therefore the demand letter is no longer effective. When this happens, the bank has failed to meet a condition precedent to its lawsuit and a requirement of the mortgage.

If the bank never sent the homeowner a demand letter, this could mean that the bank is permitted to accelerate the loan without any prior notice. The mortgage will usually specify the bank's obligations as to notice of acceleration. The bank may sometimes still send the borrower a demand letter even though it is not required to do so, and a payment made after the foreclosure action is filed may not affect the bank's rights to proceed. The answers to these questions will usually be revealed by the client's loan documents.

If you find that a payment was made and accepted by the bank after the demand, and that the demand letter is no longer good, then you have a solid defense against foreclosure because a crucial condition precedent has no longer been met. When to raise this defense may be a tactical decision. You could raise it early on, in a motion to dismiss, for example, or wait until the summary judgment stage.

---

13. *Id.* at *13.
14. *Id.* at *14.

Chapter 12

Fair Debt Collection Practices Act

The Fair Debt Collection Practices Act (FDCPA) gives important rights to a property resident facing foreclosure, as well as consumers in general. One provision of the FDCPA is that a debt collector cannot use abusive, deceptive, and unfair debt collection practices. In 1978, Congress recognized that abusive debt collection practices were contributing to the destruction of peoples' marriages, loss of jobs, bankruptcy filings and personal privacy.[1] Abusive debt collectors still cause the same problems today, and in addition only aggravate the overwhelming strain on Americans in foreclosure. These practices are illegal, and, as explained herein, a consumer may possibly recover legal damages against a debt collector who violates the FDCPA.

Some courts have held that a foreclosure plaintiff (the bank, lender, or owner of the loan who brings the foreclosure action) is not considered a debt collector under the FDCPA when the bank is the original creditor seeking to enforce its own debt and not "regularly engaged in the debt collection business."[2] However, it has also been held that the bank's foreclosure attorneys may constitute debt collectors under the FDCPA because they "regularly engage in debt

---

1. *See* 15 U.S.C. § 1692.

2. Jeliff Partners, LLC v. Brown, No. FST CV04-4001569 (Conn. Super. Ct., June 1, 2005).

99

collection activities, including foreclosures, [and therefore] are 'debt collectors' under the FDCPA and are subject to its provisions."[3] Therefore FDCPA defenses may be raised when the bank has hired attorneys who regularly engage in debt collection practices, as do most law firms that banks retain.

Under the FDCPA, a debt collector cannot just call a consumer whenever or however it pleases. For example, the debt collector cannot:

1. Call a consumer at all hours of the day or night. They are usually allowed to call the consumer between 8 a.m. and 9 p.m.[4]

2. In general, if the debt collector knows that a consumer is represented by an attorney and has that attorney's contact information, the debt collector must contact the attorney and not the consumer.[5]

3. A debt collector may not call a consumer at work if the debt collector has any reason to believe that the borrower is not permitted to receive such calls while at work.[6] If at any time the consumer advises the debt collector in writing that she is not paying a debt or she does not wish to have any further calls from the debt collector, the debt collector may not call the consumer again except to just advise her that they are terminating their collection efforts or taking other legal action.[7]

---

3. *See* Zartman v. Shapiro & Meinhold, 811 P.2d 409, 413 (Colo. App. 1990).

4. *See* 15 U.S.C. § 1692c(a)(1).

5. § 1692c(a)(2).

6. § 1692c(a)(3). In one case, the court held that it is enough to put debt collectors on notice "when a consumer states in plain English that she cannot speak to the debt collector at work." Horkey v. J.V.D.B. & Assoc., Inc., 333 F.3d 769, 773 (7th Cir. 2003). The debt collector, after the consumer had ended the conversation, called back and unleashed profane insults about the consumer to one of her co-workers. *Id.* The court found that these insults were made in connection with the violator's attempts to collect the debt, despite the debt collector's absurd insistence to the contrary. *Id.* at 774.

7. § 1692c(c).

The debt collector is permitted to communicate with only a limited number of persons regarding an alleged debt. If the debt collector calls anyone except for the consumer, the creditor, or the creditor's attorney about the debt, in general they can only verify the consumer's location.[8] The debt collector is required to identify himself, state he is trying to get the consumer's location, and give his employer's name if asked.[9] The debt collector cannot disclose to such third parties that the consumer owes any debt and usually cannot contact such persons more than once.[10] The debt collector is also prohibited from sending postcards so that information regarding the consumer's alleged debt is revealed for the whole world to see.[11] The debt collector is also prohibited from placing any information on the outside of the envelope to suggest a consumer owes a debt.[12]

Additionally, a debt collector is not permitted to harass, abuse, or mislead a consumer. For example:

1. The debt collector cannot threaten to illegally harm the consumer, his property, or reputation.[13]
2. The debt collector cannot call a consumer over and over again to intentionally annoy, harass, or abuse him.[14]
3. The debt collector cannot lie about a debt.[15]
4. The debt collector cannot assert that he is an attorney if this is not the case.[16]
5. The debt collector cannot threaten to arrest the consumer or take his property unlawfully.[17]
6. Debt collectors cannot bluff with a consumer and say they will do anything they don't really intend to do.[18]

---

8. § 1692b.
9. § 1692b(1).
10. § 1692b(3).
11. § 1692b(4).
12. § 1692b(5).
13. § 1692d(1).
14. § 1692d(5).
15. § 1692e.
16. § 1692e(3).
17. § 1692e(4).
18. § 1692e(5).

7. A debt collector is prohibited from lying to anyone about a consumer's credit.[19]

Disputing the Alleged Foreclosure Debt

Before a foreclosure action is filed, the mortgage creditor is almost always required to send the borrower a demand letter, usually pursuant to the standard language of paragraph 22 of the mortgage, as discussed in Chapter 11. The demand letter must state the amount of the debt, the name of the creditor to whom the debt is owed, and that if the borrower does not dispute the debt within 30 days, the creditor will assume the debt is valid. The demand letter usually tracks the requirements of the FDCPA, but the demand letter may not necessarily meet the FDCPA requirements for a notice of debt,[20] and often a foreclosure action will be filed without a proper FDCPA notice being provided to the borrower. A legal pleading does not constitute the initial notice of a debt required by the FDCPA.[21] If a borrower does not dispute a debt within 30 days, the debt collector cannot use this as an admission of liability that the consumer is responsible for the debt.[22]

A consumer may send the debt collector a dispute notice in writing.[23] The consumer may either dispute all or part of the debt, demand the name and address of the original creditor, or both.[24] If the consumer disputes the debt within 30 days of receiving a notice of the debt, the creditor must then stop with all debt collection activity until it can verify "the debt or a copy of a judgment, or the name and address of the original creditor, and a copy of such verification or judgment, or name and address of the original creditor, is mailed to the consumer by the debt collector."[25]

If a debt collector violates the FDCPA, it may be liable to the borrower for damages, costs, and attorney's fees.[26] In the case of an

---

19. § 1692e(7).
20. *See* § 1692g(a).
21. § 1692g(d).
22. § 1692g(c).
23. § 1692g(b).
24. *Id.*
25. *Id.*
26. § 1692k.

individual borrower, the damages are limited to those actually suffered by the borrower as a result of the collector's failure.[27] The court may also grant the borrower additional damages not to exceed $1,000.[28] If a class action has been filed against the collector, the collector may be liable for attorney's fees and actual damages of the class as well as additional damages not to exceed $500,000 or 1 percent of the debt collector's net worth, whichever is less.[29] In determining whether to award damages to a consumer, the court will look at whether the debt collector's violations were intentional and how often they committed these violations.[30]

In a foreclosure, the borrower may still seek verification of the debt after the 30-day period has expired, but the plaintiff will probably proceed with the foreclosure in the meantime. If the bank never sent the homeowner a notice of debt as proscribed by the FDCPA, that is likely an automatic violation. The initial summons and complaint do not count to satisfy such requirement. If the debt collector proceeds with the foreclosure before he has verified a timely debt dispute, he can also be liable for damages. If the plaintiff is trying to push the foreclosure toward a final judgment without having verified the homeowner's FDCPA dispute, bring this to the court's attention. You may be able to prevent the judgment from being entered until you have received proper verification, and at that time you may have strong defenses you can raise in opposition.

---

27. § 169k(a)(1).
28. § 169k(a)(2)(A).
29. § 169k(a)(2)(B).
30. § 169k(b).

Chapter 13

Notice of Appearance

With the first papers you file in opposition to the complaint, which could include a demand pursuant to the FDCPA and a qualified written request (Chapter 19), also file a notice of appearance to let all parties know that your client is represented by counsel. The bank is thereby put on notice that it is prohibited from communicating with your client without your consent. If the bank continues to communicate with your client directly without your permission, this conduct will possibly provide you with viable equitable defenses; it is acting with unclean hands by contacting your clients without authorization. A foreclosure action is intended to be an equitable proceeding, and if the bank fails to conduct itself ethically, this could also form a basis for you to seek sanctions.

Some attorneys use the notice of appearance to address other matters as well, such as a standing objection to all unilaterally scheduled hearings and proposed orders submitted ex parte, notices of unavailability, and the preferred method by which the attorney wishes to receive court documents such as e-mail, fax, regular mail, etc. Many foreclosure firms have a tendency to schedule hearings unilaterally, particularly if a party is unrepresented by counsel. Pro se defendants still have a right to have hearing dates cleared with them, but quite often this does not happen. If a court hearing was set unilaterally—especially a dispositive hearing, such as the motion for summary judgment—an objection should be raised immediately.

Bank foreclosure firms will also sometimes submit ex parte motions and orders to the court, such as motions to amend the complaint to add or drop a party, or to substitute the plaintiff when the loan changes hands. Changing the name of the party plaintiff goes to one of the ultimate issues of fact in the case; i.e., who has the right to enforce the note and mortgage. Such matters should not be decided by the court ex parte; the matter should be called up for hearing, because this is an issue to which the defense may very well object. Other jurisdictions will permit an ex parte motion to compel discovery if no response has been received,[1] but such ex parte motions have been submitted even after one party has filed a motion for extension of time, or motions that do not meet the prerequisite elements to requesting such relief.[2] Many courts will catch such improper ex parte motions and orders and set them for hearing, but sometimes such an order may be signed, and the defendant should seek to have the order vacated and set the matter for hearing, if possible.

---

1. *See* Barry K. Waters, M.D., P.A. v. American Gen. Corp., 770 So. 2d 1275, 1276 (Fla. 4th Dist. Ct. App. 2000).

2. *See* 11th Judicial Cir., Miami-Dade County, Fla., Admin. Order No. 06-09.

Chapter 14

Vacating a Default Judgment

An issue that many foreclosure defense attorneys face when first coming into a case is a default judgment against their client, because many homeowners are scared and overwhelmed by the foreclosure action and have taken no action in the case other than hiring you. If a defendant is served with a complaint and does not file a response with the court within the time specified (usually 20 days), a default judgment may be entered against the non-responding defendant. The bank in a foreclosure case will view a default judgment against the homeowner as a positive result, because it will be able to push for summary judgment and sale of the subject property much sooner. After a default judgment has been entered, the defaulted party has waived its right to defend against an action, except as to unliquidated damages.[1] However, default judgments will often be vacated; courts generally maintain a policy of deciding cases on their merits rather than technicalities.[2]

Among attorneys, it is usually common courtesy, if you know that a party is represented by counsel, to follow up with opposing counsel if they have not filed a document by a certain deadline.

---

1. *See* Kaplan v. Morse, 870 So. 2d 934, 936 (Fla. 5th Dist. Ct. App. 2004).

2. Johnson v. Johnson, 845 So. 2d 217, 220 (Fla. 2d Dist. Ct. App. 2003).

One good reason for doing this is that other attorneys will appreciate the professional courtesy and be more likely to return the favor when you need it. Another reason is that the policy of courts to decide cases on their merits is highly favored; if you aggressively seek relief against a party who has missed a deadline when you had reason to believe they intended to comply, you might waste time and resources attending a hearing and obtaining an order defaulting that party when you will only have to attend another hearing when the opposing side files its motion to vacate default, which often will be granted. This is not to say that, when a party is trying to take advantage of you or the system, there should not be limits to your good graces. When a party has shown a clear intent to disregard the tacit rules of professional courtesy or the directives of the court, you might feel it is not worthwhile to continuously remind them about deadlines that are their responsibility.

However, when a party is not represented by an attorney, the foreclosure firm will often proceed with filing a motion for default against the non-responsive parties without further warning. Sometimes the case will proceed to summary judgment and sale, and a homeowner may still receive relief from the default and perhaps from the judgment as well. In one recent Florida case, not only had a default judgment been entered against the homeowners, but summary judgment had been entered and the property had been scheduled for sale.[3] The homeowners asserted a defense that is often echoed by other borrowers in foreclosure: that the bank had given them assurances that the foreclosure would not proceed while the borrowers were under loss mitigation review.[4] The borrowers also

---

3. Palacio v. Alaska Seaboard Partners Ltd. P'ship, 50 So. 3d 54, 55 (Fla. 1st DCA 2010).

4. *Id.* This kind of representation can sometimes be one that is reasonably relied upon by homeowners. Banks sometimes use different codes in their internal systems by which they may place a file on "loss mitigation hold" and raise an alert that litigation is being placed on hold pending the review. Default law firms will sometimes have a proceed/hold department for this very reason. They field the hold/proceed instructions from the banks and in turn notify the attorneys whether to put a hold on or proceed with the court action. The court and defense counsel are sometimes notified that a case is on loss mitigation hold and that the plaintiff is not proceeding with the litigation at a given time. The plaintiff's decision to stop and start the case as it pleases is not always supported

alleged that they received no indication that the foreclosure was moving forward until they received a notice of sale on their property.[5] The borrowers supplied affidavits to the court attesting that, prior to receiving the notice of sale, they were told that the lender agreed to reinstate their loan upon receipt of an $8,500 down payment, that the principal indebtedness would be reduced from $205,000 to $150,000, and that their monthly payment would be reduced to $1,375.[6] The borrowers had even made five payments in accordance with this solution.[7] Meanwhile, however, the bank had moved for, and received, default and summary judgments.[8] Only after sending the notice of sale did the bank return the homeowners' final payment, suddenly telling them that the foreclosure was pending and the account could only be reinstated through the bank's attorney.[9]

The bank never refuted the borrowers' assertions that they reasonably understood the foreclosure to be abated as a result of the loan reinstatement that the borrowers had believed to be in place.[10] The bank argued only that that the homeowners' statements were "facially insufficient to warrant entitlement to setting aside a default judgment."[11] The appellate court held that the trial court had erred in failing to conduct an evidentiary hearing to determine the merits of the borrowers' motion to set aside the judgment.[12]

The court in the previous case made reference to another recent Florida decision where a borrower's motion to set aside a foreclosure default judgment was denied by the trial court despite uncon-

---

by the court and defense counsel. Some defense counsel ask, if the plaintiff does not wish to proceed with its case, that it file a voluntary dismissal. A court will sometimes not tolerate the arbitrary delay and set the case for trial. Refusals to recognize the loss mitigation hold can sometimes benefit the homeowner and in other cases not, if a loss mitigation review would have otherwise carried a positive result for the borrower.

5. *Id.*
6. *Id.*
7. *Id.*
8. *Id.*
9. *Id.*
10. *Id.* at 56.
11. *Id.*
12. *Id.*

tested affidavits indicating that those borrowers had entered a work-out agreement with the lender.[13] The court stated that the trial court could find upon remand that the borrowers had established "excusable neglect or some other valid basis for setting aside the default judgment."[14] The court also mentioned in dicta that the borrowers may be entitled to equitable relief, implying that the borrowers had done equity in faithfully adhering to the terms of the agreement they believed the parties had reached, while the bank had not done equity by misleading the borrowers into thinking that the matter was settled and taking their money to perpetuate this belief when the bank perhaps never intended to reinstate the loan.[15]

---

13. *Id.*, *citing* Elliot v. Aurora Loan Servs., LLC, 31 So. 3d 304 (Fla. 4th Dist. Ct. App. 2010).

14. *Id.* at 56.

15. *Id.* This scenario further underscores the necessity for caution when a homeowner or his or her attorney arranges a loan modification arrangement with the bank. In the entire foreclosure crisis, banks have revealed more than ever that their primary goal is to make money, often failing to fully consider the circumstances that have caused homeowners to go into default on their mortgages. Banks will often use a loss mitigation tool as a measure to collect even more money from the homeowner when they otherwise would not during the course of a foreclosure, as most homeowners believe that if they are in foreclosure they cannot, or at least should not, make house payments. Quite often, if a bank sees a way to both foreclose on a home and collect more money from the homeowner, it will take that opportunity, as will most operations concerned with money and not with humanity.

Chapter 15

Requirements for Service of Foreclosure Complaints

The service of the foreclosure complaint is an issue that has gained scrutiny nationwide as numerous instances in which proper service was not conducted have been discovered by investigating authorities. As reiterated elsewhere in this book, before a lender should receive the drastic remedy of foreclosure, the lender must demonstrate that it has complied with the Fifth Amendment to the United States Constitution, which guarantees that no person shall be deprived of his property without due process of law. A homeowner does not receive due process unless she receives notice of any and all documents, hearings, and proceedings relevant to a foreclosure action against her property.

It has long been held that if a defendant is "enticed into the jurisdiction of the court through fraud or trickery on the part of the plaintiff or someone acting in his behalf, in order that personal service of process upon the defendant may be obtained, the service will be set aside upon proper application therefor."[1] Recently, private process servers have been placed under scrutiny.[2] In Chicago, for example, a process server alleged that he served a homeowner with a foreclosure complaint when at the time, public records demonstrated that

---

1. 98 A.L.R.2d 554 (1964), Attack on personal service as having been obtained by fraud or trickery.

2. *See* Roger Bull, *Florida Attorney General Investigating Companies That Serve Foreclosure Papers*, FLA. TIMES-UNION, Dec. 16, 2010.

the homeowner was on a job site seven miles away.[3] A lawsuit was filed in a Chicago federal court that challenges the propriety of special process servers and that sought to obtain class-action status, which could void thousands of service returns and thereby nullify thousands of foreclosure cases that relied on such service returns.[4]

These process servers include ProVest, "one of the nation's largest process servers."[5] Courts have been discovering cases in which ProVest allegedly served a summons before the corresponding foreclosure action was even filed, as well as cases in which ProVest had signed three documents with the same name but with different signatures.[6] Process servers are an important piece of the puzzle in a bank's foreclosure case, because the service department will await notification from the process server as to when a homeowner has been served; then it can begin calculating the date by which the borrower must respond to the complaint, and if he fails to do so, the service department will likely refer the file to the default department. The court will also usually require the returns of service to be filed with the court, as many judges will not grant summary judgment without seeing returns of service and confirming that all parties have been properly served.

If the foreclosure is uncontested, many summary judgments are granted without the service or defaults even being questioned. From the court's perspective, they will most likely hold the bank's attorney responsible if the service or defaults are later shown to be improper. Before summary judgment will be considered, many courts now require the bank's attorney to complete a certification personally attesting that all the prerequisites to foreclosure, including service of all parties, have been met.[7] Therefore, summary judgments where proper service never occurred will often

---

3. Dan Mihalopoulos & Patrick Rehkamp, *Use of Private Process Servers Is Up; Concern is Too*, N.Y. TIMES, July 22, 2010.

4. *Id.*

5. *Id.*

6. *Id.*

7. For an example of the certification required from bank attorneys in Miami-Dade County, Florida, see page 7 of http://reports.jud11.flcourts.org/ Administrative_Orders/1-09-09-Revision%20Uniform%20Final%20 Judgment%20Foreclosure%20and%20Procedures.pdf (this may not be the most current version of the form).

be entered because it is incumbent on the attorneys to bring any lack of service to the judge's attention, and if they fail to do so, the courts will presume that proper service exists.

In one case, the process server failed to complete service of the complaint and summons on the homeowner, and the bank moved for summary judgment, claiming that service of process "has been properly perfected upon the Defendants herein."[8] The pro se borrower had sent an undated letter to the bank's attorney "offering to settle the parties' dispute over the subject mortgage."[9] The bank's attorney had then, without the borrower's permission, submitted to the court a "Notice of Filing Defendant's *Pro Se* Answer," attaching the letter from the borrower to the attorney.[10] The bank and the attorney argued that the homeowner had waived service of process by virtue of his "answer."[11]

However, the court rejected this argument, stating there was no basis to conclude that the homeowner had waived the defense of insufficient service or subjected himself to the jurisdiction of the court.[12] The court also noted that the undated, pro se letter "did not remotely resemble" an answer, as it contained none of the attributes required of an answer under the local rules of civil procedure, such as the caption, file number, names of the parties, and the subject matter of the paper, other than to state that the borrower wished to settle the case.[13] The court also forwarded a copy of its decision to the state bar so it could determine whether the bank's attorney had violated the rules of professional conduct.[14]

Another court was disturbed by one foreclosure firm's insistence on proceeding with summary judgment even when it had notice from a process server's notes that service of the complaint

---

8. Opella v. Bayview Loan Servicing, LLC, 48 So. 3d 185 (Fla. 3d Dist. Ct. App. 2010).
9. *Id.*
10. *Id.*
11. *Id.*
12. *Id.*
13. *Id.*
14. *Id.*

upon the homeowner was faulty.[15] In that case, ProVest's services had been engaged to complete service on the parties.[16] ProVest filed a verified return of service alleging that it had completed individual service on the homeowner.[17] However, the process server had written notes on both the front and reverse sides of the summons attached to the return of service stating that he had attempted to serve the homeowner to no avail, that he had left copies of the summons and complaint in the mailbox, and read documents aloud at the door when he saw the curtains move.[18] The homeowner later advised the court that at the time that the process server purportedly served her, she was at her mother's home recovering from surgery.[19]

The court emphasized that unless service has been obtained, a court may not proceed in the case.[20] Even though a return of service is "presumed valid absent clear and convincing evidence to the contrary," the process server's notes were considered to be an admission against the bank's interest and demonstrated the falsity of the service.[21]

The court found it to be extremely troubling that, even with notice of these discrepancies in the return of service, the bank failed to admit its mistakes to the court and instead proceeded with summary judgment.[22] The bank failed its burden to demonstrate regular service once the defect in the return of service had been established.[23] The court also excused the homeowner from having to show a meritorious defense[24] to vacate the default because no in

---

15. *See* Bennett v. Christiana Bank & Trust Co., 50 So. 3d 43, 46 (Fla. 3d Dist. Ct. App. 2010).

16. *Id.* at 44.

17. *Id.*

18. *Id.*

19. *Id.* at 45.

20. *Id.*

21. *Id.*

22. *Id.* at 46.

23. *Id.*

24. In deciding whether to vacate a judgment by default, many courts consider "(1) whether the default was willful; (2) whether defendant has a meritorious defense; and (3) the level of prejudice that may occur to the non-defaulting party if relief is granted." Speaks v. Donato, 214 F.R.D. 69, 73 (D. Conn. 2003).

personam jurisdiction had been obtained over her.[25] Therefore, the summary judgment and default were vacated, and the homeowner was then able to file a responsive pleading.[26]

Service by publication may be even more suspect. Often, when a process server cannot locate and serve a defendant, the defendant will be deemed to be served by publication. This means that instead of a process server leaving a copy of the physical complaint with a person, home, or place of business, the plaintiff will place a public notice in a newspaper advising of the foreclosure action. After the notice has run for a certain period of time, the court will consider a defendant to be served by publication, even though he may never have received a copy of the complaint. The February 11, 2010, Florida Supreme Court order states that before a defendant can be served by publication, the process server must complete an extensive "Affidavit of Diligent Search and Inquiry," which he must verify under oath. Among other things, the process server must list all efforts made to locate the defendant, and if an occupant of the property is served, the process server must ask the person if he or she knows the whereabouts of the borrower-defendant.

A private process server "is subject to substantially the same liability as imposed by the common law upon a sheriff or constable when performing similar functions."[27] An Arizona court emphasized that the "public is entitled to rely on the faithful performance of official duty and consequently *the law is strict in holding officers to a high degree of accountability for the efficient and true service of process.*"[28] The court therefore upheld a civil action for fraud against the process server, alleging that the process server knew that a return of service was false, that it contained false statements, or that the process server was "ignorant of the validity of the said affidavit and the truth of the content

---

25. *Id.* at 46.
26. *Id.*
27. Marsh v. Hawkins, 31 A.L.R.3d 1383, 1388 (Ariz. Ct. App. 1968).
28. *Id., citing* State *ex rel.* Moore v. Morant, 266 S.W.2d 723 (Mo. App. 1954) (emphasis in original).

thereof."[29] Therefore, if you believe that service of the foreclosure action was fraudulently attempted or obtained against your client, you may also consider whether a motion to quash, affirmative defenses, or counterclaim may be appropriate against the bank on these grounds.

---

29. 31 A.L.R.3d at 1387.

Chapter 16

Motion to Dismiss

The first responsive documents to a foreclosure complaint should at least include a motion to dismiss, if you are filing other papers at the same time. Although the court will usually not dismiss the action with prejudice if granted, the ball is put back into the bank's court. It will usually have to meet a deadline in which to file its amended complaint. If the bank does not meet it, other relief may be available to the homeowner, which sometimes includes a dismissal with prejudice.

A motion to dismiss is an extremely important tool in your arsenal. To be effective, as with all of your defenses, you must be specific. If your motion to dismiss is granted, the bank will usually be given leave to amend. However, if the bank has engaged in wrongful conduct, violated a crucial rule of court, or deprived the homeowner of a fundamental right, such as due process, the court may grant the extraordinary relief of dismissal of the complaint with prejudice.

Grounds for a motion to dismiss exists if the complaint does not set forth the required elements for its causes of action, is violative of court rules and procedures,[1] is too vague and unclear for a defendant

---

1. Your local rules of court and civil procedure will govern the required form of any complaint. Special rules have been formulated for foreclosure actions in certain jurisdictions. For example, in Florida all foreclosure actions against residential property must be verified. FLA. R. CIV. P. 1.110(b).

to form an appropriate response, or if a fact exists that renders the plaintiff's claims null and void. Another issue to look for is whether the bank has previously filed a foreclosure action regarding the subject loan, and whether its action was dismissed. Perhaps the court dismissed its lawsuit with prejudice, meaning that the bank is never permitted to file foreclosure on this subject loan again. The bank may also have voluntarily dismissed its own action for a variety of reasons; for example, the bank may have realized that it accepted payments from the homeowner after sending the demand letter, thereby destroying a condition precedent to foreclosure and necessitating a redemand. There is usually a limit on how many times the bank can voluntarily dismiss and refile its foreclosure before the action is deemed to be dismissed with prejudice. In the absence of a statute or rule stating otherwise, a "plaintiff may dismiss and recommence his suit as often as he chooses, subject only to payment of the cost."[2] However, the Federal Rules of Civil Procedure and counterpart state rules generally provide that "if the plaintiff previously dismissed any federal- or state-court action based on or including the same claim, a notice of dismissal operates as an adjudication on the merits."[3] In other words, the bank generally cannot refile a foreclosure action on the same loan transaction if it has already filed two voluntary dismissals.

Dissecting a Foreclosure Complaint

A boilerplate foreclosure action may look something like this:[4]

1. IN THE CIRCUIT COURT OF THE 6TH JUDICIAL
2. CIRCUIT, IN AND FOR PINELLAS COUNTY, FLORIDA
3. GENERAL JURISDICTION DIVISION
4. CASE NO:

---

2. Poplarville Sawmill Co. v. L.F. Driver & Co., 88 S.E. 36 (1916).

3. FED. R. CIV. P. 41(a)(1)(B); *see also* FLA. R. CIV. P. 1.420(a)(1); Smith v. Washington, 10 S.W.3d 877, 879–80 (Ark. 2000); Olynyk v. Scoles, 868 N.E.2d 254, 255–56 (Ohio 2007); Spokane County v. Specialty Auto and Truck Painting, Inc., 103 P.3d 792, 795 (Wash. 2004)

4. http://www.mortgage-investments.com/Real_estate_and_mortgage_Forms/formpage/2_mortgage_foreclosure_complaint.htm.

5. XXX MORTGAGE CORPORATION
6. PLAINTIFF
7. Vs.
8. ELAN KAY XXX A/K/A ELAINE K. XXXXX
9. A/K/A KAY ELAINE XXXX A/K/A ELAN KAY
10. XXXXX TRACY A/K/A KAY E. XXXXX, IF LIVING,
11. AND IF DEAD, THE UNKNOWN SPOUSE, HEIRS,
12. DEVISES, GRANTEES, ASSIGNEES, LIENOR,
13. CREDITORS, TRUSTEES AND ALL OTHER
14. PARTIES CLAIMING AN INTEREST BY,
15. THROUGH, UNDER OR AGAINST ELAN KAY
16. XXXX A/K/A ELAINE K. XXXX A/K/A KAY
17. ELAINE XXXXXX A/K/A ELAN KAY XXXXX XXXX
18. A/K/A KAY E. XXXXX; UNKNOWN SPOUSE OF
19. ELAN KAY XXXXX A/K/A ELAINE K. XXXXX
20. A/K/A KAY ELAINE XXXXX A/K/A ELAN KAY
21. BIKEL XXXXX A/K/A KAY E. XXXXX, IF ANY;
22. RUTH XXXX AS TRUSTEE OF THE RUTH XXXX
23. TRUST #XXX DATED APRIL 3, 199X; XXXXXX
24. XXXXX, AS TRUSTEE OF MINOR XXXX
25. XXXXX'S TRUST DATED OCTOBER 1,1990;
26. BEVERLY S. XXXXX; RICK KEVIN XXXX; THE
27. UNKNOWN SPOUSE OF RICK KEVIN XXXX;
28. THE UNKNOWN SPOUSE, HEIRS,
29. BENEFICIARIES, AND ALL OTHER PARTIES
30. CLAIMING AGAINST THE ESTATE OF EDGAR
31. XXXX, DECEASED; JOHN DOE AND JANE DOE
32. AS UNKNOWN TENANTS IN POSSESSION
33. DEFENDANT(S)
34. COMPLAINT TO FORECLOSE MORTGAGE AND TO RE-ESTABLISH LOST LOAN DOCUMENTS
35. Plaintiff, sues the Defendant(s) and alleges:
36. THIS IS AN ACTION to foreclose a Mortgage on real property in PINELLAS County, Florida.
37. This Court has jurisdiction over the subject matter herein.
38. On SEPTEMBER 5, 1979 BEVERLY S. XXXXX, JOINED BY HER HUSBAND, RICK KEVIN XXXX, executed and delivered a Promissory Note and a PURCHASE MONEY

Mortgage securing payment of the Note to the Payee named thereon.

39. The Mortgage was recorded on SEPTEMBER XX, 1979 in Official Records Book 4XXX at page 4XX of the Public Records of PINELLAS County, Florida, and mortgaged the property described in it, then owned by and possessed by the Mortgagors, a copy of the Mortgage AND NOTE ARE attached hereto as "Exhibit "A". Said mortgage was subsequently assigned to XXX MORTGAGE CORPORATION by virtue of an assignment recorded on MARCH 15, 199X at Book 9XXX, Page 15XX of the PINELLAS County Records, a copy of which is attached hereto as Exhibit "B".

40. The Plaintiff owns and holds the Note and Mortgage.

41. The property is now owned by the Defendant(s), ELAN KAY XXXXX A/KIA ELAINE K. XXXX A/K/A KAY ELAINE XXXX A/K/A ELAN KAY XXXXX TRACY A/K/A KAY E. XXXXX if living and if dead, the unknown spouses, heirs and beneficiaries of ELAIN KAY XXXXX A/K/A ELAINE K. XXXXX A/K/A KAY ELAINE XXXXX A/K/A ELAIN KAY XXXXX TRACY A/K/A KAY E. XXXXX who hold(s) possession.

42. There is a default under the terms of the note and mortgage for the JULY 1, 199X payment and all payments due thereafter.

43. All conditions precedent to the acceleration of this Mortgage Note and to foreclosure of the Mortgage have been fulfilled or have occurred.

44. The Plaintiff declares the full amount payable under the Note and Mortgage to be due.

45. The borrowers owe the Plaintiff $23,802.63 that is due on principal on the Note and Mortgage, interest from JUNE 1, 199X, plus the title search expense for ascertaining the necessary parties to this action, and taxes and assessments advanced by the mortgagee.

46. Plaintiff is obligated to pay its attorney a reasonable fee for his services rendered.

47. Defendants, John Doe and Jane Doe, may claim an interest in the property described in the Mortgage as tenants pursuant

to a lease agreement, either written or oral. Said interest is subject, subordinate, and inferior to the lien of the Mortgage held by Plaintiff.

48. In addition to all other named defendants, the unknown spouses, heirs, devises, grantees, assignees, creditors, trustees, successors in interest or other parties claiming an interest in the subject property by, through under or against any of said defendants, whether natural or corporate, who are not known to be alive or dead, dissolved or existing, are joined as defendants herein. The claims of any of said parties are subject, subordinate, and inferior to the interest of Plaintiff.

49. The Defendant, UNKNOWN SPOUSE OF ELAIN KAY XXXXX A/K/A ELAINE K. XXXX A/K/A KAY ELAINE XXXXX A/K/A ELAIN KAY XXXX XXXX A/K/A KAY E. XXXXX is joined because HE may claim some interest in or lien upon the subject property by virtue of a possible homestead interest. Said interest is subject, subordinate and inferior to the interest of the Plaintiffs mortgage.

50. The Defendant(s) RUTH XXXX AS TRUSTEE OF THE RUTH XXXX TRUST # 19XX DATED APRIL X, 199X IS joined because SHE may claim some interest in or lien upon the subject property by virtue of a MORTGAGE recorded in Official Records Book 98XX at Page 1XX in PINELLAS COUNTY which is inferior to Plaintiffs Mortgage described herein.

51. The Defendant(s) XXXXXX XXXXXX AS TRUSTEE OF MINOR XXXXX XXXXX'S TRUST DATED OCTOBER 1, 1990 IS joined because HE may claim some interest in or lien upon the subject property by virtue of a MORTGAGE recorded in Official Records Book 902X at Page 5XX in PINELLAS COUNTY which is inferior to Plaintiffs Mortgage described herein.

52. The Defendant(s) THE UNKNOWN SPOUSE OF RICK KEVIN XXXX IS joined because SHE may claim some interest in or lien upon the subject property by virtue of a LACK OF JOINDER OF SPOUSE IN QUIT CLAIM DEED RECORDED FEBRUARY 9, 198X in Official Records Book

569X at Page 6XX in PINELLAS COUNTY which is inferior to Plaintiffs Mortgage described herein.

53. IS. The Defendant(s) THE UNKNOWN SPOUSE, HEIRS, BENEFICIARIES AND ALL OTHER PARTIES CLAIMING AGAINST THE ESTATE OF EDGAR XXXX, DECEASED IS joined because THEY may claim same interest in or lien upon the subject property by virtue of a MORTGAGE recorded in Official Records Book 569X at Page 6XX in PINELLAS COUNTY which is inferior to Plaintiffs Mortgage described herein.

54. WHEREFORE, Plaintiff prays: That an accounting may be had and taken under the direction of this Court of what is due the Plaintiff for principal and interest on said Mortgage and Mortgage Note, and for the casts, charges and expenses, including attorneys fees and title search costs, and advancements which Plaintiff may be put to or incur in and about this suit, and that the Defendants found responsible for same be ordered to pay the Plaintiff herein the amounts so found to be due it; that in default of such payments, all right, title, interest, claim, demand, or equity of redemption of the Defendants and all other persons claiming by, through, under or again said Defendants since the filing of the Lis Pendens herein be absolutely barred and foreclosed and that said mortgage property be said under the direction of this Court; that out of the proceeds of said sale, the amounts due the Plaintiff may be paid so far as same will suffice; and that a deficiency judgment be entered if applicable, and a Writ of Possession be issued.

55. COUNT II

56. This is an action to reestablish a Promissory Note AND MORTGAGE under F.S. 71.011

57. On SEPTEMBER 5, 19XX, BEVERLY S. XXX, JOINED BY HER HUSBAND, RICK KEVIN XXXX executed and delivered a Promissory Note and a Mortgage securing payment of the Note to the payee named thereon.

58. The Mortgage was recorded on SEPTEMBER 10, 19XX in Official Records Book 49XX at page 49X, of the Public Records of PINELLAS County, Florida, a substantial copy

of the Mortgage and a copy of the Note already being attached hereto as composite Exhibit "A" to the Plaintiffs original Complaint herein.

59. The original document(s) were received by the Plaintiff at the inception of the loan or upon assignment of the note and mortgage to Plaintiff and while in its custody, the Note AND MORTGAGE WERE lost or destroyed under unknown circumstances.

60. Plaintiff knows of no parties except the Defendants who are interested in the reestablishment of said document(s).

61. WHEREFORE, Plaintiff prays that this Court re-establish the NOTE AND MORTGAGE, copy(ies) already exhibited to this Complaint.

62. XXXX XXXXXX

63. Law Offices of XXXX XXXXX, P.A.

64. Attorney for Plaintiff

65. XXX S. XXXXXXX Drive Suite XX

66. XXXXX, FL 333XX

67. (XXX) XXX-XXXX

Paragraphs 1–33 of the document above form the caption of the complaint. Foreclosure captions usually tend to be long-winded. Not only is the plaintiff's name usually extremely verbose, the bank takes a "throw everything against the wall and see what sticks" approach to naming its defendants. Even though a first mortgage is by its very nature inherently superior to other interests that might attach against the property (except for super-priority liens, to be discussed in Chapter 18), the bank often names every interest under the sun that could possibly have an interest against the property whether in the past, present, or future. These may include names that appear in its title searches of parties who sold their interest long ago.[5]

In paragraphs 35–53, we see the allegations and prayers for relief merged all together, as foreclosure complaints are often drafted. Sometimes the general or factual allegations will be labeled as such, and the causes of action or counts for relief will be itemized separately.

---

5. *See* Diane C. Lade, *Foreclosure Note [sic] Surprises Retiree: Former Owner Sold Oakland Park Condo 14 Years Ago*, Sun-Sentinel (Fort Lauderdale, Fla.) Dec. 11, 2010.

In order for a foreclosure complaint to be legally sufficient, it must state, among other things, proper jurisdiction, amount in controversy, and all necessary elements to plead a cause of action for foreclosure. The foreclosure complaint will usually satisfy the jurisdictional requirement by stating that the subject property is located within the court's jurisdiction, as this complaint does in paragraph 36.

Next, the foreclosure complaint will usually allege that the lender and the borrowers executed a mortgage and a promissory note secured by the subject property, that the borrowers defaulted on the loan, and that the lender has elected to accelerate the loan and seeks foreclosure, as this complaint does in paragraphs 38–45. Your jurisdiction may require that copies of the loan documents be attached to the complaint. However, these are all factual allegations and the borrowers may demand strict proof thereof.

Most foreclosure complaints will contain similar allegations: that the borrowers entered into the loan documents, they were required to make payments under same, they have failed to make those payments, and therefore the lender seeks foreclosure of the property secured by the mortgage. Usually the note and mortgage, and sometimes the assignment of mortgage and other documents, will be attached to the complaint. If not, you may seek to dismiss the complaint if your jurisdiction requires such documents to be attached to a foreclosure complaint.

In paragraphs 39–40 of this complaint, the plaintiff states that the mortgage was assigned to it and that it now owns the note and mortgage. Look at the date of the assignment and see if the assignment was executed after the foreclosure action was filed. If it was, you have another basis for filing a motion to dismiss (each theory for a motion to dismiss in response to this particular complaint are explained further in this chapter). A court may accept the bank's argument that it obtained physical possession of the note prior to the filing of the complaint, but the complaint does not allege this.

In paragraph 42, the plaintiff alleges that there is a default in payment as of a certain date and for all payments thereafter. You need to determine whether this is in fact the case, and whether your client made any payments within this time period that were accepted by the bank. If so, you have a potential motion to dismiss for failure of conditions precedent by the bank. The same goes for paragraph 43 of the complaint, and also if there are other conditions that the bank was required to fulfill prior to filing the complaint, such as loss mitigation procedures mandated for federally backed loans.

The complaint also contains a lost note count as its second cause of action, in paragraphs 55–61. This is another red flag that the plaintiff may not be the proper party in interest, as the real owner of the loan will usually have the original note and mortgage. The bank will likely claim that it does not have to prove ownership until the summary judgment stage, or it may come up with the originals later simply because it was in such a rush to file the foreclosure complaint that it did not want to wait until the originals were transferred to the legal department or counsel from its vault or storage facility. However, the current laws overwhelmingly require proper verification of ownership and a good basis that a foreclosure plaintiff is the real party in interest at the inception of the action. There has been an epidemic of cases in which an improper party falsely claimed the right to file foreclosure. Due to the heightened scrutiny and crisis caused by wrongful filings, there is even greater necessity to have a plaintiff make a proper showing at the inception of the case that it has a right to seek the extreme relief of foreclosure.

Is the Complaint Required to Be Verified?

If the complaint fails to comply with a law that it be verified, it is fatally deficient. It does not matter what else the complaint says; it is subject to dismissal. Some jurisdictions now require a foreclosure complaint involving residential property to be verified. As of February 2010, all actions filed to foreclose a residential mortgage in Florida are required to be verified. When verification of a document is required, the document filed shall include an oath, affirmation, or the following statement: "Under penalty of perjury, I declare that I have read the foregoing, and the facts alleged therein are true and correct to the best of my knowledge and belief."[6]

This new rule of civil procedure is the result of a Florida Supreme Court opinion which drastically changed the rules governing

---

6. Fla. R. Civ. P. 1.110(b).

the filing of foreclosure complaints and other foreclosure matters that became final on June 3, 2010.[7] Despite this rule, myriad foreclosure complaints that fail to comply have been filed in the courts. These complaints are easy targets for motions to dismiss. If the complaint was not verified when it was required to be, the court should grant the dismissal of the complaint on this basis alone.

Other documents may be required to be filed along with the initial foreclosure complaint as well. A local rule in Summit County, Ohio, requires that counsel for a foreclosure plaintiff file a Certificate of Readiness certifying that the foreclosure plaintiff "is the owner of the note and mortgage upon which the complaint is founded, that all supporting documents necessary to establish separate chains of ownership are attached to the complaint, and that all assignments shown on the preliminary judicial report bear a date prior to the filing date of the complaint."[8] The rule provides that if these requirements are not met, the action may be dismissed without prejudice.[9]

Similarly, a New York local rule of court compels a foreclosure plaintiff's counsel to:

> state that he or she communicated on a specific date with a named representative of plaintiff [], who informed counsel that he or she: (a) has personally reviewed plaintiff's documents and records relating to this case; (b) has reviewed the Summons and Complaint, and all other papers filed in this matter in support of foreclosure; and, (c) has confirmed both the factual accuracy of these court filings and the accuracy of the notarizations contained therein. Further, plaintiff's counsel, based upon his or her communication with plaintiff's representative named above, must upon his or her "inspection of the papers filed with the Court and other diligent inquiry, . . . certify that, to the best of [his or her] knowledge, information, and belief, the Summons and Complaint

---

7. http://www.floridasupremecourt.org/decisions/2010/sc09-1460.pdf.

8. Argent Mortgage Co., LLC v. Phillips, 2010 Ohio 5826 at *2 (Ohio 9th App. Dist. 2010).

9. *Id.*

filed in support of this action for foreclosure are complete and accurate in all relevant respect."[10]

This local rule was prompted by the crisis that emerged during the summer of 2010 concerning the nationwide discovery of "failure of plaintiffs and their counsel to review documents and files to establish standing and other foreclosure requisites; filing of notarized affidavits which falsely attest to such review and to other critical facts in the foreclosure process; and 'robosigning' of documents by parties and counsel."[11] The New York court found that the plaintiff's counsel had submitted a false certificate purporting to meet the requirements of the rule; the complaint contained a fraudulent verification, and the plaintiff representative with whom the attorney claimed to have spoken was apparently never employed by the plaintiff.[12]

In another New York case, the judge sharply criticized one bank's excuse for failing to comply with this local rule because it "did not have the procedures in place" to comply with the administrative order.[13] The court emphasized that it "does not work for CITI and cannot wait for CITI, a multibillion-dollar financial behemoth, to get its 'act' together."[14] The court dismissed the complaint there

---

10. Wash. Mutual Bank v. Phillip, 2010 N.Y. slip op. 52034U at *2 (N.Y. App. Div. 2010).

11. *Id.* at *3.

12. *Id.* at **4–5.

13. CitiMortgage, Inc. v. Nunez, 2010 N.Y. slip op. 52142U at *1 (N.Y. App. Div. 2010).

14. *Id.* The extent to which some banks believe they are above the law is one of the things that makes me wonder if this so-called democracy has really become an oligarchy. The length of time it takes for a case to travel through the court process is often unacceptable to a bank's guidelines, and some seem to actually believe that the courts should cater to the bank's guidelines and not vice-versa. Quite often, the soonest date available for a hearing will be several months away, and yet the bank's guidelines compel it to constantly demand statuses when there is nothing new to report. Others will reenter a property while title is still in a homeowner's name, change the locks, and employ a self-help eviction process, as discussed in Chapter 11, Shotgun Foreclosures. A foreclosure defense attorney should bear in mind that the parties across the table are often puppets pulled by the strings of mindless and inhumane policies.

without prejudice, pending the plaintiff's compliance with the administrative order.[15] In making these rulings, the court continued that:

> We cannot allow the courts in New York State to stand by idly and be party to what we now know is a deeply flawed process, especially when that process involves basic human needs—such as a family home—during this period of economic crisis. This new filing requirement will play a vital role in ensuring that the documents judges rely on will be thoroughly examined, accurate and error-free before any judge is asked to take the drastic step of foreclosure.[16]

The "deeply flawed process" has been created in part by the frenzy of banks and their foreclosure counsel to treat troubled loans like a goldmine and think of as many ways as possible to sidestep and dodge applicable laws. Many of the parties involved in this new gold rush know that if they do not collect the treasure first, somebody else will. So they attempt to circumvent the laws regulating who has the right to file foreclosure actions.

Lack of Standing/Improper Plaintiff

As discussed earlier in the book, one reason for the enormous uproar regarding foreclosures lately has been the issue of whether the plaintiff in a foreclosure action is the true owner of the loan and has the right and standing to prosecute a foreclosure action. It is often hard to tell, because mortgages are often packaged and sold in bulk within securitized trusts, and numerous investors may own a piece of such assets. With increasing frequency, when a plaintiff is required by the court at the outset of the case to put its cards on the table and satisfy the court that it is the proper party to file the lawsuit, the plaintiff cannot deliver.

If the foreclosure plaintiff does not own the loan, it cannot maintain a foreclosure action based on same. The court may consider this an issue of fact to be determined at summary judgment or trial.

---

15. *Id.* at *4.
16. *Id.* at *3.

However, if the complaint is legally insufficient to show a required allegation for a foreclosure action, such as ownership, the court may dismiss the complaint due to the plaintiff's lack of standing.[17]

On August 10, 2010, the Florida Attorney General, Bill McCollum, announced that he was launching an investigation into three of the largest default law firms in the state.[18] This investigation was in response to revelations that plaintiffs' court filings or evidence were fabricated or fraudulent. Examples of the fraud include assignments or affidavits notarized by an entity that was not in existence when the document was executed. Subpoenas were served on all three law firms demanding a vast scope of information and documents, such as all employees for the past five years, a list of all corporations located outside of the United States associated with these firms, a list of all notaries and persons involved with the preparations of assignments, an explanation of any bonus program associated with the time incurred to complete a foreclosure case, etc.[19]

A job for foreclosure defense counsel is to test the truth of the allegations contained in the complaint through the discovery process, and with depositions if at all possible. For example, does the plaintiff actually have authority to pursue the foreclosure action, even though it may purportedly be acting on behalf of the actual owner of the loan? Examine the relationship between the plaintiff and the actual owner. A deposition is the best way to present specific questions and nail down facts and disputes thereto for summary judgment and trial. The banks' entire foreclosure strategy usually depends on getting a rubber-stamped summary judgment. However, the law is very clear that summary judgment should not be granted if a genuine issue of material fact exists, and presumptions that issues of fact exist are in favor of the non-movant.[20] Strategies for opposing summary judgment will be discussed further in Chapter 21.

---

17. LNV Corp. v. Madison Real Estate, LLC, 2010 N.Y. slip op. 33376U (N.Y. App. Div. 2010).

18. Todd Ruger, *State Subpoenas Records from "Foreclosure Mills,"* HERALD-TRIBUNE (Sarasota, Fla.), Aug. 10, 2010.

19. Copies of the subpoenas served on the three law firms can be viewed at http://4closurefraud.org/2010/08/10/kaboom-florida-law-firms-subpoenaed-over-foreclosure-filing-practices/.

20. *See* Desmond v. Varrasso (*In re* Varrasso), 37 F.3d 760, 763 (Bankr. 1st Cir. 1994).

It is beyond the scope of this book to explain the bank process by which loans are bundled and constantly transferred. What matters from a foreclosure defense perspective is whether, under the laws of your jurisdiction, the plaintiff owns the loan and has standing and authority to prosecute the foreclosure action. Some defendants have successfully argued that a plaintiff does not have standing because a written assignment of the note and mortgage to the plaintiff was not executed prior to the foreclosure action being filed, though plaintiffs sometimes successfully counter this argument, as recent case law underscores the proposition that the plaintiff is the owner of the loan by virtue of possession.[21] In many jurisdictions, the Uniform Commercial Code provides that the party who physically holds a promissory note has the right to enforce that document.[22] In other words, if the plaintiff holds physical possession of the promissory note, it also holds ownership and the right to enforce the terms of this document.[23] Therefore, if the plaintiff holds the original note and produces it for your inspection, it may have proper standing.

However, when the very allegations of the complaint rely upon a written assignment as the basis for the plaintiff's ownership, the plaintiff has admitted that its ownership hinges on this assignment, and this would be a case where the bank should have a written assignment executed on or before the date of a foreclosure action filing before it can be entitled to pursue such action. Look for allegations such as "Plaintiff owns the Note and Mortgage by virtue of a written assignment dated XX and recorded at Book XX and Page XX in the Public Records of XX County, Florida." When such an allegation is contained in the complaint, the plaintiff has necessitated the existence of a written assignment at the time it files its complaint; otherwise, an essential element of its case does not exist, and the defendant should move for dismissal on that basis.

Ultimately, the plaintiff must also prove that it is the owner of the subject note and mortgage and has a right to file the foreclosure action. The chain of title in a foreclosure action can be very unclear,

---

21. *Id.*

22. *Id.*; *see also* WM Specialty Mortgage, LLC v. Salomon, 874 So. 2d 680, 682 (Fla. 4th Dist. Ct. App. 2004).

23. *Id.*

and plaintiffs are often not compelled to demonstrate sufficient proof of their ownership. The court will usually find that plaintiffs have met their burden of proof if they can produce the original note. However, foreclosure plaintiffs will frequently include a "lost note" count in their complaints. They will claim that they cannot find the original note but that they are still the owner of the loan and are entitled to foreclosure. This could be a red flag to indicate an improper plaintiff who has no right to institute a foreclosure action.

If a Plaintiff Cannot Prove Ownership or Enforcement Rights at the Time It Files Foreclosure, It Has No Standing

A recent federal decision lends authority to a number of matters central to resolving issues relevant to standing and clarifying that a plaintiff cannot maintain a foreclosure action if it does not have right to enforce the debt at the inception of the action.[24] That case described a confusing transfer history of a note and mortgage alleged to have been defaulted on by the mortgagor.[25] The mortgage had been placed in a Real Estate Investment Conduit (REMIC)[26] pursuant to a Pooling and Servicing Agreement and sold together with a bundle of securitized mortgages.[27] For part of the case, the bank confused itself into thinking that it no longer owned the note and mortgage, but then changed its mind and pursued summary judgment, arguing that it did own these documents after all.[28] However, there were multiple security interests competing against the bank's interest, including a federal tax lien, and all other lienors were also seeking summary judgment.[29]

The bank asserted that its lien against the property was superior to all others and that it had standing to pursue the foreclosure action

---

24. Merrill Lynch Credit Corp. v. Lenz, No. 09-CV-60633 at *7 (S.D. Fla. Nov. 3, 2010).

25. *Id.* at **1–6.

26. A REMIC is a "type of special-purpose vehicle used for the pooling of mortgage loans and issuance of mortgage-backed securities." http://en.wikipedia.org/wiki/Real_Estate_Mortgage_Investment_Conduit.

27. *Lenz* at *2.

28. *Id.* at *5.

29. *Id.*

when it was first filed.[30] This argument was refuted by the other defendants, who maintained that the bank could not prove its standing, and the United States asserted that the bank did not have a perfected security interest in the property, therefore rendering the bank's purported interest inferior and subordinate to the federal tax lien.[31]

The federal court then began an instructive legal review on standing and chain of title.[32] The question of who owns a note and mortgage is determined by who has standing to foreclose on the property collateral thereto.[33] If the plaintiff does not have standing at the inception of the lawsuit, it has no authority to maintain the action.[34]

The court held that the bank could not prove that it owned the note, even after the court had granted the bank numerous chances to correct factual inconsistencies regarding its purported standing.[35] The subject note contained a special endorsement, defined by the court as an endorsement that is made by the holder of an instrument to be payable to either an identified person or to a "bearer" who is specifically identified.[36] The endorsement in this case made the note payable to Banker's Trust, a party to the pooling and servicing agreement.[37] An instrument with a special endorsement can only be negotiated by the party named in the endorsement.[38] Therefore, according to the plaintiff's own exhibit, it was not the proper plaintiff to foreclose on the mortgage, as the allegations of the complaint conflicted with the terms apparent on the face of the exhibits to the complaint.[39] The contents of exhibits to a complaint control over the allegations contained therein.[40]

---

30. *Id.* at *7.

31. *Id.*

32. *Id.*

33. *Id.*

34. *Id.*; *see also* U.S. Bank Nat'l Ass'n v. Duvall, 2010 Ohio 6478 at *14 (Ohio App. 2010); U.S. Bank Nat'l Ass'n v. Perry, 2010 Ohio 6171 at **20–21 (Ohio App. 2010); *In re* Foreclosure Cases, 521 F. Supp. 2d 650, 653 (S.D. Ohio 2007).

35. *Id.* at **7–8.

. 36. *Id.* at *9.

37. *Id.* at *8.

38. *Id.* at *9.

39. *Id.* at *8.

40. *Id.*

The bank nonetheless argued that there was sufficient circumstantial evidence to prove its standing and to receive summary judgment, assuming that a valid transfer or assignment of the note existed when the bank filed its amended complaint.[41] However, the court did not accept this attempt to circumvent well-settled law that summary judgment "is appropriate only upon record proof, not assumptions."[42]

The bank also tried to establish standing by suddenly producing an unauthenticated allonge[43] that reflected an endorsement of the note to itself, attaching this document to its motion for summary judgment.[44] However, interestingly enough, the allonge had neither been in the court file nor mentioned in any pleadings, nor referenced in any discovery, nor previously disclosed to the court or opposing parties.[45] Furthermore, the court held that the bank could not cure its defect in standing subsequent to the inception of the lawsuit and could not "rely on the unauthenticated allonge to retroactively claim enforceable foreclosure rights."[46] Therefore, the bank's amended complaint was dismissed without prejudice.[47]

As noted previously, a court may recognize that the date on which a foreclosure plaintiff obtains ownership of a note is not when a written assignment is executed, but when the plaintiff obtains physical possession of the document.[48] One Florida case holds that, pursuant to Florida's Uniform Commercial Code, a plaintiff who physically holds a note with a blank endorsement is entitled to enforce the note as a negotiable instrument by virtue of possession.[49] In this method, a foreclosure plaintiff may successfully argue that it

---

41. *Id.*

42. *Id.*

43. Defined by the court as "a slip of paper sometimes attached to a negotiable instrument for the purpose of receiving further indorsements when the original paper is filed with indorsements." *Id.* at **9–10, n.5, *citing* BLACK'S LAW DICTIONARY (9th ed. 2009).

44. *Id.* at **9–10.

45. *Id.* at *10.

46. *Id.*

47. *Id.*

48. *See* Riggs v. Aurora Loan Servs., LLC, 36 So. 3d 932, 933 (Fla. 4th Dist. Ct. App. 2010).

49. *Id.*

was entitled to enforce the note and mortgage at the time it filed its action, even though this may precede the date of a written assignment of the note and mortgage.

However, if a plaintiff cannot prove that it possessed the note at the time the foreclosure was filed, then a court may still find that it lacks standing.[50] Like the Florida court, a Connecticut court held that a foreclosure plaintiff need not have a written assignment of mortgage as long as it physically holds the note, as the mortgage follows the note.[51] However, before judgment can be entered in the plaintiff's favor, the court must make a factual determination as to when the plaintiff acquired the note.[52]

In the Connecticut case, the defendant saw an opportunity to present a motion to dismiss based on lack of subject matter jurisdiction revealed by the plaintiff's exhibits to its motion for summary judgment.[53] The defendant noted that the date that the foreclosure action was filed preceded that date of the assignment of mortgage, and the plaintiff presented no evidence that it owned the note prior to the filing of the action.[54] Accordingly, the appellate court reversed the summary judgment and remanded the case for an evidentiary hearing to determine when the plaintiff acquired ownership and enforcement rights of the note and, consequently, the mortgage.[55]

A New York appellate court upheld the trial court's denial of summary judgment when the bank could never prove that the note and mortgage were delivered to it prior to the commencement of the action.[56] The borrower had raised lack of standing as an affirmative defense.[57] The bank then moved for summary judgment and, in support thereof, submitted an affidavit from its vice president alleging that the note had been physically delivered to the bank prior to the commencement of the action but failed to state when.[58]

---

50. *See* Deutsche Bank Nat'l Trust Co. v. Bialobrzeski, 123 Conn. App. 791, 792 (Conn. App. 2010).

51. *Id.* at 797.

52. *Id.*

53. *Id.* at 799.

54. *Id.* at 794.

55. *Id.* at *800.

56. U.S. Bank, N.A. v. Collymore, 68 A.D.3d 752, 754 (N.Y. App. Div. 2009).

57. *Id.* at 753.

58. *Id.* at 754.

The court held that it is incumbent upon the bank to prove its standing before it can be entitled to foreclosure.[59] The bank could establish standing by showing it was the holder or assignee of the note and mortgage at the inception of the foreclosure action,[60] or by being the assignee or holder of the note alone at the filing of the action, as "the mortgage passes with the debt as an inseparable incident" to the transfer of the note.[61]

However, the bank in that case "failed to demonstrate its prima facie entitlement to judgment as a matter of law because it did not submit sufficient evidence to demonstrate its standing as the lawful holder or assignee of the subject note on the date it commenced this action."[62] The bank's affidavit with no date of when the note was transferred to it "failed to establish that the note was physically delivered to it prior to the commencement of the action."[63] Therefore, the court held that the motion for summary judgment had been properly denied.[64]

An Ohio court recently reached a similar conclusion due to the lack of an acquisition date.[65] The bank had filed a motion for summary judgment and an affidavit in support which alleged that it was holder of the subject note and mortgage and attached alleged copies of the original note and mortgage.[66] However, the court noted that the affidavit lacked an affirmation that the plaintiff was the holder of the note and mortgage at the time the foreclosure action was filed.[67] The complaint had also been filed the same day as a written assignment of mortgage was executed.[68] The court then reversed the entry of summary judgment and directed the trial court to dismiss the complaint without prejudice.[69]

---

59. *Id.* at 753.
60. *Id.*
61. *Id.* at 754.
62. *Id.*
63. *Id.*
64. *Id.*
65. U.S. Bank Nat'l Ass'n v. Worley, 2010 Ohio 6171 (Ohio App. 2010).
66. *Id.* at *17.
67. *Id.* at *18.
68. *Id.* at *19.
69. *Id.* at *20.

The Plaintiff May Have No Relationship to the Loan at All

Massachusetts rang in the New Year with a decision on a closely followed case with numerous amici curiae briefs.[70] In this case, both U.S. Bank and Wells Fargo were seeking declarations from the court that they possessed clear title on two properties on which they had already foreclosed.[71] U.S. Bank claimed that it acquired the first loan (the Ibanez mortgage) when the mortgage was transferred together with 1,220 other loans into "a trust and converted into mortgage-backed securities that can be bought and sold by investors—a process known as securitization."[72] However, U.S. Bank never presented any evidence to the court that the Ibanez mortgage was included within this particular trust.[73] The only document providing any specific link between U.S. Bank and the Ibanez mortgage was an assignment executed more than one year after the foreclosure sale took place.[74]

The relationship between Wells Fargo and the loan it sought to enforce (the LaRace mortgage) was essentially the same. The LaRace mortgage was allegedly packaged together with other mortgages in bulk pursuant to a pooling and servicing agreement (PSA) and acquired by Wells Fargo.[75] However, Wells Fargo could produce no evidence that included the LaRace mortgage within the PSA.[76] Wells

---

70. U.S. Bank Nat'l Ass'n v. Ibanez, 458 Mass. 637 (Jan. 7, 2011).

71. *Id.* at 638. From a strategical standpoint, the bank opened a can of worms when it sought this relief from the court. After all, one of the rulings in a foreclosure judgment is usually that all other liens on the property are extinguished in favor of the plaintiff's mortgage (except for super-priority liens). One can only surmise that the title departments of Wells Fargo and U.S. Bank were concerned with the fact that the assignments had been recorded subsequent to the sale. However, in light of their own argument that their post-sale assignments were proper under the local real estate bar association rules, it seems that the banks really shot themselves in the foot, to the advantage of possibly countless homeowners.

72. *Id.* at 641.

73. *Id.* at 642.

74. *Id.* at 643.

75. *Id.* at 643.

76. *Id.* at 644.

Fargo then obtained an assignment of mortgage for the subject loan 10 months after the foreclosure sale was completed.[77]

When the *Ibanez* plaintiffs came before the court to request their relief of quiet title, the court necessarily examined the plaintiffs' "authority to foreclose under the power of sale and [] their compliance with the requirements on which this authority rests."[78] The court defined an assignment of mortgage as "a conveyance of an interest in land that requires a writing signed by the grantor."[79] Under Massachusetts law, the plaintiffs were required to possess valid assignments of mortgage at the time of foreclosure in order to obtain title to the subject properties.[80] This law differs from that of Florida and other jurisdictions, which hold that "the mere transfer of the debt [note], without any assignment or even mention of the mortgage, carries the mortgage with it . . . ."[81] Massachusetts law provides that a transfer of the note without the mortgage causes the mortgagee to "hold the legal title in trust for the purchaser of the debt, and that the latter might obtain a conveyance by a bill in equity."[82]

Therefore, the plaintiffs could not prove ownership of the subject mortgages simply because they possessed the original notes.[83] There was also no evidence directly linking the subject mortgages to the bulk loan packages to which the plaintiffs claimed interest.[84] The *Ibanez* court accordingly affirmed the trial court's ruling that the two foreclosure sales on the subject properties were invalid because the notices of sale falsely represented that the plaintiffs were the mortgage holders.[85] The court also denied the plaintiff's plea that the decision had only prospective application; therefore, it may be found in the coming months that a plethora of other foreclosure sales are void for the same reasons.[86] The court also denounced the

---

77. *Id.* at 645.
78. *Id.* at 648.
79. *Id.* at 649.
80. *Id.* at 651.
81. *Id.* at 652–53, *citing* Young v. Miller, 6 Gray 152 (1856).
82. *Id.* at 653.
83. *Id.* at 653–54.
84. *Id.* at 649–50.
85. *Id.* at 638.
86. *Id.* at 654–55.

"utter carelessness with which the plaintiff banks documented the titles to their assets."[87]

The Mortgage Electronic Registration Systems

Mortgage Electronic Registration Systems (MERS) is frequently used as a conduit to transfer loans from one bank to another. However, the issue of whether MERS has the proper authority to transfer ownership of loan documents has been sharply criticized in recent cases. The authority of MERS to assign mortgages was discredited by a New York court decision that reviewed the history of MERS, stating that MERS was created in 1993 "by several large participants in the real estate mortgage industry to track ownership interests in residential mortgages. Mortgage lenders and other entities, known as MERS members, subscribe to the MERS system and pay annual fees for the electronic processing and tracking of ownership and transfers of mortgages."[88] One reason for the inception of MERS was that often county clerks were no longer able to keep up with recording property interests and were sometimes two years behind in recording mortgages.[89] To avoid the lost profits caused by this slow process, banks sold the loans to Wall Street, "which bundles them into investments through a process known as securitization."[90] However, the legal research that determined whether MERS could properly operate nationwide was flawed; the law firm conducting the research had failed to examine the requirements of real estate laws on a state-by-state basis.[91]

The New York Code of Civil Practice Law and Rules (CPLR) provides that "a defendant may seek dismissal of a claim if the plaintiff cannot show that it has legal capacity to sue."[92] To foreclose on a

---

87. *Id.* at 655 (Cordy, J., concurring).

88. LPP Mortgage Ltd. v. Sabine Properties, LLC, 2010 N.Y. slip op. 32367U at *3 (N.Y. App. Div. 2010), *citing* MERSCORP, Inc. v. Romaine, 8 N.Y.3d 90, 96, 861 N.E.2d 81, 828 N.Y.S.2d 266 (N.Y. App. Div. 2006).

89. Michael Powell & Gretchen Morgenson, *MERS? It May Have Swallowed Your Loan*, N.Y. Times, Mar. 5, 2011.

90. *Id.*

91. *Id.*

92. LNV Corp. v. Madison Real Estate, LLC, 2010 N.Y. slip op. 33376U at *3.

mortgage, a foreclosure plaintiff must also have the right to enforce the underlying note.[93] In one New York case, the foreclosure plaintiff claimed the right to sue based on an assignment from MERS.[94] However, the assignment from MERS only indicated transfer of the mortgage to the plaintiff.[95] MERS did not hold title to the note and could not transfer any rights in same to the plaintiff.[96] Therefore, the plaintiff had no ownership or enforcement rights in the note and had no standing to pursue a foreclosure of the subject loan.[97] The court granted dismissal of the action on this basis.[98]

In another New York case, a pro se defendant also presented a motion to dismiss pursuant to the CPLR based on the plaintiff's lack of standing.[99] The assignment once again was granted to the plaintiff from MERS.[100] However, this time the court did not discuss the issue of whether the note had been transferred or not, but instead focused on the issue of whether MERS even had authority to execute the subject assignment.[101] The court stated that an assignment of mortgage by an agent of the owner is not proper without a power of attorney from the owner that demonstrates "how the agent is vested with the authority to assign the mortgage."[102] The plaintiff had submitted no evidence to show that the mortgagee had authorized MERS, its nominee, to execute the assignment.[103]

The court cited to the *Black's Law Dictionary* definition of "nominee": a "person designated to act in place of another, usually in a very limited way."[104] The bank in that case had failed to adduce any

---

93. *Id.* at *5.
94. *Id.* at *3.
95. *Id.* at *2.
96. *Id.* at *5.
97. *Id.* at *6.
98. *Id.*
99. HSBC Bank USA v. Squitieri, 2010 N.Y. slip op. 52000U at *1 (N.Y. App. Div. 2010).
100. *Id.* at *2.
101. *Id.* at *4.
102. *Id.*, *citing* HSBC Bank USA, N.A. v. Yeasmin, 866 N.Y.S.2d 92 (N.Y. App. Div. 2008).
103. *Id.*
104. *Id.*

evidence that it had conferred any assignment authority upon MERS.[105] The court explained that one obvious policy behind ensuring that assignors have appropriate authority is to protect the title of future purchasers if the lender ever elected to challenge the assignment.[106]

In the current foreclosure crisis, MERS has been used as a vehicle to transfer mortgages often without question as to whether it actually has authority to assign such interests. However, as another New York court held, "[T]here are no allegations or evidence that MERS was the owner of the note such that it could assign it to LPP. Thus, the assignment from MERS was insufficient to confer ownership of the note to LPP and it has no standing to bring this action."[107] The court also found that there was no indication that MERS had transferred the note, even though it purported to transfer the mortgage.[108] The court then entered a ruling directing the clerk to enter judgment dismissing the complaint.[109]

These cases demonstrate some of the problems posed to banks attempting to foreclose when they make the decision to file a lawsuit against the homeowners but do not have the loan documents in their hands or even the legal right to enforce them. Therefore, the banks shoot first and answer questions later, hoping the questions will never be asked. Without the assistance of MERS, banks doubtless would not be able to transfer loans around to suit their whims, and they expect the courts to comply with their system, not the other way around.[110]

---

105. *Id.*

106. *Id.*

107. *Id.* at *6; *see also* Deutsche Bank Nat'l Trust Co. v. Merrill, No. CUMre-10-248 at *4 (Me. Oct. 14, 2010).

108. *Squiteri* at **4–5.

109. *Id.* at *7.

110. Walter Hackett, a former banker and managing attorney at Inland Counties Legal Services in Riverside, California, has commented, "For 20 years I've watched bankers try to find ways around the rules. They are adept." Nelson D. Schwartz & David Streitfeld, *Mortgage Modification Overhaul Sought by States*, N.Y. TIMES, Mar. 4, 2011.

Chapter 17

Foreclosures Against Parties with No Interest in the Property

As a bank attorney, I would sometimes be contacted by people who asked me why they were getting all the foreclosure mailings and irately demanded that I take them off my mailing list. These calls could sometimes be the result of sloppy work by the title department responsible for finding all parties who could possibly have interest in the subject property and naming them so that they could be foreclosed out. Sometimes it was a corporation that had a similar name to the real party in interest. It might also be a person who sold or relinquished his or her interest in the property years before—for example, the divorced spouse of one of the parties whose interest in the property was extinguished by the dissolution of marriage. Ultimately, such a party is usually dropped from the case. However, this could possibly damage an innocent party's credit or have other adverse effects from being named in a lawsuit.

Because the banks' goal is to push foreclosures through as quickly as possible, they often prosecute foreclosures with a one-size-fits-all approach. For example, when naming defendants to the foreclosure action, the foreclosure title department will run a search to look for anyone and everyone who might have the slightest interest in the property.

The "main" defendants will be the actual homeowners and borrowers on the loan. Others may be creditors of the borrowers who are able to, or have already, placed a lien against the subject property. These may include private individuals and lenders, second mortgagees, homeowners' associations, governmental entities, and so forth. Some of these liens against the property take "super-priority" over the bank's first mortgage, which will be discussed in more detail in Chapter 18. Other defendants may be referred to as "unknown tenant in possession" or "John/Jane Doe." These nomenclatures are intended to be a catch-all for any tenants living in the property who have a leasehold or possessory interest that would not necessarily appear in a title search. Foreclosure defense counsel should check local laws to determine whether these designations are even permitted in their jurisdiction.

Recently, the issue of individuals who have been named in a foreclosure action, but have no actual or potential interest in the subject property whatsoever, has been in the news.[1] In this particular news story, a woman who had sold a property 14 years previously and had no interest in the property since then was named in a foreclosure action.[2] The practical effect of this in terms of such an individual's need to defend against the foreclosure action is negligible. The bank's goal in the foreclosure action is to extinguish all interests in the property other than its own. If a defendant's interest in the property has already been extinguished before the foreclosure was filed, then that person's being named is simply redundant and does not change the status quo regarding his or her non-interest in the property.

Being named in a lawsuit, however, has implications against a person's background and credit reports. If a person has been needlessly named as a defendant in a lawsuit, he or she may have an action for defamation against the plaintiff. Often the bank will file a notice dropping parties they have deemed unnecessary to the

---

1. *See* Diane C. Lade, *Foreclosure Note [sic] Surprises Retiree: Former Owner Sold Oakland Park Condo 14 Years Ago*, SUN-SENTINEL (Fort Lauderdale, Fla.), Dec. 11, 2010.

2. *Id.*

foreclosure action, such as when unknown tenants have been named but, according to the process server's reports, no such parties exist, because the property is owner-occupied. A person who has been wrongfully named to a foreclosure action could contact the plaintiff's counsel and ask that he or she be dropped; however, even if that request is granted, the damage to that person's name may already have been done.

In one New York case, a court issued sanctions against a plaintiff's counsel who filed a frivolous action to foreclose a mortgage that had already been satisfied.[3] The presiding judge had searched the public records and found a satisfaction of mortgage issued from the predecessor plaintiff, Argent, to the successor plaintiff, American Home Mortgage Servicing, Inc. (AHMSI).[4] The judge noted that plaintiff's counsel lacked the professionalism and integrity to notify the court of the satisfaction of mortgage, and that the attorney had wasted valuable court resources and time, could possibly have damaged the wrongfully named defendant's credit, and placed a wrongful cloud on the current property owner's title.[5] And, of course, successor plaintiff AHMSI lacked standing to maintain the foreclosure action ever since the satisfaction of mortgage was executed.[6] The court therefore dismissed the foreclosure action and lis pendens with prejudice, and summoned the plaintiff and its counsel to a hearing to show cause why sanctions should not be issued against each of them.[7]

If your client has been wrongfully named as a foreclosure defendant, you might begin by calling the bank's attorney and politely requesting that your client be dropped from the lawsuit. If opposing counsel complies and your client has not suffered any discernible damage, this may resolve the problem. However, if your client's credit has been damaged or he or she has suffered other actionable injury as a result of being wrongfully named, you might consider filing a lawsuit against the bank and/or its attorneys for

---

3. Argent Mortgage Co., LLC v. Maitland, 2010 N.Y. slip op. 51482U at *1 (N.Y. App. Div. 2010).

4. *Id.* at *2.

5. *Id.* at *3.

6. *Id.*

7. *Id.* at **7–8.

malicious prosecution, for which the following elements must be demonstrated:

- The institution or continuation of original judicial proceedings by, or at the instance of, the defendant.
- The termination of such proceedings in the plaintiff's favor (or, in some jurisdictions, in a manner not unfavorable to the plaintiff).
- Malice in instituting the proceedings.
- Lack of probable cause for the proceedings.
- The suffering of injury or damage as a result of prosecution or proceeding.[8]

Therefore, before a wrongfully named party may begin an action for malicious prosecution against the bank, the proceedings must end favorably for that party. One way this can be accomplished is to drop such party from the suit. Banks will often drop unnecessary parties from a foreclosure action so they will not have to fill out certifications as to whether those parties were properly served, filed an answer, are not in bankruptcy, are not in the military, etc., for summary judgment purposes, as courts now often require. Dropping such parties from the suit is beneficial for the bank's purpose of pushing summary judgment through as quickly as possible. If the bank will not voluntarily agree to drop your client from the lawsuit, you may have to seek such relief from the court. Once the court orders that your client be dropped from the suit and the case is otherwise resolved favorably for your client, you will have obtained a necessary prerequisite for a malicious prosecution action.

You must also establish that the bank acted with malice in naming your client in the foreclosure. Malice may mean that that the bank acted with "ill will, evil motive, gross indifference, or reckless disregard of the rights of others."[9] While a court may not find that the bank acted with a specifically evil motive in naming someone who has no interest in the subject property, it may be easier to show

---

8. 52 AM. JUR. 2D *Malicious Prosecution* § 8.
9. *Id.* § 46.

that the banks and their attorneys have acted with "gross indifference or reckless disregard of the rights of others" in being primarily concerned with the quantity of foreclosures they can generate and not whether all parties to the lawsuit have been properly named. You might also consider pursuing a motion against both the bank and its attorneys for asserting frivolous claims that have no basis in fact or law, and for which both parties should pay monetary sanctions to your client.[10]

---

10. *See* FED. R. CIV. P. 11; FLA. STAT. § 57.105.

Chapter 18

Super-Priority Liens

Some defendants named in a foreclosure action have super-priority liens (SPL), meaning that their lien is superior to the foreclosure plaintiff's first mortgage. Questions have increasingly arisen as to whether such liens include those of homeowners' associations (HOA) for unpaid dues. In states where it does not, such as Florida, an HOA can foreclose on its lien and take the property all the way to sale, but whoever buys the property will not receive clear title because an inferior lien cannot extinguish a superior lien. The first mortgage lien will remain on the property, making it still subject to foreclosure until that lien is satisfied.

Similarly, a first mortgage lien cannot extinguish an SPL. These superior liens often include those placed against title by the government; i.e., municipalities, counties, state, and federal. Examples may include IRS liens, violations of local ordinances and county codes, or state child support liens.

Sometimes a foreclosure mill will not only take a case to summary judgment without addressing all litigated issues in the file, they will also fail to address SPLs against the property. Although there is no established precedent as of yet, this could create an opportunity for the homeowner. If the SPL were to foreclose against the property and the homeowner was the successful purchaser of the property at the SPL sale, the homeowner could end up owning his home free and clear for the price of the SPL, and his former mortgage would now be extinguished. SPLs are often a small fraction of the first mortgage amount; this is why you see properties sometimes being sold for $2,000 at a tax deed sale.

In a recent federal court decision, which ruled that a bank could not maintain a foreclosure action if it did not possess the note at the inception of the action even though it acquired it later, the court also turned to the issue of whether a federal tax lien was superior to the bank's claimed first mortgage lien.[1] If a security interest exists prior to the recording of a tax lien, it may be superior to the tax lien if it is "protected under state law" and the holder of the interest has "parted with money in connection with that interest."[2]

The court held the purported transfer of the note to the plaintiff had no legal effect and was insufficient to put creditors or subsequent purchasers on notice unless it was memorialized by a written assignment titled as such and properly recorded.[3] The bank failed to present any evidence that the transfer by which it purportedly received the loan documents was documented or recorded.[4] The United States was not charged with notice of the bank's claimed equitable interests by either express actual notice, implied actual notice, or constructive notice, as there was nothing in the public records that would have indicated that the loan was transferred to the bank when it said it was.[5] Nor could the United States have known that the bank claimed ownership to the note by virtue of mere possession of same, or even by the fact that it paid taxes on the property for six years, as in Florida these payments are not reflected in the chain of title.[6] Therefore, the court denied all pending motions for summary judgment except for that filed by the United States.[7] The court granted the United States' motion for summary judgment, finding that the bank's "equitable interest

---

1. Merrill Lynch Credit Corp. v. Lenz, No. 09-CV-60633 at *10 (S.D. Fla. Nov. 3, 2010).
2. *Id.* at *11.
3. *Id.*
4. *Id.* at *12.
5. *Id.* at **12–13.
6. *Id.* at **13–14.
7. *Id.* at **14–15.

is not a 'perfected security interest' and that therefore the federal tax lien was entitled to priority over the mortgage."[8]

It might be a good idea to perform your own title search to ascertain what other parties may have liens against the property and whether the plaintiff has named them all. If the plaintiff has not, then you may have a ground to dismiss the complaint, as the plaintiff has failed to join all indispensable parties. This defense should be in your first response to the complaint; it is usually one of the defenses that is waived if not made before pleading or a subsequent motion.[9] If an SPL has not been satisfied, you might also assert that the bank has failed to meet all conditions precedent to foreclosure because it is responsible for curing the defects in the property that could lead to fines, and it would not be equitable to grant the bank relief before it has cured these defects.

---

8. *Id.* at *14.
9. *See* FED. R. CIV. P. 12(b).

Chapter 19

Affirmative Defenses

If a response to a complaint by a motion to dismiss is no longer available or appropriate, a defendant may file an answer with affirmative defenses. By filing an answer to the complaint, "a defendant concedes that the complaint states a claim, but contends that other facts nonetheless defeat recovery."[1] The scope of successful affirmative defenses to foreclosure has greatly increased proportionately with current public policy. Traditionally, the only defenses to foreclosure have been limited to payment, discharge, release or satisfaction, or lack of a valid lien.[2] According to one Connecticut court:

> The purpose of a special defense is to plead facts that are consistent with the allegations of the complaint but demonstrate, nonetheless, that the plaintiff has no cause of action. A valid special defense at law to a foreclosure proceeding must be legally sufficient and address the making, validity or enforcement of the mortgage, the note or both. Where the plaintiff's conduct is inequitable, a court

---

1. Flasza v. TNT Holland Motor Express, 155 F.R.D. 612, 613 (N.D. Ill. 1994).
2. Household Realty Corp. v. Kujawski, No. CV-08-5004992S (Conn. Super. Ct., Sept. 3, 2010).

may withhold foreclosure on equitable considerations and principles. Connecticut's courts have permitted several equitable defenses to a foreclosure action. If the mortgagor is prevented by accident, mistake or fraud, from fulfilling a condition of the mortgage, foreclosure cannot be had. Other equitable defenses that have been recognized in foreclosure actions include unconscionability, abandonment of security, and usury.[3]

Affirmative defenses, or special defenses as referred to by Connecticut courts, can prevent a bank from obtaining summary judgment if they are "legally sufficient and address the making, validity or enforcement of the mortgage, the note or both," not general and boilerplate as demonstrated by so many current foreclosure defense forms.[4] One reason that affirmative defenses should be limited to the making, validity, and/or enforcement of the mortgage and/or note is that other issues may not have any connection "with the subject matter of the foreclosure action and as such do not arise out of the same transaction as the foreclosure action," and similarly, an affirmative defense "cannot attack some act or procedure of the lienholder."[5]

As a foreclosure case is an equitable proceeding, courts permit defenses of unconscionability, abandonment of security, usury, equitable estoppel, violations of unfair and deceptive trade practice statutes, laches, breach of implied covenants of good faith and fair dealing, deed-in-lieu of foreclosure, inequitable bank refusal to allow sale of property to a third party, and lack of consideration.[6] Affirmative defenses may also properly address matters other than the origination or enforcement of the note and mortgage, such as payment.[7] In many cases, affirmative defenses must be made against an assignee of the original lender, as many loans change hands in ownership. An "assignee stands in the shoes of

---

3. *Id.*, *citing to* CONN. GEN. PRAC. BOOK, R. Super. Ct. § 10-50.

4. *See id.*

5. Webster Bank v. Linsley, No. CV-97-0260406S (Conn. Super. Ct., Aug. 9, 2001).

6. *Id.*

7. *Id.*

the assignor and 'succeeds to no greater rights than those possessed by the assignor.'"[8] Additionally, "it is a universal and uncontroversial tenet of contract law that an assignee of a claim takes the same subject to all defenses that could validly have been raised by the defendant against the assignor at the time of the assignment."[9] Therefore, if a homeowner could have asserted a defense against the original lender, he should be able to assert it against the successor transferees of the loan.

Plaintiff's Motion to Strike Affirmative Defenses

Sometimes, instead of responding to the borrower's affirmative defenses, a bank will file a motion to strike the affirmative defenses. This is often because the foreclosure law firm has too many cases to pay attention to individual affirmative defenses, wants to sweep them under the carpet to make way for summary judgment, and hopes the court will too. Sometimes such motions to strike are successful if the defenses are overly vague and conclusory. Many courts will not grant plaintiff's motions to strike homeowners' affirmative defenses because the striking of claims and defenses is an extreme sanction usually reserved as punishment for misconduct of a party. It is one thing if a homeowner knowingly raises frivolous claims and defenses for which sanctions are appropriate. But if the borrower raises affirmative defenses for which she can provide at least a few facts that she believes in good faith to exist, these defenses should not be subject to the extreme sanction of being stricken.

To the extent a pleading is required only to put the opposing party on notice, "affirmative defenses need only apprise the plaintiff of the nature of the defense."[10] Affirmative defenses that are inartfully pled may still be sufficient; facts may be implied in a defense without being expressly alleged.[11] In ruling on a motion to

---

8. Sovereign Bank v. Gawron, 13 Pa. D. & C. 5th 71, 81 (Pa. Ct. Comm. Pl. 2010).

9. *Id.*, *citing* N. Chicago Rolling Mill Co. v. St. Louis Ore & Steel Co., 152 U.S. 596 (1894).

10. Flasza v. TNT Holland Motor Express, 155 F.R.D. 612, 613 (N.D. Ill. 1994).

11. DGG Props. Co., Inc. v. Lanier, No. CV-00-0093788S (Conn. Super. Ct., Sept. 13, 2002).

strike affirmative defenses, the court must construe the defenses "in the light most favorable to sustaining [their] legal sufficiency."[12] A proponent of a motion to strike affirmative defenses "bears the burden of demonstrating that the affirmative defense is 'without merit as a matter of law.'"[13] The court must liberally construe the pleadings in favor of upholding affirmative defenses and "if there is any doubt as to the availability of a defense, it should not be dismissed."[14]

However, "affirmative defenses must set forth a 'short and plain statement' of the defense asserted."[15] Therefore, if an affirmative defense is insufficient on its face or just asserts conclusions of fact or law, it must be stricken.[16] Affirmative defenses may also be stricken if they add clutter, confusion, reargue issues that have already been ruled upon, or are moot, cumulative, immaterial, or misleading.[17] Additionally, affirmative defenses may not "contact affirmative factual assertions which could only be proven by evidence."[18]

In a foreclosure case where a defendant alleged that a refinance of her loan occurred without her consent or signature on any of the documents, she raised proper affirmative defenses and "genuine equitable issues relating to the making, validity or enforcement of the plaintiff's note and mortgage."[19] The court there held that "[i]n construing the defendant's factual allegations for purposes of testing the legal sufficiency of a special defense, the court must view

---

12. T.D. Bank, N.A. v. J&M Holdings, LLC, No. WWW-CV-10-6001479S (Conn. Super. Ct., Nov. 29, 2010).

13. Emigrant Mortgage Co., Inc. v. Fitzpatrick, 29 Misc. 3d 746, 752 (N.Y. App. Div. 2010), *citing* Vita v. N.Y. Waste Serv., LLC, 34 A.D.3d 559 (2d Dep't 2006).

14. *Id.* at 752.

15. T.D. Bank, N.A., *citing to* FED. R. CIV. P. 8(a).

16. T.D. Bank, N.A.; *see also* Webster Bank v. Linsley, 2001 Conn. Super. LEXIS 2407 at *6 (2001).

17. Imperial Constr. Mgmt. Corp. v. Laborers' Int'l Union, 818 F. Supp. 1179, 1186 (N.D. Ill. 1993).

18. New S. Fed. Savings Bank v. Gabriel, No. 0121453 (Conn. Super. Ct., Mar. 23, 1995).

19. Centex Home Equity Co., LLC v. Jarrett, No. CV-03-0195133S (Conn. Super. Ct., Apr. 28, 2004).

the facts 'in a broad fashion, not strictly limited to the allegations, but also including the facts necessarily implied by and fairly probable under them.'"[20]

Of course, the best way to avoid a boilerplate motion to strike from the bank is to craft your affirmative defenses carefully, citing to at least a few specific facts from your case that give some meat to the defenses and foreclose any good-faith claim from the bank that your defenses are too vague and conclusory. For example, a court will sometimes strike a defense which alleges no more than "The Plaintiff is not entitled to foreclosure by virtue of the doctrine of estoppel" because this defense is obviously conclusory, and it will look to the court like a boilerplate assertion that may have no relation to the present case whatsoever.

Additionally, in opposition to a bank motion to strike, you should prepare a written response that cites to the abundance of case law demonstrating the certain limited circumstances where the striking of pleadings should be granted and distinguishing your case from those circumstances.

Sample Excerpt of Answer and Affirmative Defenses: JP Morgan Chase Bank, N.A. v. Knowles, Manatee County, Florida Case No. 41-2009-CA-001051 (included on the form CD)

This excerpt of an answer and affirmative defenses was selected from the millions of foreclosure filings in Florida, from the on-line records of Manatee County, where the court docket is not only on-line, like most counties, it also permits the viewing of most documents filed in the case.[21] As attorney Carol C. Asbury did here, the allegations of the foreclosure complaint are mostly denied, or lack of knowledge is claimed in the answer portion of the document. However, Ms. Asbury also adds argument to numerous denials, as in paragraph 12, where she disputes the authenticity of any signatures or endorsements on the documents transferring the note to the plaintiff; in paragraph 14, where she raises lack of standing and

---

20. *Id.*, *citing* Dennison v. Klotz, 12 Conn. App. 570 (1987).

21. Only the first eight pages of the answer and affirmative defenses are included here, but the full document may be viewed by looking the case up at the Manatee County, Florida, Clerk Court Records Search at http://www.manateeclerk.org/PublicRecords/CourtRecordsSearch/tabid/57/Default.aspx.

conditions precedent to preclude the plaintiff's claim of default; and in paragraph 16, where lack of standing, accounting, inaccurate sums, and payment are advanced to refute plaintiff's claim of sums due and owing.

The affirmative defenses are factually brief in some instances; in others they cite case law and are presented in memorandum form. In the first affirmative defense, the defendant merely alleges that the plaintiff cannot produce any documents to evidence its right to enforce the loan documents. This affirmative defense is not merely a conclusion of law because it is supported by the defendant's factual argument that the defendant cannot prove its standing.

Frequently, affirmative defenses allege unclean hands without providing any facts that describe the allegedly inequitable conduct. However, in paragraph four of these affirmative defenses, the defendant states that the plaintiff failed to properly apply payments, brought a wrongful foreclosure action, and caused unwarranted fees, which form the underlying conduct of the defense.

In her eighth affirmative defense, the defendant raises interesting arguments that challenge the right of the plaintiff to transfer the loan into a mortgage-backed loan without the consent of the defendant, claiming that such transfer placed a cloud on the defendant's title by virtue of numerous unknown parties who would now claim partial ownership in the loan. The defendant also argues that the plaintiff has unfairly obscured the ownership of the debt obligation, thereby eliminating mutuality of obligation and remedy, and the defendant's ability to "deal with his property or mitigate his loss."

In her ninth affirmative defense, the defendant also offers case law and even a circuit court–level order rejecting the authenticity or validity of the signatures on the mortgage assignments, endorsements, and allonges. This issue has been a central concern to those investigating the sufficiency of documents in foreclosure cases nationwide, as with cases in which the court has rejected the purported authority of MERS to execute assignments on behalf of the document owner.[22]

---

22. *See* HSBC Bank USA v. Squitieri, 2010 N.Y. slip op. 52000U at *1 (N.Y. App. Div. 2010); LPP Mortgage Ltd. v. Sabine Props., LLC, 2010 N.Y. slip op. 32367U at *6 (N.Y. App. Div. 2010).

The defendant's tenth affirmative defense is more appropriately made as a motion to dismiss. If this defense had first been initiated as a motion to dismiss and the court had found that the plaintiff failed to plead all the essential elements of a foreclosure count, then the complaint could have been dismissed, but an answer accepts the technical sufficiency of the causes of action pled.[23]

Affirmative defenses 11 and 12 assert that the plaintiff has not met the condition precedent that requires it to send the borrower a demand letter compliant with the subject mortgage prior to instituting a foreclosure action. Sometimes the demand letter is included as an exhibit to the complaint. Other times the homeowner will need to request the demand letter through discovery. You will need to compare the demand letter, or lack thereof, against the terms of the mortgage, as discussed further in Chapter 11.

Deceptive and Unfair Trade Practices and Subprime Loans

As discussed, a foreclosure is both a legal and equitable proceeding. In order to receive the partially equitable relief of foreclosure, the bank should have done equity. For example, if the bank is leading homeowners to believe that the foreclosure has been stopped and a deal has been worked out for the homeowners to resume payments, while at the same time the bank is proceeding with the foreclosure action and pushing toward sale of the property, this is not equitable conduct. Unfortunately, this kind of scenario is all too common, and borrowers frequently are not represented by an attorney who can outline the inequitable conduct to the court in the detail necessary to prevent summary judgment or sale.

A homeowner may plead the equitable doctrine of unclean hands as an affirmative defense to foreclosure.[24] Before a bank can be entitled to the equitable relief of foreclosure, it must show that its "conduct has been fair, equitable and honest" and that it "comes into court with clean hands."[25] A Connecticut court explained that

---

23. Flasza v. TNT Holland Motor Express, 155 F.R.D. 612, 613 (N.D. Ill. 1994).

24. EMC Mortgage Corp. v. Shamber, No. CV-07-5001252S (Conn. Super. Ct., Nov. 12, 2009).

25. *Id.*

the clean hands doctrine is not intended for the protection of the litigants but to protect the court, to better ensure that the court's decisions will advance the interests of justice.[26] In order for a homeowner to show that the bank is guilty of unclean hands, he must demonstrate that the bank had engaged in willful misconduct ("intentional conduct designed to injure for which there is no just cause or excuse") in alleging entitlement to foreclosure.[27]

The laws of local and state governments may protect borrowers against deceptive trade practices. In some cases, the homeowners can be protected from foreclosure actions arising from such wrongful practices as in one Connecticut case.[28] The bank in that case failed to provide the borrower with a legally sufficient demand letter prior to acceleration of the loan.[29] The homeowner had filed a counterclaim against the bank, arguing in part that the bank had violated Connecticut General Statutes Chapter 735a against Unfair Trade Practices (CUTPA).[30] The court held that under Connecticut case law, homeowners may propound foreclosure counterclaims based on allegations that a lender has violated CUTPA.[31] Therefore, the court denied the plaintiff's motion for summary judgment as to the defendant's CUTPA counterclaim.[32] Breach of the implied covenant of good faith and fair dealing is a recognized defense to a foreclosure action."[33] Furthermore, another court has held that a borrower asserted a viable affirmative defense for negligent infliction of emotional distress based on the bank's breach of its statutory duty under CUTPA to protect the interests of its customers.[34]

In a New York case where a bank extended a "sub-prime/high-cost" loan to the borrower, the court upheld the borrower's claims

---

26. *Id.*

27. *Id.* at *3.

28. U.S. Bank, N.A. v. Suvemay, No. CV-08-5014358S (Conn. Super. Ct., Oct. 4, 2010).

29. *Id.*

30. *Id.*

31. *Id.*

32. *Id.*

33. DGG Props. Co., Inc. v. Lanier, No. CV-00-0093788S (Conn. Super. Ct., Sept. 13, 2002).

34. Webster Bank v. Linsley, No. CV-97-0260406S (Conn. Super. Ct., Aug. 9, 2001).

that the loan was unconscionable and that the lender had engaged in unfair and deceptive trade practices.[35] There, the defendant had alleged that the loan was substantively unconscionable because the monthly payments of principal, interest, and taxes were in excess of the defendant's fixed monthly income, that the bank knew or should have known at the time of the loan transaction that the defendant's income was insufficient to support the loan, and that the bank had failed to verify or even inquire into the borrower's income.[36] The defendant also alleged that the loan was procedurally unconscionable "due to the unequal bargaining power and imbalance of the knowledge and understanding of the parties."[37] The homeowner also alleged that the bank had engaged in unfair and deceptive trade practices by virtue of its conduct of extending the loan to the borrower without determining her ability to pay when a reasonable person would expect such an established bank as the plaintiff would offer the borrower a loan that she could afford.[38] The homeowner had lived in her home for 22 years and further stated that the bank's conduct could potentially damage other similarly situated consumers.[39]

Though a party "is under an obligation to read a document before he or she signs it" and cannot be excused from his or her obligations under a contract simply because he or she "did not read it or know its contents," "[t]here are situations where an instrument will be deemed void because the signer was unaware of the nature of the instrument he or she was signing, such as where the signer is illiterate, or blind, or ignorant of the alien language of the writing and the contents thereof are misread or misrepresented to him by the other party, or even by a stranger."[40] The definition of an unconscionable contract "is one which is so grossly unreasonable or unconscionable in the light of the mores and business practices of the time and place as to be unenforceable according to its literal

---

35. Emigrant Mortgage Co., Inc. v. Fitzpatrick, 29 Misc. 3d 746, 754–55 (N.Y. App. Div. 2010).
36. *Id.* at 748.
37. *Id.*
38. *Id.*
39. *Id.* at 748–49.
40. *Id.* at 752–53.

terms."[41] A court will consider whether a contract was unconscionable "against the backdrop of the contract's commercial setting, purpose and effect."[42]

In this particular case, the plaintiff admitted that the loan was a "no income-documentation mortgage" in which program the bank does not independently verify whether the borrower will be able to make the regularly scheduled loan payments.[43] This loan product was customarily offered almost exclusively "in commercial business lending to provide working capital," though this particular loan was extended in a residential property transaction.[44] Furthermore, as the transaction involved a high-cost home loan, the bank had obligations to ensure that the loan was made with "due regard to repayment ability, based upon consideration of the resident borrower or borrowers' current and expected income, current obligations, employment status and other financial resources . . . as verified by detailed documentation of all sources of income and corroborated by independent verification."[45] Since the bank admitted that it had not complied with these requirements, the court denied the bank's motion to dismiss the homeowner's affirmative defense alleging "that the loan was procedurally unconscionable due to the unequal bargaining power and imbalance of the knowledge and understanding of the parties."[46] The court also upheld the homeowner's affirmative defense alleging unfair and deceptive trade practices, citing its concern that the bank very well could repeat its surreptitious practices with other consumers.[47]

In one Pennsylvania case, the court found that the homeowners raised valid affirmative defenses related to whether they could void and rescind a mortgage agreement based on predatory lending, holding that "Pennsylvania law prohibits the use of fraudulent appraisals in connection with residential mortgages and recognizes that a mortgage agreement may be voidable based upon

---

41. *Id.* at 753.
42. *Id.*
43. *Id.* at 754.
44. *Id.*
45. *Id.* at 754–55, *citing* Banking Law § 6-1(2)(k).
46. *Id.* at 748, 755.
47. *Id.* at 755.

fraud in the inducement involving the assignor lender or its agent."[48] In that case, the mortgage broker who procured the loan produced an appraisal that set the value of the property at five times its actual amount.[49] The borrowers also alleged a payment defense, asserting they had made all payments based on the true value of the residence and denied any default.[50] The borrowers further alleged that they had been fraudulently induced into accepting the loan transaction.[51]

The mortgage broker in that case had also been indicted for mail fraud and allegedly "instructed others to conduct false and fraudulent appraisals of properties, produce false and fraudulent documents, supplied those false and fraudulent appraisals, and supplied software to accomplish false and fraudulent appraisals."[52] In opposition to the bank's motion for summary judgment, the borrowers stated that there were "genuine issues of material fact concerning 'the value of the property in light of the misrepresentations of the lender and mortgage broker.'"[53]

The court examined the homeowners' fraud in the inducement defense and noted that "if a party is fraudulently induced to enter an agreement (i.e., 'but for' fraudulent misrepresentation(s) the contract would not have been executed by the innocent party), the agreement is void or voidable at the option of the injured party."[54] The court held that if the borrowers have raised valid questions of fact as to whether they were fraudulently induced into accepting the mortgage, "they have asserted a valid defense to the foreclosure and summary judgment in favor of the lender is not appropriate."[55]

Next, the court observed that other jurisdictions have permitted allegations of predatory lending to afford relief to homeowners in

---

48. Sovereign Bank v. Gawron, 13 Pa. D. & C.5th 71, 72–73 (Pa. Ct. Comm. Pl. 2010).

49. *Id.* at 73.

50. *Id.* at 74.

51. *Id.*

52. *Id.* at 75.

53. *Id.* at 76.

54. *Id.* at 78, *citing* Youndt v. First Nat'l Bank of Port Allegheny, 868 A.2d 539 (Pa. Super. 2005).

55. *Id.* at 78.

foreclosure actions, including creating genuine issues of fact to pre-clude summary judgment for the bank.[56] The court held that if the homeowners were able to demonstrate that the mortgage broker fraudulently induced them into the loan agreement, they might be able to void and rescind the contracts thereto.[57] However, the court cautioned that if the homeowners succeed in this regard, it could be a pyrrhic victory, because they might then have to return borrowed proceeds as part of that rescission, as "equitable rescission is a form of retroactive relief that returns the parties as nearly as possible to their original positions."[58]

The Truth In Lending Act

The Truth In Lending Act (TIL) is a potentially sophisticated and effective defense available to homeowners. TIL relief may include a rescission of the loan to place the parties back in the position they were in before the transaction was completed; damages to the ho-meowner if certain disclosures about the loan transaction were not provided to them; and in some cases, cancellation of the loan debt so that the borrower will own a property free and clear.

TIL is intended to enhance economic stabilization and compe-tition between lenders "by the informed use of credit."[59] TIL gov-erns most residential mortgage transactions and requires the lenders to make certain disclosures to borrowers.[60] For example, "[t]he terms 'annual percentage rate' and 'finance charge'[61] shall be disclosed more conspicuously than other terms, data, or information provided in connection with a transaction, except information relating to the identity of the creditor."[62] If the lender has the borrower sign a form acknowledging receipt of disclosures required by TIL, this does no

---

56. *Id.* at 79.
57. *Id.* at 80–81.
58. *Id.* at 83.
59. *See* 15 U.S.C. § 1601(a).
60. *Id.*
61. Finance charge is defined by TIL as "the sum of all charges, payable directly or indirectly by the creditor as an incident to the extension of credit." 15 U.S.C.A. § 1605(a).
62. 15 U.S.C. § 1632(a).

more than create a rebuttable presumption of delivery thereof."[63] A creditor may not make TIL-required disclosures "on two separate documents at two separate times."[64] Additionally, TIL disclosures must be delivered to the consumer "not less than 3 business days prior to consummation of the transaction."[65]

A creditor or assignee of a loan cannot be held liable for TIL violations when a preponderance of the evidence shows that "the violation was not intentional and resulted from a bona fide error notwithstanding the maintenance of procedures reasonably adapted to avoid any such error."[66] The penalty for a willful and knowing failure to provide disclosures required by TIL or misrepresentation of such required information may be a fine of up to $5,000 or imprisonment of up to one year.[67]

Certain provisions in mortgages are prohibited, such as:

1. With some exceptions, no "prepayment penalty for paying all or part of the principal before the date on which the principal is due";[68]
2. The interest rate may not be raised after default;[69]
3. No balloon payments; i.e., a mortgage with a term of less than five years "may not include terms under which the aggregate amount of the regular periodic payments would not fully amortize the outstanding principal balance";[70]
4. No negative amortization; i.e., a principal balance on a mortgage may not increase because the periodic loan payments are insufficient to cover the interest due;[71]
5. The consumer cannot be compelled to make more than two periodic payments prior to receiving loan proceeds;[72] and

---

63. 15 U.S.C. § 1635(c).
64. Shepeard v. Quality Siding & Window Factory, 730 F. Supp. 1295, 1300–01 (D. Del. 1990).
65. 15 U.S.C. § 1639(b)(1).
66. 15 U.S.C.A. § 1640(c).
67. 15 U.S.C. § 1611.
68. 15 U.S.C. § 1639(c)(1)(A).
69. 15 U.S.C. § 1639(d).
70. 15 U.S.C. § 1639(e)
71. 15 U.S.C. § 1639(f)
72. 15 U.S.C. § 1639(g).

6. "Prohibition on extending credit without regard to payment ability of consumer: A creditor shall not engage in a pattern or practice of extending credit to consumers under mortgages . . . based on the consumers' collateral without regard to the consumers' repayment ability, including the consumers' current and expected income, current obligations, and employment."[73]

If the creditor extends a mortgage to the consumer that contains a prohibited provision under section 1639, this "shall be deemed a failure to deliver the material disclosures required" by TIL.

When, in a "consumer credit transaction," a lender will acquire an interest in "property which is used as the principal dwelling of the person to whom credit is extended," the borrower has the right to rescind the loan transaction "until midnight of the third business day following the consummation of the transaction or the delivery of the information and rescission forms required under this section together with a statement containing the material disclosures required under this subchapter, whichever is later . . . ."[74] A borrower may also rescind the loan transaction after a foreclosure action has been filed if:

(A) a mortgage broker fee is not included in the finance charge in accordance with the laws and regulations in effect at the time the consumer credit transaction was consummated; or

(B) the form of notice of rescission for the transaction is not the appropriate form of written notice published and adopted by the Board or a comparable written notice, and otherwise complied with all the requirements of this section regarding notice.[75]

However, certain transactions are exempted from rescission, including:

---

73. 15 U.S.C. § 1639(h).
74. 15 U.S.C. § 1635(a).
75. 15 U.S.C. § 1635(i).

1. A purchase money transaction where the "security interest is created or retained against the consumer's dwelling to finance the acquisition or initial construction of such dwelling"; in other words, where the loan is being used for the initial purchase of the home;[76]
2. A refinance by the original lender on the same property;[77]
3. "[A] transaction in which an agency of a State is the creditor";[78] or
4. "[A]dvances under a preexisting open end credit plan if a security interest has already been retained or acquired and such advances are in accordance with a previously established credit limit for such plan."[79]

If the consumer exercises this right of rescission, "the creditor shall return to the obligor any money or property given as earnest money, down payment, or otherwise, and shall take any action necessary or appropriate to reflect the termination of any security interest created under the transaction."[80] The application of a homeowner's right of rescission requires that the parties be restored to the status quo, or position they were in prior to the transaction.[81]

Only after the creditor has performed its obligations under this section must the borrower "tender the property to the creditor, except that if return of the property in kind would be impracticable or inequitable, the obligor shall tender its reasonable value."[82] Ownership of the subject property will vest in the borrower if the creditor does not take possession of it within 20 days of the borrower's tender.[83] With certain exceptions, the statute of limitation for the right of rescission is "three years after the date of consummation of the transaction or upon the sale of the property, whichever occurs first,"

---

76. *See* 15 U.S.C. § 1602(w).
77. *See* 15 U.S.C. § 1635(e)(2).
78. 15 U.S.C. § 1635(e)(3).
79. 15 U.S.C. § 1635(e)(4).
80. 15 U.S.C. § 1635(b).
81. EMC Mortgage Corp. v. Shamber, No. CV-07-5001252S (Conn. Super. Ct., Nov. 12, 2009).
82. *Id.*
83. *Id.*

regardless of whether all required TIL disclosures have been delivered to the borrower.[84]

The exercise by a homeowner of his right to rescission under TIL bars enforcement of a mortgage and therefore precludes foreclosure.[85] A homeowners' assertion of rescission as an affirmative defense is properly made if he asserts a proper right to rescind and timely election of that right.[86] Furthermore, rescission can properly be asserted as a counterclaim to foreclosure because rescission "directly affects the enforcement of the mortgage and thus, can be said to arise from the same transaction which is the subject of the foreclosure action."[87]

To determine whether or not the borrower still has the right to rescind the loan, you will need to look at whether the loan was a purchase money or refinance transaction. The answer to this will usually be contained in the loan application or HUD-1 Settlement Statement. In the Uniform Residential Loan Application, Fannie Mae form 1003, there is a section where one will indicate the purpose of the loan and whether the loan is for a purchase, refinance, construction, construction-permanent, or other.[88] Additionally, you may look at the HUD-1 Settlement Statement.[89] You may ascertain whether this is a refinance and whether other loans are being paid off by the lines 504 and 505, which state the amount of the closing funds being routed for the satisfaction of these other loans. You will also be able to tell if this is a purchase-money loan if there is nothing listed in line 203, "Existing loan(s) taken subject to."

If the loan is a qualifying refinance, you will need to see whether you are still within the three-year period reserved for your client to make a rescission claim. The circumstances of whether the creditor complied with TIL may very well provide you with genuine issues of material fact by which you may defeat summary judgment, as

---

84. *See* 15 U.S.C. § 1635(f).

85. EMC Mortgage Corp. v. Shamber, No. CV-07-5001252S (Conn. Super. Ct., Nov. 12, 2009).

86. *Id.* at *9.

87. *Id.* at *19.

88. You may view a Fannie Mae Form 1003 at https://www.efanniemae.com/ sf/formsdocs/forms/pdf/sellingtrans/1003.pdf.

89. Sample at http://www.hud.gov/offices/adm/hudclips/forms/files/1.pdf.

borrowers did who raised affirmative defenses that the bank failed to make required TIL disclosures and circumvented the borrower's right to rescind the loan, and also raised the question of whether the bank committed racketeering activity in violation of the Racketeer Influenced and Corrupt Organizations Act (RICO).[90]

Home Owner's Equity Protection Act

"The HOEPA [Home Owner's Equity Protection Act] . . . was enacted as an amendment to [TIL] to provide increased protection to consumers entering into predatory and high interest loans ('HOEPA loans') as defined under 15 U.S.C. § 1602(aa)."[91] HOEPA loans are defined as consumer credit transactions[92] secured by the consumer's principal dwelling[93] and must be a second or subordinate mortgage as opposed to a residential mortgage transaction,[94] a reverse mortgage,[95] or an open-end credit plan.[96] Also, "either the annual percentage of interest at consummation of the loan transaction must exceed certain levels"[97] or the "'total points and fees' payable by the borrower at or before closing must exceed the greater of 8% of the total loan amount or $400."[98] HOEPA prohibits increased interest rates upon default and, with certain exceptions, prepayment penalties.[99]

A homeowner may show that a lender violates HOEPA if the creditor engages "in a pattern or practice of extending credit to consumers under mortgages . . . based on the consumers' collateral without regard to the consumers' repayment ability, including the consumers' current and expected income, current obligations, and

---

90. Bank of New Haven v. Liner, No. CV-91-034516S (Conn. Super. Ct., Nov. 9, 1993).

91. *In re* Vincent, 381 B.R. 564, 570 (Bankr. Mass. 2008).

92. 15 U.S.C. § 1602(h).

93. 15 U.S.C. § 1602(v).

94. 15 U.S.C. § 1602(w).

95. 15 U.S.C. § 1602(bb).

96. 15 U.S.C. § 1602(i); Bankers Trust Co. of Cal., N.A. v. Payne, 188 Misc. 2d 726, 730 (N.Y. App. Div. 2001).

97. 15 U.S.C. § 1602(aa)(1)(A).

98. 15 U.S.C. § 1602(aa)(1)(B); Payne, 188 Misc. 2d at 731.

99. 15 U.S.C. § 1639(c)–(d).

employment."[100] HOEPA damage claims are governed by a one-year statute of limitation.[101] Also, a HOEPA violation may constitute a defense for the homeowner against foreclosure.[102]

In one New York case that examined a HOEPA loan, the note provided that the interest rate would rise to 24 percent on default by the borrower.[103] The note also included that there would be a prepayment penalty of 5 percent of the loan principal.[104] Further, the borrower claimed that the creditor "did not ask him for verification of his income or otherwise certify the loan's affordability, and, therefore, extended credit to him without regard to his repayment ability. . . ."[105]

The court therefore found that the loan documents contained HOEPA violations on their face.[106] The court noted the undisputed facts between the parties that the plaintiff was a "creditor" as defined by TIL, that the transaction was subordinate financing to another loan, that it involved a "consumer credit transaction," and that the total points and fees charged to the defendant were in excess of the legal limit set by HOEPA.[107] In light of the bank's HOEPA violations, in addition to other grounds, the court upheld the lower tribunal's decision to refuse entry of summary judgment to the bank.[108]

Real Estate Settlement Procedures Act

The Real Estate Settlement Procedures Act of 1974 (RESPA) governs multiple aspects of real estate transactions; one significant benefit that RESPA offers to homeowners facing foreclosure is the ability to demand detailed accountings about their loans from servicers (explained further in the discussion about qualified written requests

---

100. 15 U.S.C. § 1639(h); *Payne*, 188 Misc. 2d at 732.
101. 15 U.S.C. § 1640(e).
102. Payne, 188 Misc. 2d at 730.
103. *Id.* at 731.
104. *Id.* at 732.
105. *Id.*
106. *Id.*
107. *Id.*
108. *Id.* at 733.

(QWR)). Also significant in foreclosure cases is the way RESPA governs the transfer of loan servicing and the inherent notices to borrowers that are required. The congressional intent behind RESPA is to:

> (1) bring about more effective advance disclosure of settlement cost to home buyers and sellers; (2) eliminate kickbacks and referral fees that tended to increase the cost of settlement services; (3) reduce sums that home buyers were required by lenders to place in escrow accounts to insure payment of real estate taxes and insurance; and (4) significantly reform and modernize local record keeping of land title information.[109]

According to RESPA, the Secretary of HUD shall "prepare and distribute booklets to help persons borrowing money to finance the purchase of residential real estate better to finance the purchase of residential real estate settlement services."[110] The lender must provide the borrower, together with such information booklet, a "good faith estimate of the amount or rate of charges for specific settlement charges the borrower is likely to incur in connection with the settlement."[111]

The lender must also inform the borrower at the time of loan application "whether the servicing of the loan may be assigned, sold or transferred to any other person at any time while the loan is outstanding."[112] If the loan is later transferred to another party, the servicer must "notify the borrower in writing of any assignment, sale, or transfer of the servicing of the loan."[113] With a few exceptions, this written notice must be provided to the borrower "not less than 15 days before the effective date of transfer of the servicing of the mortgage loan."[114] The transferee servicer of such loan, again with a few exceptions, shall provide the borrower with

---

109. 12 U.S.C.A. § 2601.
110. 12 U.S.C.A. § 2604(a).
111. 12 U.S.C.A. § 2604(c).
112. 12 U.S.C.A. § 2605(a).
113. 12 U.S.C.A. § 2605(b)(1).
114. 12 U.S.C.A. § 2605(b)(2)(A).

written notice of the transfer within 15 days after thereof.[115] This notice must include the effective date of the transfer; the name, address, and toll-free or collect-call number of the transferee servicer; the dates on which the transferor and transferee, respectively, will cease and begin to accept payments; any effect the transfer may have on continued availability of mortgage, life, disability, or other kind of optional insurance; and a statement that the transfer will not affect the terms of the loan documents, except for those provisions which relate to servicing.[116]

The letter received from the transferee servicer is often called the "welcome letter." Welcome letters are fairly consistently sent, but notices from the outgoing servicers seem less common. Of course, a borrower needs to receive both if their servicer changes, and if they do not, grounds for a RESPA violation may exist. A servicer must use "reasonable care and diligence" to send notices to the correct last known address for the borrower, otherwise the servicer may not be deemed to have complied with RESPA.[117] RESPA does not specifically require that a borrower receive required notices,[118] but the servicer "must exercise reasonable care and diligence in determining the correct address of the borrower," and to make use of both actual and constructive knowledge in determining same.[119] In one California case, the court determined that the servicer had failed to establish that it had no actual knowledge of the borrower's actual address or that it would not have been able to obtain the address through reasonable care and diligence.[120] As for the servicer's motion for the summary judgment (the plaintiff and servicer were the same in this case), the court held that genuine issues of fact remained as to the scope of information the servicer should have searched and what it would have found if it had conducted such a search.[121]

---

115. 12 U.S.C.A. § 2605(c)(2)(A).

116. 12 U.S.C.A. § 2605(b)(3).

117. Wanger v. EMC Mortgage Corp., 103 Cal. App. 4th 1125, 1137 (Cal. App. 2002).

118. *Id.* at 1133.

119. *Id.* at 1135.

120. *Id.* at 1136.

121. *Id.*

Qualified Written Requests

Under RESPA, through qualified written requests (QWR), a borrower may obtain useful information and build specific defenses to foreclosure.[122] A QWR is an official written letter or notice sent to the servicer by the borrower.[123] It must be titled as a "qualified written request." The QWR must include the borrower's name and account number, or enough information for the servicer to identify it.[124] The QWR must also include a statement of why the borrower believes the account to be in error, or be specific as to other information the borrower seeks.[125]

Frequently, borrowers will send a QWR to the foreclosure plaintiff's attorney (usually the plaintiff is the lender or servicer). The federal statute governing QWRs provides that the QWR must be sent to the servicer.[126] There are a few courts that have allowed the QWR to be sent to the servicer's attorney, but it is best to be on the safe side and follow the exact requirements of the statute.

The servicer must acknowledge receipt of the QWR within 20 business days.[127] An exception to this is when the servicer grants the borrower's requests prior to the 20-day deadline.[128] Within 60 business days of receiving the QWR, the servicer must do one of three things:

1. Make necessary corrections to any errors in the borrower's account;
2. After making an investigation, explain to the borrower why there are no errors in the account; or
3. After making an investigation, explain to the borrower why the requested information cannot be obtained by the servicer.[129]

---

122. 12 U.S.C. § 2605(e).
123. 12 U.S.C. § 2605(e)(1)(B).
124. 12 U.S.C. § 2605(e)(1)(B)(i).
125. 12 U.S.C. § 2605(e)(1)(B)(ii).
126. 12 U.S.C. § 2605(e)(1)(A).
127. *Id.*
128. *Id.*
129. 12 U.S.C. § 2605(e)(2).

In all three situations the servicer must also provide the borrower with the name and telephone number of its representative who can further assist the borrower.[130] For the duration of the 60-day period, the servicer is not permitted to report overdue payments relating to the QWR to any consumer reporting agency.[131]

If a servicer fails to comply with these provisions, it may be liable to the borrower for damages, costs, and attorney's fees.[132] In the case of an individual borrower, the damages are limited to those actually suffered by the borrower as a result of the servicer's failure.[133] The court may also grant the borrower additional damages not to exceed $1,000.[134] If a class action has been filed against the servicer (meaning a lawsuit filed on behalf of numerous persons in a similar situation), the servicer may be liable for attorney's fees and actual damages of the class, as well as additional damages not to exceed $500,000 or 1 percent of the servicer's net worth, whichever is less.[135]

However, a servicer will not be liable for failing to comply with the above requirements if it took action to correct an error in the borrower's account within 60 days after discovering it, before a QWR or written notice of the error is filed.[136] The servicer must notify the borrower, make necessary corrections to the account, and make sure that unnecessary fees or costs will not be assessed against the borrower.[137]

If you send the QWR to a plaintiff's attorney instead of the servicer itself, the attorney may file a motion with the court to strike the QWR, meaning the servicer would not have to comply with the requests contained in your notice. Other times, a plaintiff's attorney may ask the court the strike the QWR because it is too vague and not detailed enough, and because borrowers cannot file a general laundry list of grievances. You may not know whether certain errors exist, and the

---

130. *Id.*
131. 12 U.S.C. § 2605(e)(3).
132. 12 U.S.C. § 2605(f).
133. 12 U.S.C. § 2605(f)(1)(A).
134. 12 U.S.C. § 2605(f)(1)(B).
135. 12 U.S.C. § 2605(f)(2).
136. 12 U.S.C. § 2605(f)(4).
137. *Id.*

servicer is in the only position to know. However, questions seeking information on how the plaintiff obtained ownership of the loan and the servicer's right to manage the loan should be fair game, since ownership of the loan is the cornerstone to the plaintiff's case.

A court has upheld a homeowner's counterclaim for statutory negligence against a bank, alleging that the bank breached its duty to notify him where to send his payments pursuant to § 2605(b)(1) and that consequently he suffered actual damages, including late charges and damage to his credit.[138] The well-established elements required for a negligence claim are duty, breach of that duty, causation, and actual injury.[139] The *Restatement (Second) of Torts* has established a four-part test of when statutory provisions may be used to establish a "reasonable person's standard of conduct" for purposes of determining whether negligence has occurred:

> The court may adopt as the standard of conduct of a reasonable [person] the requirements of a legislative enactment . . . whose purpose is found to be exclusively or in part (a) to protect a class of persons which includes the one whose interest is invaded, and (b) to protect the particular interest which is invaded, and (c) to protect that interest against the kind of harm which has resulted, and (d) to protect that interest against the particular hazard from which the harm results.[140]

The court noted that a primary goal of RESPA is to "insure that consumers throughout the Nation are provided with greater and more timely information on the nature and costs of the settlement process and are protected from unnecessarily high settlement charges caused by certain abusive processes that have developed in some areas of the country."[141] The court held that the homeowner had pled a proper claim for statutory negligence by virtue of the

---

138. EMC Mortgage Corp. v. Shamber, No. CV-07-5001252S (Conn. Super. Ct., Nov. 12, 2009).

139. *Id.* at *28.

140. Hansen v. Friend, 118 Wn. 2d 476, 480 (Wash. 1992), *citing* RESTATEMENT (SECOND) OF TORTS § 286 (1965).

141. *Shamber, citing* 12 U.S.C. § 2601.

bank's violation of RESPA because "he is a member of the class protected by RESPA, i.e., consumers/borrowers, and the alleged injuries are of the type that RESPA was intended to protect, i.e., late fees and damages to a consumer's credit."[142] Furthermore, the borrower had alleged that his damages of late fees and derogatory credit reports were proximately caused by the bank's breach of its statutory duty of care.[143] Therefore, the court denied the bank's motion to strike the homeowner's counterclaim for statutory negligence.[144]

Fraud

Affirmative defenses are frequently raised alleging that the bank promised the borrower something that contradicts the terms of a written agreement between the parties. In many cases, such claims will be barred by the parol evidence rule, which "generally prohibits the introduction of extrinsic evidence, including evidence of any prior or contemporaneous oral agreement, to vary, alter, or add to the terms of an integrated written instrument."[145] When a contract contains an integration clause, it is a "complete and final embodiment" of the agreement between the parties.[146]

However, a party may have a court consider parol evidence when that party alleges he was fraudulently induced into signing a contract.[147] A party alleging fraud must demonstrate that "a material representation of a past or existing fact was made which was untrue and known to be untrue by the party making it or else recklessly made and that another party did in fact rely on the representation and was induced thereby to act to his detriment."[148] A drafter of a contract commits fraud when he and another party to the contract "have a prior understanding about the contract's terms, and the party responsible for drafting the contract includes contrary terms

---

142. *Id.* at *31.

143. *Id.*

144. *Id.* at *32.

145. Riverland Cold Storage, Inc. v. Fresno-Madera Prod. Credit Assoc., 191 Cal. App. 4th 611, 616 (Jan. 3, 2011).

146. *Id.* at 617, *citing* Masterson v. Sine, 436 P.2d 561 (Cal. 1968).

147. *Id.*

148. People's Trust & Sav. Bank v. Humphrey, 451 N.E.2d 1104, 1112 (Ind. Ct. App. 1983).

and then allows the other party to sign it without informing him of changes."[149]

One California case examined a situation in which plaintiffs appealed a summary judgment against them denying their claims that the defendant had fraudulently induced them to enter into a forbearance agreement on a loan held by defendant.[150] The plaintiffs alleged that prior to and at the time they entered into the forbearance agreement, the defendant orally represented that it would forbear from collection for two years in exchange for additional security.[151] The plaintiffs admitted that based on these representations, they did not read the written agreement.[152] The defendant then sought summary judgment, alleging that plaintiffs failed to comply with the forbearance agreement.[153] The forbearance also contained an integration clause, and the court found it was a complete and final embodiment of the agreement between plaintiffs and defendant, barring any parol evidence to vary the terms of the agreement.[154]

However, the court closely reviewed applicable law on the fraud exception to the parol evidence rule, which holds that evidence to show that a contract was induced by fraud is admissible.[155] The court performed a detailed analysis of *Bank of America v. Pendergrass*, 48 P.2d 659 (Cal. 1935), one of whose central holdings was that the fraud exception to the parol evidence rule does not "authorize admission of parol evidence to prove an oral promise made without intent to perform it, where the promise directly contradicted the provisions of the written agreement."[156] While the court noted that the *Pendergrass* decision had been subject to scholarly attack, the opinion also has the effect of preventing countless contractual disputes from spawning unwarranted allegations of fraud, and curtailing a slippery slope that would lead to litigants improperly claiming the protections of the fraud exception.[157]

---

149. *Id.*
150. *Id.* at **1–2.
151. *Id.* at **2–3.
152. *Id.* at *3.
153. *Id.*
154. *Id.* at *8.
155. *Id.* at *9.
156. *Id.* at **9–10.
157. *Id.* at *13.

A true instance of the fraud defense and when evidence may be admissible in support thereof was defined as when one party "makes an independent promise without intention of performing it" to induce another party to sign a contract, but does not vary or contradict the matters covered by the main agreement.[158] In other words, when a written agreement is procured by a misrepresentation of how a party should interpret terms of the contract, made contemporaneously with the execution of the contract, evidence of such events may be admissible as an exception to the parol evidence rule.[159] The court noted that this exception would not swallow the parol evidence rule because parties claiming this defense would also need to prove reasonable reliance on such misrepresentations that caused them to execute a contract.[160] Therefore, the defendant's motion for summary judgment on plaintiffs' causes of action based on defendant's alleged fraud should not have been granted because a triable issue of material fact existed.[161]

One Indiana court found that a bank had represented one set of contract terms to homeowners and thereafter, unbeknownst to the homeowners, changed the contract to include predatory loan terms and induced the homeowners to sign the predatory version of the contract.[162] Later, the bank had held two of the borrowers' mortgage payments without crediting them to the loan balance or returning the checks.[163] Furthermore, the bank clouded the homeowners' title by filing a baseless foreclosure action when the homeowners were current on their payments.[164]

---

158. *Id.* at **16–17.

159. *Id.* at *21.

160. *Id.* at **24–25.

161. *Id.* at **29–30; *see also* Bankers Trust Co. of Cal., N.A. v. Payne, 188 Misc. 2d 726, 730 (N.Y. App. Div. 2001) (homeowner had submitted sworn affidavit making detailed allegations about how he relied upon misrepresentations of the bank in his execution of the mortgage and that its predatory practices had damaged many other homeowners; affidavit helped created a genuine issue of material fact to defeat the bank's motion for summary judgment).

162. *Id.* at 1113–14.

163. *Id.* at 1114.

164. *Id.*

The court found that punitive damages were appropriate against the bank because it found "clear and convincing" evidence to support an imposition of such damages; there was also no indication that the bank's "tortious conduct was the result of a mistake of law or fact, honest error of judgment, over-zealousness, mere negligence or other such non-iniquitous human failing."[165]

Failure to Comply with Conditions Precedent

Most foreclosure complaints will contain the legally sufficient, albeit conclusory recitation that "all conditions precedent to the filing of this action have been met or waived." Many conditions precedent to the foreclosure action are established by the language of the loan documents themselves, such as the mortgage and note. For example, most residential mortgages require that a borrower receive a demand letter—i.e., notice of a default and intent to accelerate the balance due on the loan—before the lender can file a foreclosure action against that borrower, as discussed in Chapter 11. If the lender fails to send the homeowner a demand letter when it is required, the lender has failed to meet a condition precedent to foreclosure.

One Maine court reversed a summary judgment and order of sale in favor of the bank, finding that genuine issues of material fact remained as to whether the borrowers received proper notice of default and their right to cure.[166] At the time that the bank filed its motion for summary judgment, it was required to establish "the amount owed on the mortgage note and evidence of properly served notice of default and the right to cure."[167] The borrowers alleged in their opposition to summary judgment that the bank had improperly accelerated the note before giving them the required notice and right to cure.[168] The court found that the record contained "competing versions of the truth whether [the homeowners] were served proper notice of default and the right to cure before Chase accelerated the note, such that there is a genuine issue as to this material fact."[169]

---

165. *Id.*
166. Chase Home Finance LLC v. Higgins, 985 A.2d 508, 509 (Me. 2009).
167. *Id.* at 511.
168. *Id.* at 512.
169. *Id.*

Other conditions precedent may be established by the loan documents if, for example, the parties entered into a federally backed loan and the loan servicer was required to make certain loss mitigation efforts prior to foreclosure. For example, the *Knowles* affirmative defenses, included on the form CD to this book, assert in paragraph 13 that the bank is not entitled to foreclose without complying with requirements established by the U.S. Department of Housing and Urban Development (HUD). The failure of the bank to satisfy HUD requirements can be fatal to a bank's motion for summary judgment of foreclosure. In one Indiana case, a homeowner successfully argued that the bank was not entitled to pursue foreclosure because it:

> (1) did not engage in loss mitigation in a timely fashion as required by 24 C.F.R. § 203.605(a); (2) did not have a face-to-face meeting or make a reasonable effort to have a face-to-face meeting "before three full monthly installments due on the [M]ortgage [were] unpaid" as required by 24 C.F.R. § 203.604(b); and (c) did not accept partial payments as required by 24 C.F.R. § 203.556.[170]

The court was not persuaded by the bank's argument that these regulations applied only to "the relationship between the mortgagee and the government" or its assertions that a borrower is not entitled to allege noncompliance with HUD as an affirmative defense.[171]

The Indiana court discussed the background of HUD, stating that it was established by the Federal Housing Authority, which was created by the National Housing Act of 1934 and, according to the HUD website, "is the largest government insurer of mortgages in the world."[172] The congressional intent behind HUD was to provide "a decent home and suitable living environment for every American family."[173]

---

170. Lacy-McKinney v. Taylor, Bean & Whitaker Mortgage Corp., 937 N.E.2d 853, 859 (Ind. Ct. App. 2010).
171. *Id.*
172. *Id.* at 860.
173. *Id., citing to* 12 U.S.C. § 1701t.

The court proceeded to list obligations imposed upon servicers by Title 24, Part 203 (Single Family Mortgage Insurance), Subpart C (Servicing Responsibilities) of the Code of Federal Regulations (CFR), including but not limited to:

1. "A mortgagee must initiate face-to-face contact with the mortgagor prior to foreclosure";
2. "Before four full monthly installments due on the mortgage have become unpaid, the mortgagee shall evaluate on a monthly basis all of the loss mitigation techniques";
3. A mortgagee must "accept any partial payment from the mortgagor and either apply it to the mortgagor's account or identify it with the mortgagor's account and hold it in a trust account pending disposition."[174]

HUD further provides that "[i]t is the intent of the Department that no mortgagee shall commence foreclosure or acquire title to a property until the requirements of [Subpart C] have been followed."[175]

The Indiana court held that borrowers may raise a lender's non-compliance with HUD relating to an FHA-insured loan as an affirmative defense to foreclosure.[176] The court also noted that "the states of Florida, Maryland, and New York have likewise held that HUD servicing responsibilities may be raised as an affirmative defense in foreclosure actions even though the regulations do not create a private right of action."[177] The public policy of HUD would be circumvented without "mandatory regulations for HUD-approved mortgagees to insure that objectives of the HUD program are met."[178]

The court then held that the bank was not entitled to summary judgment, as the court agreed with the homeowner and found that a genuine issue of material fact remained as to whether the plaintiff

---

174. *Id.* at 861.
175. *Id., citing to* 24 C.F.R. § 203.500.
176. *Id.* at 861–62.
177. *Id.* at 862–63.
178. *Id.* at 863, *citing to* Associated E. Mortg. Co. v. Young, 394 A.2d 899 (N.J. Super. Ct. Ch. Div. 1978).

had "complied with the conditions precedent to foreclosure" prior to acceleration of the loan and filing of a foreclosure action.[179]

In an Ohio case where the mortgage was a federally insured loan and subject to the regulations of HUD, the court found that compliance with HUD was a condition precedent to foreclosure on the mortgage.[180] That court also rejected the bank's attempts to characterize its notice of default to the borrower as also meeting all HUD conditions precedent to its foreclosure action.[181] The bank had failed to establish that it made any attempt to schedule a face-to-face interview as required by HUD, or make "a reasonable effort to arrange the interview before bringing the foreclosure action."[182] Accordingly, the entry of summary judgment in favor of the bank was reversed.[183]

One bank attempted to excuse itself from the HUD requirement to arrange a face-to-face meeting with the borrower, which attempt must be evidenced by at least one certified letter to the borrower seeking to arrange such meeting.[184] Wells Fargo had tried to sidestep this requirement by sending the borrower a letter giving her a toll-free number by which she could discuss her financial situation by phone.[185] The borrower acknowledged having received the letter but noted the bank's failure to comply with HUD.[186]

The bank would have been excused from meeting with the borrower if it had not had a branch office within 200 miles of the mortgaged property.[187] The bank did not dispute the fact that it did have a branch office within that range, but claimed that it did not have to perform the face-to-face meeting because "it did not have a branch office with competent servicing personnel within 200 miles of the property."[188]

---

179. *Id.* at 866–67.
180. U.S. Bank, N.A. v. Detweiler, 2010 Ohio 6408 at **57–58 (Ohio App. 2010).
181. *Id.* at *58.
182. *Id.* at *57.
183. *Id.* at *60.
184. Wells Fargo Bank, N.A. v. Isaacs, 2010 Ohio 5811 at *6 (Ohio App. 2010), *citing* 24 C.F.R. § 203.604.
185. *Id.*
186. *Id.*
187. *See id.* at *7, *citing* 24 C.F.R. § 203.604.
188. *Id.* at *8.

Wells Fargo suggested that it had the authority to follow its own interpretation of § 203.604 because it claimed that the term "branch office" was ambiguous, and that "where a regulation is ambiguous, the court should look to the agency's interpretation of its regulations."[189] However, the Ohio court referred to another decision where a court had also considered whether the term "branch office" as used in § 203.604 means "service branch office."[190] Both courts held that the term "branch office" is not ambiguous and that the court "need not look to external sources to define the regulation's terms."[191] Since Wells Fargo itself admitted that it had branch offices within 200 miles of the subject property, the court held that "the regulation unambiguously required Wells Fargo to make a reasonable attempt to schedule a face-to-face meeting with Isaacs."[192] Therefore, the appellate court held that the trial court had properly denied the bank's summary judgment motion and granted summary judgment in the homeowner's favor.[193]

In New York, the Home Equity Theft Prevention Act (HETPA) creates conditions precedent with which banks must comply before filing foreclosure actions.[194] HETPA was enacted in 2006 and was intended to "afford greater protections to homeowners confronted with foreclosure."[195] HETPA "requires the foreclosing party in a residential mortgage foreclosure to provide specific notice to a homeowner in order to proceed with a foreclosure action."[196] This statutory notice must be delivered together with the summons and complaint and "shall be in bold, fourteen-point type and shall be printed on colored paper that is other than the color of the summons and complaint, and the title of the notice shall be in bold, twenty-point type. The notice shall be on its own page."[197]

---

189. *Id.* at *9.

190. *Id.* at *10.

191. *Id.*

192. *Id.*

193. *Id.* at *11.

194. First Nat'l Bank of Chicago v. Silver, 73 A.D.3d 162, 613 (N.Y. App. Div. 2010).

195. *Id.* at 166.

196. *Id.* at 165.

197. *Id.*

A New York court noted that other courts have "consistently interpreted HETPA's notice requirement as a mandatory condition or condition precedent . . . . [T]he foreclosing party has the burden of showing compliance therewith and, if it fails to demonstrate such compliance, the foreclosure action will be dismissed."[198] In that case, the court found that the bank had failed to comply with the notice provisions of HETPA and therefore reversed the trial court's entry of summary judgment.[199]

Payment

A strong defense to foreclosure may exist if your client has made consistent payments to the bank before, during, and after the foreclosure, and this defense is even better if the bank has accepted the payments. It does not matter what the bank has done with the money[200]—if it took money during the foreclosure or the events leading thereto, the homeowner may have a good argument that he is not in default and that the bank has failed to meet conditions precedent, undoing an essential element to the bank's case. Your client should assert a payment defense if, at any time after he received the demand letter, he made a payment that was accepted in any way by the bank.

If the facts indicate that the borrowers may have a payment defense, their attorney should request and obtain a full accounting. You will need to obtain all records your clients may have relating to payments they ever made to the bank, and obtain a payment history for the period in question from the bank that adequately explains the bank's position on how the borrower can be in default after the payments were accepted. It can be difficult to obtain any documents from the bank voluntarily, so you will probably need to get the loan payment history through a request for production.

---

198. *Id.*

199. *Id.* at 169.

200. Some banks might claim that accepted payments do not defeat their foreclosure action because they did not apply the payments to the loan principal and interest, but instead applied it differently, such as placing it in a suspense account.

Counterclaims

Sometimes, instead of filing merely an answer and affirmative defenses, a homeowner may wish to also file a counterclaim if the circumstances give rise to at least one cause of action against the bank. Many courts will require the homeowner to include the appropriate filing fee together with her counterclaim, as it is a separate action seeking affirmative relief against the bank and not just affirmative defenses. Causes of action for violations of RESPA and TIL, along with fraud, often form bases of foreclosure counterclaims. The test for whether a cause of action is appropriate as a foreclosure counterclaim is whether it meets the "transaction test"; i.e., "whether the same issues of fact and law are presented by the complaint and the counterclaim and whether separate trials on each of the respective claims would involve a substantial duplication of effort by the parties and the courts."[201]

Foreclosure cases are usually decided by a judge and no jury, by virtue of the facts that foreclosure is an equitable proceeding and the terms of the mortgage usually contain a jury trial waiver.[202] In one Connecticut case, the homeowners had placed the foreclosure case on the jury docket because they raised legal issues in their affirmative defenses and counterclaim.[203] The bank opposed having the case determined by jury trial, but asked in the alternative that the court sever the equitable issues from the jury trial so that the equitable issues could be determined by the judge alone.[204] The judge removed the foreclosure action from the jury docket, as it ruled that "[a]n action of foreclosure is peculiarly equitable and the

---

201. EMC Mortgage Corp. v. Shamber, No. CV-07-5001252S (Conn. Super. Ct., Nov. 12, 2009).

202. Chase Home Finance LLC v. Higgins, 985 A.2d 508, 512 (Me. 2009). Furthermore, most mortgages are executed with the Single Family–Fannie Mae/Freddie Mac Uniform Instrument, which provides, in paragraph 25: "**Jury Trial Waiver**. The Borrower hereby waives any right to a trial by jury in any action, proceeding, claim, or counterclaim, whether in contract or tort, at law or in equity, arising out of or in any way related to this Security Instrument or the Note."

203. Bank of New Haven v. Liner, No. CV-91-034516S (Conn. Super. Ct., Nov. 9, 1993).

204. *Id.*

court may entertain all questions which are necessary to be determined in order that justice may be done between the parties."[205]

However, in a later Connecticut case, the court did grant a motion to sever a homeowner's counterclaim from the foreclosure action and set it for jury trial, though interestingly the motion was made by the bank, not the homeowner.[206] When several causes of action are joined in a case and it "appears to the court that they cannot all be conveniently heard together, the court may order a separate trial of any such cause of action."[207] When solely equitable facts and law are presented to a court, the court may exercise its equitable powers to determine the issues without a jury, but when a party presents issues that are "properly cognizable in an action at law, either party has the right to have the legal issues tried by a jury."[208] Because all six causes of action presented in the counterclaim were legal in nature and stated claims for damages cognizable at law, the court therefore determined that the homeowner was "entitled, as a matter of constitutional right, to a jury trial on her counterclaim."[209]

However, due to the solely equitable nature of the bank's complaint for foreclosure, the court retained the foreclosure action to be determined solely by the judge.[210] The appellate court commented that "the trial court will necessarily have to weigh the possible preclusive consequences that may attach to a decision on the merits of the foreclosure action in advance of a jury trial on the counterclaim."[211]

Class-Action Complaint

Some homeowners have elected to file their own actions against the banks, not only on behalf of themselves but as a class action, in favor of all similarly situated individuals. A class-action suit "is a procedural device designed to promote efficiency and fairness in

---

205. *Id.*
206. Webster Bank v. Linsley, No. CV-97-0260406S (Conn. Super. Ct., Aug. 9, 2001).
207. *Id.* at **39–40.
208. *Id.* at *40.
209. *Id.* at *41.
210. *Id.*
211. *Id.* at **41–42.

the handling of large numbers of similar claims,"[212] and "an exception to the usual rule that litigation is conducted by or on behalf of the individual named parties only."[213] In order for a class-action lawsuit to proceed, "there must be an ascertainable class and there must be a well-defined community of interest in the questions of law and fact involved affecting the parties to be represented."[214] In deciding whether to certify a class, a court should "accord plaintiffs every favorable view of the complaint and record,"[215] and a "class action should lie unless it is clearly infeasible,"[216] as the "class action's 'historic mission of taking care of the smaller guy' has been widely recognized."[217]

It has been held that in order for a class to be certified, six factors must be demonstrated: "(1) numerosity; (2) commonality; (3) predominance; (4) typicality; (5) superiority; and (6) adequacy."[218] "Numerosity and commonality concern the entire class, while typicality and adequacy concern the nexus of the named class representatives with the class itself."[219] For numerosity, the size of the class must be so large "that joinder of all members is impracticable."[220] Commonality means that "there are questions of law or fact common to the class."[221] Predominance means that "the questions of law or fact common to the members of the class predominate over any question affecting only individual members."[222]

---

212. Lilian v. Commw., 354 A.2d 250, 253 (Pa. 1976).

213. Iliadis v. Wal-Mart Stores, Inc., 922 A.2d 710, 718 (N.J. 2007).

214. Gerhard v. Stephens, 442 P.2d 692, 728 (Cal. 1968), *citing* Daar v. Yellow Cab Co., 433 P.2d 732 (Cal. 1967).

215. Iliadis v. Walmart Stores, Inc., 922 A.2d 710, 714 (N.J. 2007); *citing* Riley v. New Rapids Carpet Ctr., 294 A.2d 7 (N.J. App. Div. 1993).

216. *Iliadis*, *id.* at 718, *citing* Riley, 294 A.2d 7.

217. *Iliadis*, *id.* at 719, *citing* Marvin E. Frankel, *Amended Rule 23 from a Judge's Point of View*, 32 ANTITRUST L.J. 295, 299 (1966).

218. Williamson v. Sanofi Winthrop Pharmas., Inc., 60 S.W.3d 428, 432 (Ark. 2001).

219. Atlanta Cas. Co. v. Russell, 798 So. 2d 664, 666 (Ala. 2001), *citing* Warehouse Home Furnishing Distribs., Inc. v. Whitson, 709 So. 2d 1144 (Ala. 1997).

220. BPS, Inc. v. Richardson, 20 S.W.3d 403, 406 (Ark. 2000), *citing* ARK. R. CIV. P. 23(a)(1).

221. *Id.*, *citing* ARK. R. CIV. P. 23(a)(2).

222. *Id.*, *citing* ARK. R. CIV. P. 23(b)

Typicality means that the claims held by the representative parties would be typical of the claims of the proposed class.[223] Superiority means that the class action must "be superior to other available methods for the fair and efficient adjudication of the controversy."[224] Finally, adequacy means that "the representative parties [will] fairly and adequately represent the class."[225]

Recently, a group of borrowers successfully obtained the certification of a class-action lawsuit against a Florida law firm that has repeatedly come under fire for numerous alleged wrongful practices in the course of its business as a foreclosure and default law firm for banks,[226] with the class being defined as "all persons in the State of Florida to whom THE LAW FIRM sent reinstatement letters on behalf of WELLS FARGO Bank, N.A., and who either reinstated their mortgages by paying the reinstatement charges, or who lost their property . . . "[227] The defendants fought the class certification, urging that the court should distinguish between those borrowers who reinstated their mortgages and those who lost their homes.[228]

The class's causes of action were based on their claims that the law firm sent borrowers reinstatement letters "demanding payment for fees and costs which . . . were unreasonable, excessive or 'not currently due and owing,'" such as service of process, title, and attorneys' fees and other charges.[229] The class met the certification requirements of Florida Rule of Civil Procedure 1.220(b)(3) because:

> [T]he members share common characteristics, and common questions of law and fact predominate over any individual

---

223. *BPS, Inc.*, 20 S.W.3d at 412.

224. *Id.*, *citing* ARK. R. CIV. P. 23(b)

225. *BPS, Inc.*, 20 S.W.3d at 412.

226. The embattled law firm ceased "the practice of law with respect to all pending foreclosure matters in the State of Florida as of March 31, 2011." Peter Franceschina, *David Stern Foreclosure Firm Closing at End of Month*, SUN-SENTINEL (Fort Lauderdale, Fla.), Mar. 7, 2010.

227. Law Offices of David J. Stern, P.A. v. Banner, 50 So. 3d 1221, 1222 (Fla. 4th Dist. Ct. App. 2010).

228. *Id.*

229. *Id.* at 1221.

issues, since "[t]he nature of this case and the elements of [plaintiffs'] claims primarily involve issues focusing on THE LAW FIRM's acts and not those of the class members. It was stipulated and shown that THE LAW FIRM's activities and practices in attempting to collect charges related to the reinstatement of the residential mortgages were common practices to all class members, and it is alleged that these activities violate [the Florida Consumer Collection Practices Act and the Florida Deceptive and Unfair Trade Practices Act].[230]

The court was not concerned that there would be a lack of commonality between class members as a result of individualized damage issues.[231] The court held that for those class members who had reinstated their loans, their damages could be "determined by a relatively simple and mechanical computation," and noted that the majority of the class members would be entitled to request statutory damages and injunctive relief.[232]

As this case demonstrates, distressed homeowners who, for example, are all victims of a specific fraudulent practice may consider seeking relief by way of a class action. The foreclosure mills have sometimes churned out fraudulent paperwork so quickly that the damage caused is far-reaching and extends to possibly thousands of homeowners. For example, the office manager of one foreclosure law firm that is closing amid government investigations "testified in depositions that she routinely signed hundreds of affidavits a day swearing to the accuracy of foreclosure paperwork without reviewing the contents of the documents."[233]

Since class members must show commonality that dominates over any individual questions of fact, a potential class should start with narrow issues that potentially affect all class members. If the scope of a potential class action becomes too broad, then there may be too many individual issues that defeat the requirements of commonality. In the case of robo-signed affidavits, the potential class

---

230. *Id.* at 1222.

231. *Id.*

232. *Id.*

233. Peter Franceschina, *David Stern Foreclosure Firm Closing at End of Month*, SUN-SENTINEL (Fort Lauderdale, Fla.), Mar. 7, 2010.

should review the affidavits to ascertain whether there are consistent misrepresentations of fact or law, and the sort of damage that has been caused by the misrepresentations.

The foreclosure mills operate on a volume business, with their profits usually commensurate to the number of foreclosures generated. This business model largely depends on scientific management,[234] uniformity, and boilerplate forms from which deviation is discouraged, if not prohibited. Because these practices are deployed on such a uniform basis against distressed homeowners, this uniformity of foreclosure prosecution may well provide required elements for additional foreclosure class-action suits.[235]

234. Frederick Winslow Taylor coined the term "scientific management" to describe his theories to optimize production of factory workers. *See* Deborah Stead, *Back in Time With America's Time-and-Motion Man*, N.Y. TIMES, Apr. 6, 1997.

235. *See* Atlanta Cas. Co. v. Russell, 798 So. 2d 664, 666 (Ala. 2001), *citing* Warehouse Home Furnishing Distribs., Inc. v. Whitson, 709 So. 2d 1144 (Ala. 1997).

Chapter 20

Discovery

One purpose of discovery is to test the strength and weaknesses of opponents' positions, and sometimes reveal additional claims and defenses that a party did not have at the beginning of its lawsuit. Another function of discovery is to "to remove surprise from trial preparation so the parties obtain evidence necessary to evaluate and resolve their dispute."[1] The discovery process may even facilitate settlement, as discovery helps to establish where each party stands in terms of its potential success or failure in the case.[2]

The discovery methods permitted by the Federal Rules of Civil Procedure are depositions, interrogatories, production of documents or things (including requests to enter lands, sample products, etc.), physical and mental examinations, and requests for admission. A party is permitted to use cumulative methods of discovery in conjunction with each other and usually in any order, rather than having to choose between methods.[3] A party can be required to produce documents or information even if they are available from some other source, which is useful in the foreclosure arena, as many

---

1. Ragge v. MCA/Universal, 165 F.R.D. 601, 603 (C.D. Cal. 1995).

2. *See* Greyhound Corp. v. Super. Court of Merced County, 56 Cal. 2d 355, 377 (1961).

3. *See* Pulsecard, Inc. v. Discover Card Servs., 168 F.R.D. 295, 305 (D. Kan. 1996).

documents may be available in the public record but are difficult to find.[4] This places the burden on the banks to locate the documents instead of the homeowner, which is usually fairer, as the bank has more resources to locate documents and usually has most of the documents relevant to the foreclosure in its possession anyway.

Some jurisdictions require the parties to lay certain cards on the table. Cases governed by the Federal Rules of Civil Procedure require the parties to disclose certain matters without awaiting a discovery request, which include the names of potential witnesses, copies of documents supportive of each party's claims or defenses (or a description of their contents and location), computations of the parties' damages, and copies of any insurance agreements that may be used to satisfy a judgment.[5] The Federal Rules, as well as some jurisdictions, also require a party to supplement discovery disclosures if he learns that his initial response is now incomplete or incorrect.[6] When no minimum discovery or supplementation of responses is required, it is up to the parties to craft the methods to best ferret out the information they need from the other side, which more often than not the other side does not want to reveal.

A great deal of time can be wasted in discovery; but on the other hand, time wisely spent in this stage of the litigation can make all the difference for a homeowner defending against foreclosure. Courts often have a great deal of respect for litigants who are able to negotiate the discovery process without court intervention. Courts often do not like to be called upon to resolve discovery disputes, as this is often a sign to the court of a lack of professionalism on one or both sides, especially if the discovery requests are reasonable. One thing to keep in mind is that even if information is produced to the other side in discovery, it cannot necessarily be introduced as evidence in support of summary judgment or trial, as parties may keep certain matters out through motions in limine.

In the foreclosure arena, the bank is usually not interested in propounding discovery on the defendants. For one thing, it is a volume

---

4. *See* Wright v. Patrolmen's Benevolent Ass'n, 72 F.R.D. 161, 164 (S.D.N.Y. 1976).

5. *See* Fla. R. Civ. P. 26(a)(1).

6. *See* Fed. R. Civ. P. 26(e).

business for the bank and its foreclosure counsel, and the bank is signing on to the inherent delays of discovery if it serves its own discovery on homeowners, and knows it has to wait at least 30 days before it will receive results. Banks usually want instant gratification and want to avoid voluntarily submitting themselves to this kind of waiting. Their prevalent goal is to file the minimum amount of documents needed to win judgment—i.e., the complaint, summons, and any supporting documents; a motion for default; and a motion for summary judgment and any corresponding affidavits and notice of hearing. For another, from the bank's point of view, its case is usually established merely by the fact that the borrowers failed to make payments on the loan, and the bank feels it does not need any further discovery to prove the elements of its foreclosure case.

Banks will often resist giving homeowners documents and other discovery which lawyers and the courts, according to general litigation principles, consider discoverable as a matter of course. However, as most lawyers know, the Federal Rules of Civil Procedure, whose provisions have been adopted by most state courts, provide that "parties may obtain discovery regarding any matter, not privileged, that is relevant to the claim or defense of any party, including the existence, description, nature, custody, condition, and location of any books, documents, or other tangible things and the identity and location of persons having knowledge of any discoverable matter."[7] The federal definition of "relevant evidence" is also extremely broad, as it encompasses "evidence having any tendency to make the existence of any fact that is of consequence to the determination of the action more probable or less probable than it would be without the evidence."[8] "Relevant information need not be admissible at trial, if the discovery appears reasonably calculated to lead to the discovery of admissible evidence."[9]

For the borrower, discovery can be an extremely useful tool in thwarting the bank's goal to push the case through the foreclosure mill as quickly as possible, but discovery should not be used merely for delay tactics. Delay can seem to be the sole effect of truckloads

---

7. FED. R. CIV. R. 26(b)(1).
8. FED. R. EVID. 401.
9. FED. R. CIV. P. 26(b)(1).

of boilerplate discovery. Some defense law firms propound close to 100 requests for production and then never use any of the documents they obtain in favor of their client's case. For each piece of information or document you request from the other side, ask yourself why you or your client needs it, and what this information could do for your case if you get it.

A borrower is entitled to have the bank produce evidence that proves or disproves the allegations set forth in the complaint.[10] Therefore, the homeowner should be entitled to proof that, for example, the homeowners entered into a loan agreement with the plaintiff; whether or not the plaintiff is the owner of the note and mortgage; a complete loan transaction history, including all payments and how they were applied; whether the plaintiff has possession of the original note; whether the borrowers actually defaulted on the loan or whether the bank wrongfully refused to apply the borrower's payments properly, etc. If the complaint contains vague and conclusory allegations, discovery intended to clarify those allegations should not be objected to on the grounds that the discovery is itself vague and conclusory.[11] Allegations such as "the borrower defaulted on the loan" or "plaintiff is the lawful owner and holder of the note" are inherent conclusions of both fact and law, as default and ownership are both questions of law, and these statements beg fact-intensive questions as to how the plaintiff's allegations could be true.

If a borrower has potential affirmative defenses or counterclaims that involve specific individuals at the bank, he or she should be able to obtain those names in discovery.[12] The exact structure of the bank as it relates to a homeowner's loan is rarely known to anyone except for the bank, and the borrower should be able to ascertain what was done or not done among these individuals to cause the foreclosure to be filed.[13] A homeowner should also be entitled to obtain the names of all potential witnesses who might give testimony relevant in the

---

10. *See* Brown v. Waco Fire & Casualty Co., 73 F.R.D. 297, 298–99 (S.D. Miss. 1976).

11. *See* B-H Transp. Co. v. Great Atl. & Pac. Tea Co., 44 F.R.D. 436, 438–39 (N.D.N.Y. 1968).

12. *See* Bluefield Supply Co. v. Broome, 121 W. Va. 584, 588 (1939).

13. *See id.*

case.[14] Whereas such a list may be relatively easy to ascertain in other varieties of cases, such as personal injury, it may be more difficult in a foreclosure case, because anyone at the bank who reads the loan notes, usually contained in an on-line computer platform, may then become a witness to the case. The business records doctrine is usually central to how any one bank representative claims knowledge about a foreclosure case. Most likely, no one representative at a bank has much more knowledge about any one foreclosure case than another, except for perhaps the upper management and officers of the bank who understand the larger picture and behind-the-scenes information. This is why sometimes a bank manager attempts to appear at a deposition in place of a lower-level employee who may have been summoned, so as to attempt to avoid more damaging statements being made by someone who would not know any better.[15]

The privileges that may limit the production of relevant evidence include marital communications, physician-patient, psychotherapist-patient, attorney-client, cleric-congregant, journalist, trade secret, and work product.[16] Some documents or information that a borrower might wish to collect would be the guidelines by which the bank would determine whether the borrower qualifies for a certain loss mitigation program. Sometimes these requests are met with an objection that the defendant is seeking trade secrets of the bank. However, "there is no absolute privilege for trade secrets and similar confidential information."[17] To avoid producing such information, the opponent to the discovery must prove that the information

---

14. *See* Atl. Greyhound Corp. v. Lauritzen, 182 F.2d 540, 542 (6th Cir. 1950).

15. I have attended the deposition of affiants whose sole responsibilities were to execute affidavits of indebtedness on behalf of the bank in support of summary judgment. In each case, the witnesses were not native Americans, did not speak English as their primary language, and had no prior experience with litigation before. The depositions also revealed that they had no information about the case other than what their job functions entailed to complete the affidavits of indebtedness. Since they executed many affidavits per day (although they may not have been robo-signers), they did not have any independent recollection about the subject cases.

16. 23 AM JUR 2D *Depositions and Discovery* § 27.

17. *In re* Continental Gen. Tire, 979 S.W.2d 609, 612 (Tex. 1998), *citing* Fed. Open Mkt. Comm. v. Merrill, 443 U.S. 340 (1979).

constitutes a trade secret; if they meet this burden, the opposing party must then prove that it needs the information in order for its claims to be fairly adjudicated.[18] A homeowner should be able to meet this burden when it comes to obtaining internal guidelines of the bank by which banks select borrowers for approval in various loss mitigation programs. Borrowers may know that they fit the guidelines for HAMP, but they may not know all of the programs in which the bank participates, the criteria the borrower must meet to qualify for each one, whether two borrowers with exactly the same qualifications might not both be approved for the same program and why, whether the bank exercises arbitrary criteria, etc. Having this information is essential to a fair adjudication of a homeowner's case, because it will save borrowers and their counsel from going on a wild-goose chase to litigate their case when the case could simply be settled, precious court time and resources could be preserved, and unnecessary attorney's fees to both sides avoided.

Interrogatories

Interrogatories are a good tool for ascertaining facts, obtaining admissions and factual positions from the opposing party, procuring evidence, and obtaining descriptions and locations of other evidence.[19] As with other methods of discovery, the scope of information obtainable through interrogatories is very broad, "in the interest of a fair trial, eliminating surprise and achieving substantial justice."[20] In ruling on objections to interrogatories, a court should consider not whether the question calls for an opinion, but whether an answer would serve any legitimate purpose to either lead to new evidence or narrow the issues, and if the latter is the case, the court should compel an answer to the interrogatories.[21] An interrogatory may properly ask for an opinion if it is "phrased with particularity" and if "the need for the information outweighs the prejudice and burden to the interrogated party in divulging it."[22]

---

18. *Id.* at 613.
19. *See* United States v. Purdome, 30 F.R.D. 338, 340 (W.D. Mo. 1962).
20. *Id.*
21. *Id.* at 341.
22. McClain v. Mack Trucks, 85 F.R.D. 53, 59 (E.D. Pa. 1979).

In most foreclosure cases, the bank does not propound interrogatories on the borrower, as this just delays the bank's time lines, and the bank usually has all the information about the borrower it feels it needs. I mention the broad scope of discovery here once again to reiterate that advantage from a foreclosure defense perspective. You might want to use interrogatories with a deposition follow-up so that you will have good starting point for questioning in the deposition and, hopefully, save yourself time in getting to the real issues. You might use interrogatories subsequent to the deposition as more of an admission-gathering tool to confirm and crystallize information obtained during the deposition. Or you may use interrogatories standing on their own. Interrogatories that might properly request the bank's opinion could include questions relating to how the borrower might qualify for a loss mitigation solution, or what factors the bank considers in whether to grant a reduction in principal balance.

Even though the Federal Rules carry a policy in favor of full and open disclosure of non-privileged information, responses to interrogatories, just as with other forms of discovery, are often evasive and non-responsive. However, proper answers to interrogatories must be "responsive, full, complete and unevasive," and the answering party must not "ignore information immediately available to him or under his control."[23] The scope of knowledge and resources that a bank must utilize to supply responses to interrogatories extends to the bank's "attorney, investigators employed by or on behalf of the party, the party's insurer, and agents or representatives of the party."[24] Furthermore, if the bank representative chosen to respond to the interrogatories does not have sufficient knowledge of all the matters raised therein, it is the bank's responsibility to "make a conscientious good faith effort to designate the persons having knowledge of the matters sought by the discovering party and to prepare those persons in order that they can answer fully, completely, unevasively, the questions posed by the discovering party as to the relevant subject matters."[25]

---

23. Miller v. Doctor's Gen. Hosp., 76 F.R.D. 136, 140 (W.D. Okla. 1977).
24. *See* Wycoff v. Nichols, 32 F.R.D. 370, 372 (W.D. Mo. 1963).
25. *See* Barron v. Caterpillar, Inc., 168 F.R.D. 175, 176–77 (E.D. Pa. 1996).

The information available to banks is often contained within their online case management platform, granting them the means to answer most reasonable questions that a borrower would pose to them. Foreclosure defense counsel should take measures to ensure that the responses to the interrogatories encompass the knowledge and resources of the bank and *all* of its required agents, not just those of the attorney who drafts the responses to the interrogatories, who may know nothing about the loan beyond the limited documents usually provided by the bank, such as the mortgage, note, loan payment history, demand letter, and assignment of mortgage.[26] Furthermore, a deposition may be necessary to subpoena the representative who executed the interrogatories to ascertain whether they truly have sufficient knowledge of the matters they attested to, so that foreclosure defense counsel may obtain the names of additional bank representatives who have the appropriate knowledge to fill in any gaps.[27]

It is common to not have questions answered sufficiently through interrogatories, so you may use them as a springboard for a deposition, where you may examine the person who executed the interrogatories more thoroughly about her answers or lack thereof. Advantages of interrogatories include the ability to establish facts—or the nonexistence thereof—without the time, expense, and tediousness of a deposition, to obtain court orders compelling the bank to respond properly if it fails to do so, and to obtain sanctions against the bank if it still refuses, potentially crippling its foreclosure action.

---

26. *See Wycoff*, 32 F.R.D. at 372.
27. *See Barron*, 168 F.R.D. at 176–77.

Sample Interrogatories

When did the plaintiff acquire ownership of the note and the mortgage?

Is the note lost?

Can the plaintiff properly account for the loss?

Has the mortgage been satisfied or paid off?

What is the relationship between the plaintiff and the original lender?

What are current reinstatement and payoff amounts?

What does the bank consider the current market value of the property to be?

What are the bank's criteria for the borrower to qualify for any loss mitigation program which the bank currently utilizes?

Give any reasons why the borrower does not qualify for any loss mitigation program, and what factors would need to change to allow the borrower to qualify?

Requests for Production

Often you will need to compile all relevant documents to the subject loan and property through requests for production. Many lender firms may balk at your requests. However, the discovery rules in most jurisdictions entitle you to a broad scope of discovery and to receive all information or documents that may lead to relevant evidence. Some lender firms may claim that you are only entitled to a limited scope of documents, such as the note, mortgage, assignment of mortgage, demand letter, and payment history. However, your investigation into the case must start at the very beginning, and that is with the loan origination file.

The loan origination file usually includes the loan application, the HUD settlement statement, the Truth-in-Lending disclosures, a title insurance policy, the note, mortgage, warranty deed, and various other documents. However, there are certain things you should focus on in examining the loan origination file.

First, look at the loan application. This will tell you whether the loan is a purchase-money mortgage or a refinance. Determine also whether the property is your client's primary residence or secondary property, such as for investment purposes. Many loss mitigation programs and certain legal relief are available only for primary residences. Also, the type of loan will determine certain rights under the Truth In Lending Act, whose disclosures you should look for next. For the Truth In Lending Act (TIL) there are two important disclosures: the adjustable rate disclosure and Notice of Right to Cancel. If required disclosures were not provided to your client, you may have additional TIL defenses, as discussed further in Chapter 19.

You also need to request all correspondence between your client, the plaintiff, and the servicer. If opposing counsel tries to get away with simply giving you the demand letter, persist. Many important facts and rights lie within the correspondence. For example, you also need to look for a "welcome letter" or lack thereof for possible RESPA violations (Chapter 19). A welcome letter is a notice to the borrower that the servicer of the loan has changed. If such a change occurs, notice to the borrower is required.[28] Additionally, the bank may have

---

28.   12 U.S.C. § 2605(c)(2)(A).

granted your client a loss mitigation solution previously. The reasons for why it ended are very important. The bank may have ended it with no justification. Quite frequently, borrowers have been placed on "trial modifications" and made all payments required under that modification, only to be told that they did not qualify for a permanent loan modification. Nail the bank down as to the reasons why; it could be that the bank never had any intention of reinstating your client's loan.

This is another reason it is so important for a borrower to get any and all evidence of a loss mitigation, forbearance, workout, or any other loan solution, temporary or permanent, verbal or written. When the day of the summary judgment hearing comes, many homeowners, often showing up with their families and young children, tell the court that they have been working things out with the bank, only to still have judgment entered against them. Their verbal representations are usually not enough for the court. If the homeowner was verbally told by the bank that a loan solution was or is in progress, the homeowner needs to send the appropriate bank representative or department a letter memorializing and confirming same. Getting an e-mail address of the specific representative making such promises or assurances is even better.

If the bank did confirm an agreement in writing, such evidence must be presented to the court, together with a sworn affidavit representing the homeowner's side of the story. This kind of evidence is more likely to create a genuine issue of material fact that will defeat the bank's motion for summary judgment, much more so than verbal pleas for help, no matter how heart-wrenching.

Many bank attorneys will object to the production of their fee agreement with their client. In reality, because foreclosures are a volume business, the attorneys' fees on any one case are usually capped to a low fee, usually between $1,000 and $1,500 per foreclosure. Often, the law firm will not get paid by the bank until the property goes to sale, providing one impetus for the firm to push the foreclosures along as quickly as possible. As suggested by the subpoenas served by the Florida Attorney General's office on three of the state's largest foreclosure mills,[29] some firms may also receive bonuses based on the speed of their turnaround time on getting a foreclosure to sale. Foreclosure firms are also always pushing to meet the guidelines imposed by the banks on how long a foreclosure should take, whether or not the guidelines are realistic.

As an initial matter, fee agreements between an attorney and client are generally covered by the attorney-client and work-product privileges. However, the requester of such a document may be able to overcome these bars to production if he can show that the document is necessary to his case and he cannot get the same information from another source without undue hardship.[30] Since the bank usually claims attorneys' fees in its complaint and therefore puts the matter directly at issue in the case, homeowners should be entitled to know the basis for the fees sought to be collected from them. Quite frequently, the foreclosure attorney's fee structure is revealed anyway in her attorney's fee affidavit in support of summary judgment, which is required to show the court how much should be entered for attorney's fees in the final judgment.

---

29. Copies of the subpoenas served on the three law firms can be viewed at http://4closurefraud.org/2010/08/10/kaboom-florida-law-firms-subpoenaed-over-foreclosure-filing-practices/.

30. *See* Va. Elec. & Power Co. v. Sun Shipbuilding & Dry Dock Co., 68 F.R.D. 397, 410 (E.D. Va. 1975).

Sample Requests for Production

Produce all correspondence between you and any party to the litigation.

Produce copies of the original note, together with any endorsements or allonges thereto.

Produce all documents containing or reflecting the date on which you obtained physical possession of the note and mortgage.

Produce the right to cancel and notices of adjustable rate mortgage pursuant to the Truth in Lending Act provided to the homeowner at closing.

Produce all documents reflecting the names of all loss mitigation programs in which you participate and the qualification criteria for each.

Produce all documents relating to any loan modification, forbearance, or repayment plan which you offered or implemented for the homeowner.

Produce a life of the loan payment history for the loan which fully accounts for how each payment made by the borrower was applied, together with an explanation of any codes or abbreviations used therein.

Provide all documents reflecting the name, address and telephone number for any and all current investors on the loan.

Provide copies of all appraisals ever performed on the subject property.

Request for Admissions

One purpose of a request for admission is to produce an "unassailable statement of fact that narrows the triable issues in the case."[31] "Admissions are sought, first to facilitate proof with respect to issues that cannot be eliminated from the case, and secondly, to narrow the issues by eliminating those that can be eliminated."[32]

One challenge in crafting an effective request for admission is to phrase it so that it does not call for legal conclusions and it pins the recipient down to a yes or no answer. This can be difficult in a foreclosure case, where some of the ultimate questions of fact depend on ownership of the loan, which can be at least partially a legal issue. You may ask the recipient to declare that no written assignment was executed transferring the note and mortgage to the plaintiff before the foreclosure action was filed, but in some states ownership can turn on whether the plaintiff "holds" the note prior to the foreclosure to establish proper standing. Or you may ask the bank to admit that it accepted payments from the borrower after the foreclosure action was filed, but whether this negated the bank's satisfaction of all conditions precedent to filing the foreclosure action may be a question of law.

As a request for admission is usually limited to a specific, discrete factual issue, such demands as "Admit that the Plaintiff is not the owner and holder of the note and mortgage" may properly be met with an objection on the grounds that the demand calls for a legal conclusion. A request might be better phrased as "Admit that you have the original note in your possession," "Admit you obtained ownership of the mortgage via a written assignment of mortgage." Following are additional examples of requests for admission.

---

31. Howell v. Maytag, 168 F.R.D. 502, 504 (M.D. Pa. 1996), *citing* Langer v. Monarch Life Ins. Co., 966 F.2d 786 (3d Cir. 1992).

32. *Id.*, *citing* FED. R. CIV. P. 63, 1970 advisory committee notes.

Sample Requests for Admissions

When the Plaintiff filed this action, there was no written assignment transferring the note and mortgage to the Plaintiff.

The subject mortgage is not included in the securitized trust for which the Plaintiff is the trustee.

The Plaintiff has accepted payments for the Defendant on the subject loan subsequent to the filing of this action.

The Plaintiff cannot produce any evidence that it had possession of the note and mortgage on the date this action was filed.

The Plaintiff has previously filed a dismissal of a complaint to foreclose this same loan.

The Plaintiff or its predecessors in interest on the subject loan received funds under the federal Troubled Asset Relief Program.

Depositions

Depositions are a unique discovery tool that can create advantages for the homeowner in ways that no other discovery method can. If possible, you should depose the person who will be signing and notarizing the affidavit of indebtedness (AOI). You want to find out how true her statement of personal knowledge of all matters contained within the affidavit really is. Also look at the local requirements for affidavits in your jurisdiction. Is the affiant signing under penalty of perjury, subject to fines, imprisonment, or both? Does the affidavit contain conclusions of law or fact, and is the affiant qualified to make those conclusions?

The bank will usually file a motion for protective order in an attempt to avoid the deposition. As mentioned earlier, depositions can be disastrous for customer relations between the bank and their counsel because depositions can be contentious and emotional. According to the Federal Rules of Civil Procedure, a party can obtain a protective order that limits the discovery or depositions it must produce to the opposing side:

> The court may, for good cause, issue an order to protect a party or person from annoyance, embarrassment, oppression, or undue burden or expense, including one or more of the following:
>
> (A) forbidding the disclosure or discovery;
> (B) specifying terms, including time and place, for the disclosure or discovery;
> (C) prescribing a discovery method other than the one selected by the party seeking discovery;
> (D) forbidding inquiry into certain matters, or limiting the scope of disclosure or discovery to certain matters;
> (E) designating the persons who may be present while the discovery is conducted;
> (F) requiring that a deposition be sealed and opened only on court order;
> (G) requiring that a trade secret or other confidential research, development, or commercial information not be revealed or be revealed only in a specified way; and
> (H) requiring that the parties simultaneously file specified documents or information in sealed envelopes, to be opened as the court directs.[33]

Foreclosure firms will frequently argue to the court that a deposition is far too invasive and unnecessary for the foreclosure procedure. Some will cite case law that stands for the proposition that if less invasive means of discovery are available, a party is required to utilize those methods of discovery instead. However, as noted

---

33. FED. R. CIV. P. 26(c)(1).

earlier, a party is free to choose which methods of discovery she wishes to employ, and in what order.[34] Furthermore, a request to vacate a notice of taking deposition is usually not well received by a court due to the policy in favor of "full discovery of relevant facts and the broad statement of scope in [Federal] Rule 26," as well as the court's ability to control the manner in which depositions are taken.[35] An oral deposition is a discovery tool which may reveal information that other methods cannot because it is a live, ongoing, interactive process. If a witness does not answer a question or resolve a matter to an attorney's satisfaction the first time, the attorney may follow up with additional questions, something that cannot be done with the static nature of written requests for production and interrogatories. Additionally, there is no written limit to the questions that may be asked in a deposition, unlike interrogatories or requests for admissions, although a deposition should not be unduly burdensome and harassing to the witness.

Under the Federal Rules, a party may also require the deponent to produce documents at the deposition.[36] However, a party should not abuse this privilege by examining numerous or complex documents at a deposition so that an undue burden is imposed on others, as a party may then request that the court require the requesting party to simply serve a request for production.[37]

In preparation for the deposition, you should obtain, at a minimum, copies of the original note, mortgage, any and all demand letters, welcome letter, a loan payment history for the life of the loan, and the loan origination file. You may want to schedule not only the deposition of the AOI affiant, but also that of the person having the most knowledge regarding the subject loan, because they may not be the same person.

For example, a bank may hire individuals whose sole job responsibility is AOIs, such as the robo-signers we have heard about

---

34. *See* Pulsecard, Inc. v. Discover Card Servs., 168 F.R.D. 295, 305 (D. Kan. 1996).

35. Investment Props. Int'l, Ltd. v. IOS, Ltd., 459 F.2d 705, 708 (2d Cir. 1972).

36. *See* FED. R. CIV. P. 30(b)(5).

37. *See* Notes of Advisory Committee on 1970 Amendments to Rule 30, FED. R. CIV. P.

in the news lately. The AOI representatives will usually review an affidavit prepared by their attorneys, notarize it, and send it back to the law office to be filed with the court. The AOI representatives are usually lower-level employees who likely do not comprehend the legal terminology that often appears in these affidavits. It is unlikely that these AOI reps have any knowledge about the subject loan other than the facts contained in their affidavit, and often not even that. On the other hand, upper management and officers of the banks have a greater in-depth knowledge of the inside information and policies that impact any given loan. Even if they are not the particular person who worked on the loan in your case, they may be able to shed light on the policies and practices of the bank that affected your client at the deposition.

Any court has a tremendous amount of power in its hands. They have the power to order any person, no matter how high ranking, to tell the truth or face contempt of court. In turn, we as attorneys possess a great deal of power which we can use for good. We can summon those high-ranking officials to testify under oath before us and to be held accountable for the allegations they have made against our clients.

This is not to say that securing such a person's presence at a deposition will not be difficult. The banks have all the money they need at their disposal to hire top guns to seclude them from such pesky matters as depositions. But once you have secured that person's presence and they are bound by law to answer your questions truthfully, you may obtain answers and defenses relevant not only to your client's case, but to many others as well.

At the deposition, the borrower's counsel should be on guard for inappropriate objections from the bank's counsel. As mentioned previously, many bank representatives still have little to no experience with litigation, much less with being personally deposed (a fact you may ascertain within your first few questions to the witness). The bank's counsel may employ speaking objections to minimize damaging statements from his or her client, such as "objection, calls for a legal conclusion/asked and answered/compound/vague and ambiguous," etc. However, any objections to deposition questions should be "stated concisely in a nonargumentative and nonsuggestive manner."[38] This means that if you were to ask the witness, "What are the guidelines with which my client must comply to be eligible for a waiver of deficiency?," the bank's attorney should not respond with, "Objection, calls for legal conclusions, my client does not have all of her guidelines in front of her, lack of foundation," etc. Or if you ask, "Would you accept a modified payment of $1,500 per month with a down payment of $5,000 in order to reinstate the loan?," the bank's attorney should not respond with "Objection, we will not agree to any settlement discussions on the record." However, just as with any deposition, if the opposing party or attorney feels that you are being abusive or harassing, or that the deposition has continued for an unnecessary amount of time, he or she may terminate the deposition. This decision to terminate the deposition is subject to review by the judge, who will determine whether or not the deponent was justified in walking out and whether discovery sanctions are appropriate.[39] However, to save everyone the time and trouble of running back to the judge over such disputes and avoiding either or both parties facing sanctions, it is obviously best to conduct depositions in a civil and professional manner in which both parties understand this is just an integral process of litigation, and which the deponent does not attempt to terminate because he knows that the court would not ratify that decision.

---

38. FED. R. CIV. P. 30(c)(2).
39. *See* FED. R. CIV. P. 30(d).

Sample Deposition Questions

What is your relastionship to the Plaintiff?

Why do feel that your are the best person to testify on behalf of the Plaintiff at this deposition?

Please describe your educational background.

Have you had any experience with litigation before?

How long have you worked for the Plaintiff?

What documents did you review in preparaton for this deposition?

Have you personally reviewed the note, mortgage, demand letter, loan payment history and assignment of mortgage (if any)?

What is the exact date that the Plaintiff acquired ownership of this loan?

Please describe the specific procedures by which the Plaintiff acquired the loan (assignment, endorsement of note, successor-in-interest)?

Please describe a "day in the life" on your job.

In the scope of your employment, how many affidavits do you execute on average, per day?

Who is the person who notarized this document for you?

Please describe the procedure by which you had this document notarized.

When you state that you have personal knowledge of all facts in this affidavit, what is your understanding of personal knowledge?

Please specifically describe the event or non-event that causes the Plaintiff to allege that the homeowner is in default on the loan.

Has the Plaintiff accepted any payments from the borrower subsequent to the filing of this foreclosure action?

If so, how were those payments applied or accounted for?

You may be able to use the bank representative's affidavit to create a genuine issue of material fact and preclude a summary judgment of foreclosure for the bank.[40] In one Florida case, the homeowner, through its counsel, asserted that summary judgment for the bank should not have been granted because the bank affiant "relies upon attorneys to draft the form affidavits in foreclosure cases, fails to understand most of the language in the affidavits she signs, and routinely signs these affidavits without personal knowledge of the facts stated therein."[41]

In this particular case, however, counsel's argument did not change the outcome of the case issued by the trial court because the appellate court did not find that the homeowner had met her burden required to set aside a judgment according to Florida law: the "motion must specify the fraud with particularity and explain why the fraud, if it exists, would entitle the movant to have the judgment set aside."[42] The homeowner had not alleged in her motion that the bank had committed fraud, did not show why any of the facts would entitle her to set aside a default judgment, did not claim that she did not default on her mortgage, or claim that the amounts set forth in the bank's affidavit of indebtedness were not accurate.[43] Additionally, the court found that the bank representative's deposition testimony was consistent with her assertion that she had personal knowledge of the amounts due and owing, and noted that she had admitted that she did not know the exact individual who had entered information about the particular loan into her case management system.[44] The court also rejected the homeowner's attempt to assert, for the first time on appeal, that the "affidavit was insufficient to satisfy the requirements for admissibility under the business records exception to the hearsay rule" when this issue had not been preserved for appellate review at the trial level.[45]

---

40. Freemon v. Deutsche Bank Trust Co. Ams., 46 So. 3d 1202 (Fla. 4th Dist. Ct. App. 2010).
41. *Id.* at 1204.
42. *Id.*
43. *Id.* at 1205.
44. *Id.*
45. *Id.*

Even though this particular court found against the borrower, it also provides guidance on how the case may very well have turned out differently if the homeowner had alleged that the affiant statements were inaccurate, provided a factual basis for such argument, and preserved the issues for appeal. Additionally, if the argument that the affidavit testimony failed to meet the standard required for the business records exception, the case may also have turned in the borrower's favor. It may very well be that we will soon see an appellate decision where defense counsel has asserted such facts that meet the standard to have a judgment overturned, or to affirm a denial of summary judgment, in such a way that create a genuine issue of material fact. Foreclosure defense attorneys everywhere may learn from this decision what information from a bank representative's deposition is most helpful to use in combating summary judgment.

Part III

Summary Judgment and Beyond

Chapter 21

Summary Judgment

Almost as important as keeping the title in your client's name is making sure a summary judgment of foreclosure is not awarded to the bank. This is one of the final nails in the coffin, barring a successful appeal. Once summary judgment is granted, the judge will usually set a sale date, which is commonly one to three months away. The judge will often give the borrower a send-off saying, "Keep trying to work things out with the bank." Though the court is only trying to be helpful, these words may be of little encouragement to a homeowner, because if the bank did not work things out with him before winning summary judgment, it is less likely this will happen when the bank has essentially already won the case.

Summary judgment is the second most important event after the sale for which a bank pushes in its foreclosure action. This is where it wants the court to put a rubber-stamp of approval on all of its allegations; i.e., that it owns the note and mortgage, the homeowners have defaulted on the loan, and the bank is entitled to a judgment of foreclosure. A bank will usually present a boilerplate motion for summary judgment alleging the bare-bones elements required for such a motion. In efforts to prove the requisite nonexistence of any genuine material fact, the bank will present an affidavit in support of its motion. The affidavit usually claims that the affiant has personal knowledge of the facts stated

213

therein, the borrower entered into a note and mortgage secured by the subject property, the borrower defaulted on the payments due on the loan, and sums of money are due, usually containing some semblance of a breakdown; i.e., title search, filing fees, interest, attorney's fees, etc. Summary judgment often breaks down to a five-minute bench trial, as "[t]here is no right to a jury trial in foreclosure proceedings,"[1] although certain legal claims may be severed for trial from an equitable foreclosure action.[2]

In their haste to push foreclosures through the system, most foreclosure law firms schedule their motions for summary judgment on uniform motion calendar dockets, or on dockets reserved for hearings five minutes in length or less, when permitted by the court. In reality, this time is usually inadequate to resolve all issues in a matter of such importance. The courts usually permit foreclosure motions for summary judgment to be scheduled on motion calendar dockets, because most jurisdictions are glutted with foreclosure cases and want to get them off judges' and court staffs' workloads.

The majority of foreclosure cases have been uncontested, and often no one complains about the foreclosure case being scheduled for motion calendar. In most cases, however, they should complain. At least one (and often more) viable defense exists for every homeowner who deserves more of the court's attention than a rushed five minutes. This, however, requires careful preparation, scheduling with the court, and compliance with its procedures.

To prevent a loss at summary judgment, your arsenal of defenses should be meticulously investigated, organized, and crafted into motions, pleadings, memoranda of law, and/or affidavits as appropriate. This is the time when you must file with the court all

---

1. Chase Home Finance LLC v. Higgins, 985 A.2d 508, 512 (Me. 2009). Furthermore, most mortgages are executed with the Single Family–Fannie Mae/Freddie Mac Uniform Instrument, which provides, in paragraph 25: "**Jury Trial Waiver**. The Borrower hereby waives any right to a trial by jury in any action, proceeding, claim, or counterclaim, whether in contract or tort, at law or in equity, arising out of or in any way related to this Security Instrument or the Note."

2. *See* Webster Bank v. Linsley, No. CV-97-0260406S (Conn. Super. Ct., Aug. 9, 2001).

your evidence in opposition by the prescribed deadlines and possibly file your own cross-motion for summary judgment. In fact, the homeowner need not wait for the bank's cue to seek summary judgment; the homeowner may decide to seek summary judgment long before the bank does, depending on the circumstances of the case, what discovery reveals, etc.

The bank's modus operandi is usually the same. It is trying to push the case toward summary judgment as quickly as possible. In opposing summary judgment, if you had to choose one time in the foreclosure case to be prepared and have all your ducks in a row, this is it. Follow your local rules of procedure as to when you need to have your evidence in opposition, as well as any cross-motion for summary judgment and notice for hearing filed and set, to be sure that your cross-motion is heard either prior to, or at the same time as, the bank's motion. Many judges have excused the requirement that foreclosure defendants have filed their opposition by the prerequisite days in advance, but do not make such a presumption with your judge. It is your responsibility, not your judge's, to prepare and argue your case, whether or not your judge chooses to fill in the blanks if you miss something.

A motion for summary judgment can only be granted if "the pleadings, affidavits and other proof submitted show that there is no genuine issue as to any material fact and that the moving party is entitled to judgment as a matter of law."[3] The movant for summary judgment must meet its initial burden to make a "*prima facie* case for entitlement to the relief sought," and a bank may meet this burden when it presents the original note together with evidence of the borrower's default on same.[4] Further, a motion for summary judgment should only be granted if "a fair and reasonable person could conclude only one way."[5] Once the movant has made a prima facie case for summary judgment, the burden shifts to the opponent to demonstrate "the existence of a triable issue of fact as to a bona fide defense to the

---

3. Wells Fargo Bank, N.A. v. Toth, No. LLI-CV-09-6001082S (Conn. Super. Ct., Oct. 15, 2010); Alejandre v. Deutsche Bank Trust Co., 44 So. 3d 1288, 1289 (Fla. 4th Dist. Ct. App. 2010).

4. Beneficial Homeowner Serv. Corp. v. Steele, 2011 N.Y. slip op. 50015U at *2 (N.Y. App. Div. 2011).

5. *Toth, supra.*

action, such as waiver, estoppel, bad faith, fraud, or oppressive or unconscionable conduct on the part of the [movant]."[6]

Local rules of civil procedure often establish a minimum number of days that must elapse after a party has filed a motion for summary judgment before a hearing can be held on such motion.[7] Because of their rush to schedule summary judgment hearings, banks often will not comply with the required time frame.[8] For example, a summary judgment of foreclosure was reversed in Ohio because the bank did not file the motion at least 14 days prior to a hearing on same, as required by the local rules of civil procedure.[9] In fact, the motion for summary judgment and proposed judgment on same were filed one day and granted the next, with no hearing on same ever set.[10] The court found that that the homeowners were deprived of their due process rights and vacated the summary judgment so that the defendants would have an opportunity to respond to the bank's motion and be heard.[11]

Before a motion for summary judgment can be granted, it must appear from the entire record that no genuine issue of material fact remains that would need to be resolved by a trier of fact. In one case, the homeowner appealed the granting of a bank's summary judgment when the bank had never filed the original note with the trial court, and a copy of the note filed by the bank indicated that

---

6. Emigrant Mortgage Co., Inc. v. Fitzpatrick, 29 Misc. 3d 746, 751 (N.Y. App. Div. 2010).

7. *See* FLA. R. CIV. P. 1.510(c) (the motion must be served at least 20 days prior to the hearing on same).

8. Many courts now do not permit a bank to schedule a summary judgment hearing before prerequisite documents are filed with the court, such as the motion, all affidavits in support, and the original note. Often, courts now will not permit the bank's counsel to schedule the hearing, directing counsel to await the hearing date to be issued from the court instead. *See* Dade County, Florida Foreclosure Master Calendar Procedures, at http://www. jud11.flcourts.org/what's_new/Foreclosure_Master_Calendar_Information.pdf.

9. BAC Home Loans Servicing, LP v. Mowery, 2010 Ohio 5570 at **4–8 (Ohio App. 2010).

10. *Id.* at *3.

11. *Id.* at *8.

another entity was the proper party in interest.[12] The court reiterated the well-established law that it must draw every possible inference in favor of the non-moving party in determining a motion for summary judgment.[13] Additionally, the court noted that to be entitled to a summary judgment of foreclosure, the bank must either produce the original note or seek to reestablish a lost note.[14] In light of the fact that the record on appeal did not contain a filing of the original note, assignment of same to the plaintiff, or an affidavit of ownership, the court found that genuine issues of material fact existed and that the summary judgment granted was improper.[15]

A bank was also not entitled to summary judgment when at the trial stage it relied on unsigned, uncancelled checks to show that the homeowner received the loan proceeds.[16] The homeowner countered that "he was defrauded in connection with the mortgage loan at issue, that [the bank] engaged in predatory lending practices, that he did not receive the funds from the loan, and that he had made timely payments under the mortgage up until the time that plaintiff commenced this foreclosure action against him."[17] Oddly enough, by the time the case got to the appellate court, the bank had magically produced signed and cancelled copies of the checks by which the loan proceeds were allegedly disbursed to the borrower.[18] The bank could not explain why it could not produce these documents at trial and could not show that these checks cleared when they first presented their motion for summary judgment.[19] In any case, summary judgment was improper even with this new evidence, because the checks were mostly payable to other parties at the closing besides the homeowner, and failed to demonstrate that the borrower had received all of the loan proceeds due to him.[20]

---

12. Servedio v. US Bank Nat'l Ass'n, 46 So. 3d 1105, 1106 (Fla. 4th Dist. Ct. App. 2010).

13. *Id.*

14. *Id.* at 1107.

15. *Id.*

16. Bankers Trust Co. of Cal., N.A. v. Payne, 188 Misc. 2d 726, 728 (N.Y. App. Div. 2001).

17. *Id.*

18. *Id.* at 730.

19. *Id.*

20. *Id.*

Affirmative Defenses May Raise a Genuine Issue of Material Fact

Affirmative defenses, including but not limited to those listed earlier in Chapter 19, may be tools with which to fight the motion for summary judgment, according to the circumstances. The difference between using these defenses to counteract summary judgment as opposed to just alleging them in an answer and stating a few facts in support is that now is the time to put your money where your mouth is. You need to find some actual evidence; whether it be by affidavit, information and documents received in discovery, deposition transcripts, or other documents filed with the court in the case that support whatever legal defense you are making, and show how the facts, law, or both create a "genuine issue of material fact" such that the bank's motion for summary judgment cannot be granted, or that your own motion for summary judgment should be granted.

The bank often fails to meet the requirement that all documents referred to in the affidavit must be attached thereto.[21] In some states, affidavits submitted in support of a motion for summary judgment must attach all documents referred to within the affidavit or file those documents together with the affidavit:

> Form of Affidavits; Further Testimony. Supporting and opposing affidavits shall be made on personal knowledge, shall set forth such facts as would be admissible in evidence, and shall show affirmatively that the affiant is competent to testify to the matters stated therein. Sworn or certified copies of all papers or parts thereof referred to in an affidavit shall be attached thereto or served therewith. The court may permit affidavits to be supplemented or opposed by depositions, answers to interrogatories, or by further affidavits.[22]

Quite often, a bank affiant will state that he has reviewed documents upon which he relied in making the affidavit, but those documents will not be attached to the affidavit, nor will they have been

---

21. *See* PHH Mortgage Corp. v. Barker, 2010 Ohio 5061 at *30 (Ohio Ct. App. 2010).

22. FLA. R. CIV. P. 1.510(e).

filed with the court in many cases. An argument that has recently been advanced is that because the vast majority of AOIs filed as of this writing fail to attach documents referenced therein, the affidavits are deficient. Therefore, summary judgment cannot be granted, because a genuine issue of material fact exists as to the facts alleged in the complaint and AOI.

Another reason that a jury trial may be favorable for your client is that you cannot cross-examine an affidavit, and the bank's evidence in favor of its summary judgment is usually presented in affidavit form, unless live testimony is required to reestablish a lost note. The affidavit is the shortcut the bank wants to take to avoid placing one of its representatives on the stand to testify in person before a judge, jury, and an entire courtroom, under oath, to be subject to direct and, if done correctly, a piercing cross-examination by the defense.

The banks' modus operandi is to file an affidavit of indebtedness (AOI), usually as its only evidence in support of a motion for summary judgment. The AOI will usually be a notarized statement of a plaintiff representative stating that it has personal knowledge of all facts contained therein. However, the affidavit (drafted by the bank's attorney) will often contain legal terms of art that neither a layperson nor the affiant can define if questioned in a deposition.

The AOI will typically provide a recap of the facts alleged in the complaint and itemize a list of the charges the plaintiff claims is due and owing. Usually, the AOI will state that the affiant has reviewed other records and that the affiant bases her personal knowledge on those records.

Often, in its rush to obtain summary judgment, the bank will either ignore or try to sidestep legitimate affirmative defenses raised by the homeowner. However, if these affirmative defenses are not addressed in such a way that removes genuine issues of material fact, summary judgment should not be granted for the bank.[23] In one case, the homeowners had raised affirmative defenses invoking the Real Estate Settlement Procedures Act (RESPA), the Truth In Lending Act (TIL), and unclean hands.[24] The court held that to

---

23. *See* Alejandre v. Deutsche Bank Trust Co., 44 So. 3d 1288, 1290 (Fla. 4th Dist. Ct. App. 2010).

24. *Id.* at 1289.

overcome these affirmative defenses, the bank must either "disprove those defenses by evidence or establish the legal insufficiency of the defenses."[25] There, the bank had done neither.[26] Therefore, the trial court's granting of summary judgment for the bank was reversed.[27]

If a borrower adduces affirmative defenses that raise disputed issues of fact that cannot be settled as a matter of law, the court will deny summary judgment to the bank. One homeowner accomplished this while raising the affirmative defense of standing.[28] The bank insisted that there was no material fact in dispute as to its ownership of the loan, because it submitted an affidavit attesting that it acquired the note prior to the filing of the foreclosure action, as well as copies of the note, mortgage, assignment from MERS, deed, and demand letter.[29] The homeowner responded that the bank had shown nothing to prove it was the owner and holder of the note other than the assignment of mortgage executed after the foreclosure action was filed.[30] The bank then alleged that it had shown by the preponderance of the evidence that it was the proper party in interest, and it was now incumbent on the borrower to produce counter-affidavits to prove the contrary.[31]

The court did not accept the mere allegation, though made by affidavit of the bank's vice president of loan documentation, that the subject note was delivered to the plaintiff "prior to the commencement of the instant foreclosure action" to satisfy proof of the bank's ownership for summary judgment purposes.[32] The affidavit was "devoid of any allegation as to the exact date that the plaintiff received the note," and this vague allegation did not satisfy to the court the plaintiff's burden of proving subject matter jurisdiction.[33]

---

25. *Id.*, *citing* Bunner v. Fla. Coast Bank of Coral Springs, N.A., 390 So. 2d 126 (Fla. 4th Dist. Ct. App. 1980).

26. *Id.* at 1290.

27. *Id.*

28. Wells Fargo Bank, N.A. v. Toth, No. LLI-CV-09-6001082S (Conn. Super. Ct., Oct. 15, 2010).

29. *Id.*

30. *Id.*

31. *Id.*

32. *Id.*

33. *Id.*

Therefore, the bank's motion for summary judgment of foreclosure was properly denied.[34]

In determining whether a motion for summary judgment should be granted, a court may look beyond the defenses raised in the pleadings to determine if there are any issues of triable fact remaining.[35] In one New York case, the bank appealed the trial court's denial of its motion for summary judgment even though it appeared from the opinion that the defendants did not raise triable issues of fact in their answer.[36] The court found nonetheless that, elsewhere in their court filings, the homeowners raised meritorious defenses as to "whether plaintiff accepted payments on the mortgage after the date of the default alleged in the complaint . . . waiver and estoppel."[37]

In another New York case, the borrower had initially filed a pro se answer but then, by the time the bank filed a motion for summary judgment, had hired counsel and submitted an affidavit in opposition of summary judgment that also contained a request to amend the pro se answer.[38] The borrower had not submitted a cross-motion for summary judgment or to amend his answer, but the court nonetheless found that "the request [was] amply supported by facts and [was] not some stalling device."[39]

The court then reviewed a number of recently publicized events regarding "the abuses of the banks in foreclosure cases," including the January 2011 decision (discussed further at Chapter 16) whereby a Massachusetts court found unanimously that "U.S. Bank and Wells Fargo [] failed to prove that they owned the mortgages when they foreclosed on the homes."[40] The borrower had also raised "robo-signing" as one of his defenses in his affidavit, which (though this

---

34. *Id.*
35. Consumer Solutions REO, LLC v. Giglio, 2010 N.Y. slip op. 8291 at *1 (N.Y. App. Div. 2010); *see also* Emigrant Mortgage Co., Inc. v. Fitzpatrick, 29 Misc. 3d 746, 751 (N.Y. App. Div. 2010).
36. *Giglio*, 2010 N.Y. slip op. 8291 at *1.
37. *Id.* at **1–2.
38. Deutsche Bank Nat'l Trust Co. v. Ramotar, 2011 N.Y. slip op. 50017U at *1 (N.Y. App. Div. 2011).
39. *Id.*
40. *Id.* at *2, *referring to* U.S. Bank Nat'l Ass'n v. Ibanez, 458 Mass. 637 (Jan. 7, 2011).

term has recently become integrated within the country's vernacular) the court defined as "the act of employees of plaintiff-institutions signing en masse mortgages' foreclosure documents without a careful evaluation of the merits of each case."[41] The New York court joined its brethren jurists in criticizing the haphazard, rabid manner in which many banks have pursued foreclosure.[42]

In light of the numerous instances in which the New York court found that banks have taken advantage of the system, the court gave the homeowner the benefit of the doubt and permitted him to expand on his defenses by way of an amended pleading.[43] The court accordingly denied the bank's motion for summary judgment.[44]

Yet another New York decision denied the bank's motion for summary judgment and scheduled a hearing to determine whether sanctions should be issued against the bank, not because of any specific affirmative defense raised by the homeowners, but because of the clear discrepancies of the documentary evidence on record.[45] The bank there had sought to enforce a loan agreement against two homeowners and offered sworn testimony that this agreement had been signed by both homeowners.[46]

However, when the court examined the loan agreement, it found that not only was just one homeowner party to the agreement, not both, the agreement had not even been signed by the homeowner.[47] The court expressed astonishment at how the bank audaciously demanded summary judgment when the evidence controverted the bank's sworn testimony.[48] The court therefore "seriously question[ed] Plaintiff's good faith in commencing this action" when the loan agreement had not been signed and ran counter to the state's statute of frauds.[49]

---

41. *Id.* at *2.
42. *Id.*
43. *Id.* at *3.
44. *Id.* at *4.
45. Beneficial Homeowner Serv. Corp. v. Steele, 2011 N.Y. slip op. 50015U at *3 (N.Y. App. Div. 2011).
46. *Id.* at **1–2.
47. *Id.* at *2.
48. *Id.* at **2–3.
49. *Id.* at *2.

In all three New York cases, the borrowers were fortunate to have a judge assigned to their case who carefully examined all the relevant documents on record to make an independent determination of the evidence, revealing discrepancies between what the bank claimed and the reality of the evidence. These are all cases in which the borrowers were perhaps not as well prepared as they should have been, because the court, in taking initiative to make sure that justice was done, read between the lines to adduce defenses that should have been promulgated by the borrowers themselves.

Chapter 22

Trial Orders

It is increasingly common to see the courts pushing foreclosure cases along on a sua sponte basis. Foreclosures have glutted the dockets and internal systems of courts nationwide, and one of the courts' primary goals is to get rid of the backlog. Sometimes a foreclosure case will sit for a while with no activity. This may be because the loan is changing hands and it has not yet made its way to the default department. Sometimes a foreclosure file will change hands from one law firm to another.[1] Sometimes a bank's loss mitigation department has voluntarily placed hold instructions on a loan, and the bank's attorneys will therefore not proceed with the foreclosure as long as the loss mitigation hold is in place.

If a foreclosure case has already been filed, however, and it is not moving for one of these or other reasons, the court will often not let it just sit. In this situation the court may issue a sua sponte trial order. A court may also issue such an order if a party, quite frequently a homeowner's association (HOA), has filed a notice of readiness for trial. HOAs will often do this because the longer a foreclosure case sits, the longer it will be deprived of association fees from the distressed homeowner who is often no longer able

---

1. Diane C. Lade & Harriet Johnson Brackey, *Mass Layoffs at Stern as Foreclosure Law Firm Loses Top Clients*, SUN-SENTINEL (Fort Lauderdale, Fla.), Nov. 5, 2010.

to pay them. HOAs in some states have attempted to hold the banks responsible for association fees during the pendency of the foreclosure, but such attempts have been unsuccessful.[2] As a result, HOAs will constantly monitor the status of the foreclosure action and be just as anxious as the bank to see it come to summary judgment and sale.

An order that may be issued by a court in these circumstances is embodied by a sample trial order, included on the form CD.[3] A trial order must be immediately prioritized because of the plethora of deadlines and requirements imposed therein. For example, in this particular order, the following actions must be taken by the parties prior to the calendar call—a brief conference between the court and the parties to ascertain whether all of the court's directions have been followed and if the case is ready to proceed to trial:

1. 60 days prior, the parties must exchange lists of their respective trial and expert witnesses and trial exhibits;
2. 45 days prior, the parties must disclose all of their rebuttal witnesses;
3. 30 days prior, the parties and their attorneys shall meet in person for a settlement and order compliance review conference;
4. 25 days prior, the plaintiff's attorney must appear before the court to advise if a pretrial stipulation has not been filed and depositions transcripts to be used, if any shall be filed;

---

2. U.S. Bank Nat'l Ass'n *ex rel.* Harborview 2005-10 Trust Fund v. Tadmore, 23 So. 3d 822, 823–24 (Fla. 3d Dist. Ct. App. 2009). In Florida, since the HOA has no recourse against the bank for condominium fees during the course of a foreclosure, some HOAs have taken this loss out on all condominium residents, even those current on their unit fees, locking everyone out of the pool, clubhouse, and other facilities simply because some six condo owners were in foreclosure and in default on their maintenance dues. Erika Pesantes, *Boynton Beach Condo Residents Locked Out of Pool and Clubhouse*, SUN-SENTINEL (Fort Lauderdale, Fla.), Feb. 2, 2010. The HOA has warned all owners that "[T]he police department will be called for anyone who creates a disturbance."

3. http://15thcircuit.co.palm-beach.fl.us/divisionan/divisionan_pretrialorder.pdf.

5. 20 days prior, joint pretrial stipulations must be filed and all discovery must be completed;

6. 15 days prior, the parties must submit objections to or additional portions of the transcripts which they deem necessary to be considered in fairness to the initial deposition transcript filings, if any, of each party;

7. five days prior to any pretrial court conference scheduled by the parties, the parties must file their joint pretrial stipulation; and

8. prior to calendar call, the parties must complete a formal mediation, submit any arguments relating to unique questions of law and motions in limine, and meet with the clerk of court and assist the clerk with the marking of all exhibits.

The same day that you receive a trial order, you or your assistant should immediately calendar these deadlines in your calendaring system. There are so many law office and case management platforms these days to help keep you organized. Some attorneys prefer the traditional method of writing everything down, calendaring all their events in their "red book,"[4] keeping everything in a paper file, handwriting all their notes, etc. Now, however, the trend has been, and still is, toward paperless files. Programs such as Amicus Attorney, Time Matters, and ProDoc enable you to have all your case files, documents, calendar, deadlines, events, messages, e-mails, notes, billing, and other information related thereto all in one place. With your standard computer backup, you are protected against loss of your files and the resultant liability.

Some attorneys say that they like to have everything on paper, that their clients require it, that they like to have an actual piece of paper in their hands, etc. This may be true in some instances, and there are certain documents of which you need the original or best paper copy, and not merely an electronic copy, such as mortgages, notes, certain contracts, documents with original seals or markings, and other evidence. But the vast majority of documents and paper associated with a case can be scanned in. Some state bars do not require that attorneys retain paper copies of most documents, and

---

4. http://www.lawdiary.com.

you should check on the requirements of your bar association. Many courts are jumping on the wireless train as well and allowing electronic paperless filing, as many federal courts have already done.

This particular trial order requires that the parties submit a joint pretrial stipulation and that unilateral stipulations cannot be submitted without leave of court. This is an instance where it pays to have a decent working relationship with opposing counsel, because if you are at each other's throats, any task that requires cooperation will be difficult if not impossible. You will also need to work together to get the mediation coordinated, and if you cannot both agree on a mediator, then this will be another matter for the court to deal with, which it may not be very happy about.

Appeal

Sometimes, despite your best efforts and preparation, summary judgment may be entered against the homeowner for any number of reasons. When this happens, and the homeowner wants to fight it, you will need to take steps to appeal the decision as soon as possible. One important thing is to file your notice of appeal right away; often you have a deadline of 30 days from when the order you wish to appeal was entered.[5] If an order granting permission to appeal from a federal district court is entered, you must pay the district court clerk any required cost bond and other fees.[6]

You must also arrange for the trial record to be sent to the appellate court, which must generally contain everything necessary to the resolution of the issues presented to the appellate court, including facts establishing personal jurisdiction, evidence, statutes or ordinances on which the parties are relying, local rules of court on which the parties rely, and written materials of any judicial action that triggered the appeal or is necessary for the resolution of the appeal.[7]

In a federal appeal, within 10 days of filing a notice of appeal or entry of a ruling on certain motions, you must either order a transcript of those portions of the proceedings you deem necessary

---

5. *See* 28 U.S.C. § 2101(a); FED. R. APP. P. 4(a)(1)(A); FLA. R. CIV. P. 9.110(b).
6. FED. R. APP. P. 5(d)(1).
7. 5 AM JUR 2D *Appellate Review* § 441.

to the appeal or file a certificate stating that no certificate will be ordered.[8] Review the issues you have preserved for appeal (hopefully you also had a court reporter at your last hearing) and begin thinking about the facts and law you will use for your appellate argument.

Sometimes you may be faced with the decision of whether to file an appeal of a non-final or interlocutory order, "one which does not finally determine a cause of action but only decides some intervening matter pertaining to the cause, and which requires further steps to be taken in order to adjudicate the cause on the merits."[9] In general, interlocutory orders are not appealable, but an interlocutory appeal may be considered if "the trial court's decision deprives the appellant of a substantial right which would be lost absent immediate review."[10] If, for example, an interlocutory order deprives your client of his home or rights thereto, you may wish to appeal such an order. Such action may be appropriate if the bank has unlawfully entered upon your client's property or deprived your client of access thereto while he still holds title, and the trial court has not afforded him relief.

The deadlines for filing your initial brief, when and how the record from the trial court must be received, and other procedural matters will be outlined in your particular appellate court's local rules. Often, the appellate court will also give you further directions once you have filed your notice of appeal.

Once you have filed your notice of appeal, it should be your responsibility to ensure that the bank does not attempt to sell the property or take any actions in furtherance of same, such as contracting with other parties or entering the property to show it to prospective buyers. Not only is ownership of the property still in dispute and maintenance of the status quo necessary until appellate review is complete, from a title perspective, but also the bank cannot guarantee clear title to a new buyer, as the appellate court may overturn the trial court's entry of summary judgment or trial verdict in favor of the bank. If the filing of an appeal in your jurisdiction does not impose an automatic stay on any sale that was scheduled

---

8. FED. R. APP. P. 10(b)(1).

9. *See* 4 AM JUR 2D *Appellate Review* § 77.

10. *Id.* at § 78.

in conjunction with entry of summary judgment, you must file a motion for stay or to abate the trial proceedings so that the sale does not proceed while you are appealing the case.

Sale

If the sale has been scheduled for a certain day, many motions to cancel sale filed by the borrower at the last minute have been granted by the court, sometimes even minutes before the sale is scheduled to take place, though the borrower should work to stop a sale as early as possible and not wait until the last minute. In some counties there have been judges assigned for this very purpose every morning that sales are scheduled. A good deal of court energy is expended to deal with motions to cancel sale, because quite often the banks are the ones who file them. The bank might want to cancel the sale because it has suddenly placed a loss mitigation hold on the file, or the loan is being transferred again and the assignment of bid is not ready.

Frequently, requests to cancel the sale of a property have been presented to the court without any reason for the party's request. In some states, motions to cancel foreclosure sales must now be supported by an explanation, so that the court can determine when the sale can be properly reset, or whether the sales process is being abused.[11] Review your jurisdiction's regulations pertaining to motions to reset or cancel foreclosure sales, if any.

The period in which the homeowner has to redeem the property from sale depends on the facts of the case and jurisdiction. As one court held, "[t]he right to redeem is 'absolute' and may be validly exercised at any time prior to the confirmation of [the foreclosure] sale."[12] The time that a homeowner has to redeem the property after sale is usually fixed by statute.[13] This statutory period cannot be extended in the absence of fraud, collusion, or deceit in the sale process.[14]

---

11. http://www.floridasupremecourt.org/decisions/2010/sc09-1460.pdf.

12. Bates v. Postulate Invs., LLC, 176 Ohio App. 3d 523, 528 (Ohio App. 2008), *citing* Women's Fed. Sav. Bank v. Pappadakes, 38 Ohio St. 3d 143 (1988).

13. Parker v. Dacres, 130 U.S. 43, 48 (1889).

14. Vangorp v. Sieff, 2001 S.D. 45 at *14 (S.D. 2001).

Sometimes a borrower can prevent her property from going to sale if she files a timely motion to set aside summary judgment and sets it for hearing prior to the sale. This may be possible if the borrower files a timely motion for rehearing, or asserts proper grounds on which to set aside the judgment, which may include:

(1) mistake, inadvertence, surprise, or excusable neglect;

(2) newly discovered evidence that, with reasonable diligence, could not have been discovered in time to move for a new trial under Rule 59(b);

(3) fraud (whether previously called intrinsic or extrinsic), misrepresentation, or misconduct by an opposing party;

(4) the judgment is void;

(5) the judgment has been satisfied, released, or discharged; it is based on an earlier judgment that has been reversed or vacated; or applying it prospectively is no longer equitable; or

(6) any other reason that justifies relief.[15]

Newly discovered evidence should not include arguments that the plaintiff is not the owner and holder of the note or other evidence that should have been ascertained during the course of the case. However, many borrowers have received relief from a sale order because the bank had led them to believe that the foreclosure had been abated pursuant to the terms of a loss mitigation plan, and the first indication that the borrowers receive that this is not the case is a notice of sale.[16] One court has held that if the borrowers have raised "a colorable entitlement to relief, a formal evidentiary hearing and appropriate discovery is required."[17] If parties are successfully able to raise such "colorable entitlement," this may also meet multiple criteria for setting aside a judgment, including newly discovered evidence, surprise, fraud, or general grounds that justify relief. Homeowners may also be able to avoid a sale by virtue of the automatic stay imposed by a bankruptcy filing, as discussed further in the next chapter.

---

15. Fed. R. Civ. P. 60(b).

16. Palacio v. Alaska Seaboard Partners Ltd. P'ship, 50 So. 3d 54, 55 (Fla. 1st Dist. Ct. App. 2010).

17. *Id.* at 56.

Chapter 23

Bankruptcy

Often, homeowners have turned to bankruptcy for no other reason than as a last resort to save their home, or be relieved of their mortgage debt. Many Americans with the goal of saving their home are willing to do almost anything to achieve that end, and the credit implications of bankruptcy seem a small loss in comparison to being able to keep their home. There are other methods to resolve debt such as credit cards, medical bills, student loans, etc., with the increasing incidence of debt relief companies, although one must be sure that they choose a reputable company. But no debt relief company can potentially provide the relief to save a home or relinquish a debt the way that bankruptcy can.

As with other debt collection processes, a foreclosure and home loan collection activity must at least momentarily cease when a homeowner files bankruptcy, due to the imposition of an automatic stay on the collection efforts of all the debtor's creditors.[1] The automatic stay provision was added to a debtor's bankruptcy protections by the 1978 Bankruptcy Reform Act.[2] Congress has recognized

---

1. *See* H.R. REP. No. 95-595, p.340 (explaining the automatic stay pursuant to 11 U.S.C. § 362).

2. Ann K. Wooter, J.D., *What Constitutes "Willful Violation" of Automatic Stay Provisions of Bankruptcy Code (11 U.S.C.A. § 362(k)) Sufficient to Award Damages—Chapter 7 Cases*, 23 A.L.R. FED. 2D 339 at § 2 (2007).

the automatic stay as a fundamental protection of the bankruptcy code, as it protects "debtors from further collection efforts by their creditors, ensuring an equitable distribution of assets by protecting the creditors, ensuring an equitable distribution of assets by protecting the creditors and making sure that no parties get more than their fair share of bankruptcy estate, and ensuring that liquidation and repayment of debts will be carried out in an orderly fashion."[3] A debtor who can prove injury due to a willful violation of the automatic stay can recover actual damages, including costs, attorney's fees, and possibly punitive damages.[4] To prove a willful violation of an automatic stay, a debtor must show that the violator had knowledge of the bankruptcy case when acting and that the violator intended to carry out the proscribed act.[5]

Another advantage of bankruptcy is that it may potentially resolve "all or most issues relevant to a debtor and that it contemplates participation by any party having an interest in any issues relating to the debtor."[6] It is not necessary for a debtor to be insolvent or show any particular level of financial difficulty in order to be eligible for bankruptcy.[7]

Bankruptcy is also intended to grant debtors a fresh start, and courts will interpret the provisions of the bankruptcy code in debtors' favor.[8] However, bankruptcy is intended to grant a fresh start to unfortunate but honest debtors, and those who attempt to defraud and abuse the bankruptcy system will not be granted that relief.[9]

There are several different filing options in bankruptcy court, but the ones most applicable as options for homeowners facing foreclosure are Chapter 7 or Chapter 13. In a Chapter 7 case, the debtor

---

3. *Id.*
4. 11 U.S.C.A. § 362(h).
5. Ann K. Wooter, J.D., *What Constitutes "Willful Violation" of Automatic Stay Provisions of Bankruptcy Code (11 U.S.C.A. § 362(h)) Sufficient to Award Damages – Chapter 13 Cases*, 8 A.L.R. FED. 2d 433 (2006).
6. *In re* St. Mary Hosp., 86 B.R. 393, 394–95 (Bankr. E.D. Pa. 1988).
7. *See* United States v. Huebner, 48 F.3d 376, 379 (9th Cir. 1994).
8. *See In re* Bammer, 112 F.3d 1355, 1357 (9th Cir. 1997).
9. *See In re* Barr, 207 B.R. 168 (Bankr. N.D. Ill. 1997).
10. 11 U.S.C. §§ 701 *et seq.*

is usually requesting liquidation of all debts.[10] In this case, if Chapter 7 relief is granted, the mortgage debt will be discharged and the homeowners will be required to tender the property back to the lender. A Chapter 7 may be preferable for debtors who do not have regular income required for the implementation of another chapter,[11] who have no non-exempt property they need to keep, and who are willing to turn all of their non-exempt property over to the bankruptcy estate.[12]

For debtors with regular income and an acceptable amount of debt, Chapter 13 may be an option if they wish to reach a solution on their mortgage payments and keep their home. With Chapter 13 relief, debtors may stay creditor actions, adjust the debtor-creditor relationship, propose a plan to pay creditors, and rehabilitate themselves financially.[13] Eligibility for a Chapter 13 does not depend on the source of the regular income, but rather its "regularity and stability," as Congress intended that the definition of regular income be interpreted liberally.[14] The advantages of Chapter 13 relief include, inter alia, (1) retention of property rather than liquidation, (2) broader range of dischargeable debts, (3) a hardship discharge may be available prior to repayment in full under an approved plan, and (4) the stigma attached is less severe than that associated with liquidation of debts as with a Chapter 7.[15]

One of the first things the bank will probably try to do in a foreclosure case after the homeowner has filed for bankruptcy is file a motion for relief from the automatic stay. The burden to show entitlement to an automatic stay is upon the debtor.[16] Relief from an automatic stay may sometimes be granted without notice to the adverse party, but only if

> [I]t clearly appears from specific facts shown by affidavit or by a verified motion that immediate and irreparable injury, loss, or damage will result to the movant before the

---

11. *See* 11 U.S.C. § 1123(a)(5).
12. *See* 11 U.S.C. § 1327(b).
13. *In re* Jones, 231 B.R. 110, 112 (Bankr. N.D. Ga. 1999).
14. *See In re* Sigfrid, 161 B.R. 220, 221 (Bankr. D. Minn. 1993).
15. *See* 9 Am. Jur. 2d *Bankruptcy* § 72.
16. *See* 9B Am. Jur. 2d *Bankruptcy* § 1877.

adverse party or the attorney for the adverse party can be heard in opposition; and (2) the movant's attorney certifies to the court in writing the efforts, if any, which have been made to give notice and the reasons why notice should not be required.[17]

For hearings on motions for relief from an automatic stay where there is notice to the debtor, the party requesting relief from the stay must prove that it has equity in the property, and the burden then shifts to the debtor to prove all other issues in opposition to relief from stay.[18] Once the movant is "able to make an initial showing of 'cause,' the burden then shifts to the debtor to demonstrate entitlement to the protection of the stay; the risk of nonpersuasion is on the debtor."[19] The court will examine the facts of the case and determine whether relief from the automatic stay is appropriate under the circumstances.[20]

To demonstrate entitlement to relief from the automatic stay "for cause" due to a lack of adequate protection for a creditor's interest, the creditor must show "(1) a debt owing from the debtor to the creditor; (2) a security interest held by the creditor that secures the debt at issue; and (3) a decline in the value of the collateral securing the debt, along with the debtor's failure to provide adequate protection of the creditor's interest."[21] "If the secured creditor meets this burden, then the debtor must establish that the creditor is adequately protected."[22]

Bankruptcy relief may still be available to a homeowner after a sale of her property has been conducted, as there is a usually a statutory period that must expire before the sale becomes final and a certificate of title is issued to the purchaser. In one Arkansas bankruptcy case when a property went to sale and the homeowner filed

---

17. 9 Am Jur 2d *Bankruptcy* § 144.

18. 11 U.S.C.S. § 362(g).

19. Chase Manhattan Mortgage Corp. v. St. Pierre (*In re* St. Pierre), 295 B.R. 692, 695 (Bankr. D. Conn. 2003), *citing In re* Fitzgerald, 237 B.R. 252 (Bankr. D. Conn. 1999).

20. *Id.* at 695.

21. *In re* Bivens, 317 B.R. 755, 770 (Bankr. N.D. Ill. 2004).

22. *Id.*

a Chapter 13 bankruptcy action before the certificate of title was issued, the court overruled the bank's objections to confirmation of the debtor's plan.[23]

The bank objected to confirmation of the debtor's plan, claiming that the sale of the home was completed before the homeowner filed bankruptcy, and therefore the homeowner was not entitled to cure the mortgage default and have the loan reinstated.[24] However, the borrower correctly argued that while the sale was conducted prior to her bankruptcy filing, the bankruptcy had still been filed before the sale of the property became final.[25]

To determine when the sale of the property became final, the court analyzed the Statutory Foreclosure Act of 1987 of the State of Arkansas.[26] Although Congress had attempted to clarify the deadline by which a mortgagor has the right to cure a default, the court noted division between multiple bankruptcy jurisdictions on this issue.[27] However, the court noted that if "Congress had intended to sever a debtor's ability to cure a delinquent mortgage on the date of the auction, which is typically only one step in the foreclosure sale process, it could have easily done so."[28] The court liberally construed the stated congressional intent of assisting homeowners even after a court has granted summary judgment and ordered a sale.[29]

In Arkansas, a sale of a property at auction does not become final until 10 days after the sale, when the "mortgagee or trustee shall execute and deliver the Trustee's Deed or Mortgagee's Deed to the purchaser."[30] At any time prior to the delivery of the deed, a successful bid at auction is subject to being rejected and payment must still be received, and the trustee has the absolute right to cancel the sale.[31] The *Jenkins* court determined that a sale has not occurred until the property has been irrevocably transferred.[32] As that

---

23. *See In re* Jenkins, 422 B.R. 175, 182 (Bankr. E.D. Ark. 2010).
24. *Id.* at 176.
25. *Id.*
26. *Id.* at 177.
27. *Id.* at 177–78.
28. *Id.* at 178.
29. *Id.* at 179.
30. *Id.* at 180.
31. *Id.* at 180–81.
32. *Id.* at 181.

had not yet occurred when the debtor had filed her bankruptcy action, the court found that she was entitled to the automatic bankruptcy stay against the foreclosure that immediately attached upon filing, and that she was entitled to the confirmation of her Chapter 13 bankruptcy plan.[33]

Therefore, bankruptcy may be an option to pursue by itself or in conjunction with other foreclosure defense methods, and may save a borrower's home as late as post-sale, as this latter case demonstrates. Bankruptcy practice is complex and may require the engagement of separate counsel who specializes in this field. However, as bankruptcy can be an important component of foreclosure defense strategies, it would benefit defense attorneys to obtain necessary education, training, and possibly certification necessary to add bankruptcy law to their practice areas. It will behoove both you and your client when you can authoritatively discuss bankruptcy remedies in addition to other available foreclosure defense strategies, and widen your arsenal of the best options for your clients.

---

33. *Id.* at 182.

Chapter 24

The Neighborhood Assistance Corporation of America

Despite the scores of disreputable loan consultants who have set distressed homeowners in their sights, there are reputable, government-approved counselors who may facilitate actual, permanent loan solutions for borrowers. One such group is the Neighborhood Assistance Corporation of America (NACA). NACA is an organization of HUD-approved loan counselors who have contractual relationships with a number of lenders, servicers, and investors. NACA currently conducts "Save the Dream" tours, holding events throughout the country where borrowers and lenders come together, often negotiating permanent modifications of troubled loans. The borrowers will provide NACA's loan counselors with all relevant documentation, and together the parties will formulate a loan solution proposal to be submitted to the lender. At NACA's live events, these proposals may be accepted on the spot by the servicer or investor.

A foreclosure defense attorney should be aware of all options available to his client, from litigation to alternative dispute resolution to bankruptcy. Working with reputable loan counselors such as NACA may be "homework" to give to clients. Mediation is also an option to litigation and may be handled by the parties themselves, but this is another opportunity that attorneys may best know how to leverage. To work with NACA, borrowers must gather all of their relevant loan paperwork and complete the workbooks provided by NACA, which include forms such as hardship letters. In these letters, the borrowers must explain in detail all events that caused them to default on their loan. These materials will then be given to NACA, which will scan them into its database and provide a specifically crafted proposal to the bank supported by the documents. The borrower will have access to an on-line account where she will be able to exchange messages with the servicer through the NACA environment.

The servicer will indicate its acceptance or rejection of the borrower's proposal through the NACA system, where it may also request additional information or documents from the borrower before making its decision. The borrower will have a record of every date he provided documents and information to the bank, so that he will have a clear history of events and all actions he took in support of loss mitigation in the event he needs to seek relief from the court and these actions are relevant.

In its Save the Dream Tour, NACA offers homeowners financial counseling and face-to-face meetings with loan servicers. Representatives from Fannie Mae and Freddie Mac may also be present at the tour stops. NACA staff advise that even if their servicer has not attended the event, borrowers may still meet with these federal corporations to discuss a loan solution.

NACA never charges the homeowners for providing loan modification services; it has a financial relationship with various servicers whereby NACA is paid if it successfully helps a homeowner reach a loan solution. An example of a loan solution NACA endeavors to provide is as follows:

> The solution for borrowers with stable income is to restructure the mortgage by permanently reducing the interest rate to 4 percent, 3 percent and as low as 2 percent and if necessary reducing the outstanding principal as well. For borrowers who are unemployed or under-employed the solution is a forbearance agreement where there is a minimal payment for a period of time while the borrower is seeking stable

income. If a lender cannot provide these solutions they need to provide NACA the opportunity to appeal the decision.[1]

Conclusion

There are new developments emerging every day in the foreclosure defense industry. Between the time that the last draft of this book is finalized and that this book goes to press, there may be another game-changing development. As of the date of this writing, multiple investigations into the foreclosure crisis continue, conducted by the Obama Administration's Financial Fraud Enforcement Task Force, the Federal Reserve, the Federal Housing Administration, the Executive Office for U.S. Trustees (part of the Justice Department), and all 50 state attorneys general.[2] Among the demands presented to the servicers by the attorneys general are that a bank may not institute foreclosure proceedings while a homeowner is actively engaged in loan modification efforts, and if any borrower successfully makes three payments pursuant to a trial modification plan, the modification will become permanent.[3]

These investigations have contributed to the drop in foreclosure activity, as evidenced by a "21 percent [drop] in November from October, the biggest monthly decline in five years."[4] This comes to the dismay of many investors who have previously capitalized on the oversupply of "product."[5] The recent article observes that

---

1. https://www.nacalynx.com/nacaWeb/Advocacy/chase-lawsuit.asp? #LawsuitBreach.

2. David Streitfeld, *Facing Scrutiny, Banks Slow Pace of Foreclosures*, N.Y. TIMES, Jan. 8, 2011.

3. Nelson D. Schwartz & David Streitfeld, *Mortgage Modification Overhaul Sought by States*, N.Y. TIMES, Mar. 4, 2011.

4. David Streitfeld, *supra* note 2.

5. *Id.* Another ugly component of human nature that emerges from the foreclosure crisis is the Darwinist preying of humans upon the misfortunes of others—individuals, couples, families, children, the elderly, etc. It is easy for investors and companies looking to capitalize off the foreclosure market to just think about money, profits, and the bottom line. Perhaps they have not seen, or are indifferent to, the endless stream of families to and from the courthouse— husbands, wives, children, sometimes babies in strollers or in mothers' arms, standing there in that courtroom holding out a hope that they can still keep their home. Perhaps this is why the banks so often rationalize by blaming the

the efforts to ameliorate the foreclosure crisis to date have only been "fitfully successful," explaining that "[l]oan servicers are not set up to identify the true financial picture of each borrower having trouble . . . and cannot easily figure out who is likely to stop paying without a modification and who will keep sending a check every month."[6] Whether the servicers could devise systems to ascertain such data, but choose not to, is another question altogether.

Other developments are landing every day. In Nevada, a non–judicial foreclosure state, a judge recently ordered that all seizures of homes by a unit of Bank of America temporarily cease.[7] The court found that irreparable injury would result to these homeowners if the seizures proceeded before determining the propriety of such actions by Bank of America's ReconTrust Company.[8] The law firm of Ice Legal in West Palm Beach recently announced that it would hold an open house for homeowners facing foreclosure and pick the 25 most compelling cases to represent on a pro bono basis, because founding partner Thomas Ice said, "It pains us to see so many good people being taken advantage of and losing their homes to the banks without putting up a fight when so many of them have valid defenses."[9] New York state has now extended the constitutional right to free counsel in criminal cases to homeowners named as defendants in foreclosure actions.[10] Legal aid organizations and other pro bono groups are stepping up to the plate to meet the needs and serve the new rights of these homeowners.

The foreclosure war is far from over, but there seems to be a call to action where new soldiers join the side of justice, myself

---

victim. For example, banks sometimes claim that to grant relief to those in need would be unfair when others have maintained their loan payments.

6. *Id.*

7. David McLaughlin, *BofA Unit Ordered to Halt Foreclosures in Nevada*, Jan. 25, 2011, at http://www.bloomberg.com/news/2011-01-25/bank-of-america-unit-ordered-to-halt-nevada-foreclosures.html.

8. *Id.* However, this argument runs counter to many banks' own actions when they received government bailouts, as such bailouts are not available to Americans in general.

9. Paul Owers, *Ice Law Firm Offers Free Foreclosure Defense to 25 Most Compelling Cases*, SUN-SENTINEL (Fort Lauderdale, Fla.), Jan. 28, 2011.

10. David Streitfeld, *New York Courts Vow Legal Aid in Housing*, N.Y. TIMES, Feb. 15, 2011.

included, each day and bring their own unique skills to help win the battle. The foreclosure mill cannot be beaten in every case, but new theories are constantly revealed in how to fight the battle and succeed. Perhaps new laws will be enacted that will render some issues in this book moot. But in the meantime, we rely on the ever-expanding compendium of our common-law system, current legislation, our court system, its officers, and the people we represent to seek for the people the same justice enjoyed by the banks.

Index

U

U.S. Bank, 136
U.S. Bankruptcy Code, 52
unconscionable contract, 159
    court consideration of, 159–60
    defined, 159
    loan agreement as, 159
unfair trade practices. *See* deceptive
    trade practices
Uniform Commercial Code,
    promissory note, holding of,
    130
unprofessional conduct, opposing
    attorney, 10–11
    complications caused by, 11
    dealing with, 10
upside-down loans
    defined, 63
    short sale option, 63

W

Wells Fargo, 136
Wright, Blair, 28
written arguments, 15–18
    analysis portion, 16
    authorities, organization of, 16
    bank relief, arguments for preclud-
      ing, 16
    boilerplate forms, avoidance of,
      15
    challenging documents, dealing
      with, 17
    IRAC case-briefing theory, use of,
      16
    Microsoft Office 2010, assistance
      with, 16
    particular facts, itemization of, 18
    preparation, importance, 17
    principles of law, deference to, 16
    research for, 15–16

About the Author

After working for foreclosure firms for about two years and seeing the real-life impact of foreclosure on individuals and families, **Rebecca A. Taylor** started a solo practice defending against foreclosures to put to use the knowledge she had gained of the system for the benefit of the people.

Ms. Taylor grew up in Newark, Delaware. She obtained a B.A. degree from Rutgers College in American Studies. After college, Ms. Taylor moved to New York City and began work as a paralegal in 1997. She completed temporary assignments with some of New York's top law firms, such as Sullivan & Cromwell, Skadden Arps, and Rogers & Wells. Ms. Taylor served in the 82d Airborne Division of the U.S. Army from 2000 to 2001 and received an honorable discharge.

Ms. Taylor entered Nova Southeastern University Shepard Broad Law Center in 2001. She earned her J.D. degree and was admitted to the Florida Bar in 2004. Ms. Taylor earned the top award for pro bono service at graduation for her services as a summer law clerk with the Palm Beach Circuit Court. Over her career as an attorney, Ms. Taylor has focused on litigation, practicing in family law, landlord-tenant law, commercial litigation, guardianships, appellate work, property rights, consumer advocacy, tort law, and foreclosures. Ms. Taylor currently resides in Hollywood, Florida, with her husband, Jim, and son, Carl. Her Facebook profile is available at www.facebook.com/pages/Rebecca-A-Taylor-Attorney-at-Law, and her website is www.rataylorlaw.com.